THE NATURE
of
VOCABULARY ACQUISITION

THE NATURE
of
VOCABULARY ACQUISITION

Edited by

Margaret G. McKeown • *Mary E. Curtis*
University of Pittsburgh *Harvard University*

LEA LAWRENCE ERLBAUM ASSOCIATES, PUBLISHERS
1987   Hillsdale, New Jersey   London

Lawrence Erlbaum Associates, Inc., Publishers
365 Broadway
Hillsdale, New Jersey 07642

Library of Congress Cataloging-in-Publication Data

The Nature of vocabulary acquisition.

   Includes bibliographies and indexes.
   1. Vocabulary—Study and teaching.   2. Language
acquisition.   3. Verbal ability in children.
I. McKeown, Margaret G.   II. Curtis, Mary E.
LB1576.N335   1987   401'.9   86-29051
ISBN 0-89859-548-7

Printed in the United States of America
10 9 8 7 6 5 4 3 2 1

Contents

List of Contributors   xi

Introduction   1

PART I: HOW KNOWLEDGE OF WORD MEANINGS
DEVELOPS

Chapter 1   Two Vocabularies for Reading: Recognition
and Meaning
Jeanne S. Chall   **7**

The Two Vocabularies   *7*
Recognition Vocabularies   *9*
Meaning Vocabularies   *10*
Conclusion   *15*

Chapter 2   Breadth and Depth of Vocabulary Knowledge:
Implications for Acquisition and Instruction
William E. Nagy and *Patricia A. Herman*   **19**

Vocabulary Size   *20*
The Nature of the Task   *27*
Conclusion   *32*

Chapter 3   Vocabulary Testing and Vocabulary Instruction
Mary E. Curtis   **37**

What Do Vocabulary Tests
Measure?   *38*

The Diagnostic Value of
    Vocabulary Tests   *45*
The Implications for Vocabulary
    Instruction   *47*
Conclusions   *48*

Chapter 4   Cognitive Processes in Learning Word Meanings
Marianne Elshout-Mohr and *Maartje M. van
Daalen-Kapteijns*   **53**

Verbal Comprehension: An Outline
    of the Skill   *53*
Verbal Comprehension: Cognitive Processes
    in Learning Vocabulary From
    Context   *58*
Promoting Vocabulary Learning   *65*

Chapter 5   Learning Word Meanings From Written Context
Priscilla A. Drum and *Bonnie C. Konopak*   **73**

Sources for Meaning   *74*

PART II: HOW KNOWLEDGE OF WORD MEANINGS
            CAN BE PROMOTED

Chapter 6   Most Vocabulary is Learned From Context
Robert J. Sternberg   **89**

Three Basic Facts About
    Vocabulary   *89*
An Explanatory Framework for
    the Three Basic Facts   *90*
Implications of the Facts and Framework
    for the Teaching and Learning
    of Vocabulary   *94*
Data Testing the Theory of Learning
    Vocabulary From Context   *97*
Conclusions   *103*

Chapter 7   Remembering Versus Inferring What a Word Means:
Mnemonic and Contextual Approaches
Michael Pressley, Joel R. Levin, and
Mark A. McDaniel   **107**

Introduction to Vocabulary-Remembering
    Approaches   *108*

Mnemonic Versus Contextual
Vocabulary-Remembering Strategies   *111*
Vocabulary-Inferring Strategies   *120*
Final Words on Keyword
Versus Context   *122*

Chapter 8   Issues in the Design of Vocabulary Instruction
Edward J. Kameenui, Robert C. Dixon, and
Douglas W. Carnine   **129**

Toward a New Perspective of Vocabulary
Learning and Reading Comprehension   *130*
Toward a Comprehensive Vocabulary and
Reading Comprehension Training
Program   *140*

Chapter 9   The Effects and Uses of Diverse Vocabulary
Instructional Techniques
Isabel L. Beck, Margaret G. McKeown, and
Richard C. Omanson   **147**

The Relationship Between Vocabulary and
Reading Comprehension   *147*
Design of a Vocabulary Program   *149*
Results of Implementing the
Program   *150*
A Study to Compare Type and Frequency
of Instruction   *152*
The Role of Rich Instruction   *154*
An Intermediate Grade Vocabulary
Program   *157*

Chapter 10   The Roles of Instruction in Fostering Vocabulary
Development
Michael F. Graves   **165**

Learning Words   *167*
Learning to Learn Words   *172*
Learning About Words   *177*
Concluding Remarks   *181*

Author Index   **185**
Subject Index   **191**

List of Contributors

Isabel L. Beck, *University of Pittsburgh*
Douglas W. Carnine, *University of Oregon*
Jeanne S. Chall, *Harvard University*
Mary E. Curtis, *Harvard University*
Robert C. Dixon, *University of Illinois*
Priscilla A. Drum, *University of California, Santa Barbara*
Marianne Elshout-Mohr, *University of Amsterdam*
Michael F. Graves, *University of Minnesota*
Patricia A. Herman, *Kamehameha Schools, Honolulu, Hawaii*
Edward J. Kameenui, *Purdue University*
Bonnie C. Konopak, *Louisiana State University*
Joel R. Levin, *University of Wisconsin*
Mark A. McDaniel, *University of Notre Dame*
Margaret G. McKeown, *University of Pittsburgh*
William E. Nagy, *University of Illinois at Urbana-Champaign*
Richard C. Omanson, *University of Pittsburgh*
Michael Pressley, *The University of Western Ontario*
Robert J. Sternberg, *Yale University*
Maartje M. van Daalen-Kapteijns, *University of Amsterdam*

Introduction

John Carroll (1971) pinpoints vocabulary acquisition as one of the most basic objectives of schooling.

> Although a considerable amount of vocabulary learning is associated with primary language learning in the early years, the acquisition of most of the vocabulary characteristic of an educated adult occurs during the years of schooling, and in fact one of the primary tasks of the school, as far as language learning is concerned, is to teach vocabulary. (p. 121)

As such, it is easy to understand why the need to answer questions like "How does word knowledge develop?" and "How can its growth be promoted?" is of such importance to educators. Less understandable, perhaps, is why these questions have proven to be so difficult to answer. Uncertainty about vocabulary acquisition seems not to stem simply from neglect on the part of researchers to study it. Indeed, quite the opposite seems to be the case. To date, a substantial amount of research effort has been devoted to this topic. In a bibliography of vocabulary studies, published by Edgar Dale and Taher Razik (1963), over 3,000 titles were included. Since that time, authors of over 2,000 more articles have used "vocabulary development" as a descriptor in the Educational Resources Information Center (ERIC) database. Clearly, missing answers have not resulted from a reluctance to search for them.

Instead, although the study of vocabulary learning has been an ongoing one (as old as educational psychology itself), it seems to suffer from a lack of a framework powerful enough to organize and allow for interpretation of all the available evidence. As a consequence, research studies that use different approaches and/or focus on different issues often can lead to differing conclusions about the most effective instructional practices. Without a framework, these opposing conclusions are difficult to reconcile.

The goal of this volume has been to move beyond a collection of the most recent studies in the area of vocabulary learning. Toward that end, we have brought together the work of researchers who, although they may differ in their views on vocabulary acquisition and instruction, acknowledge that many of the same questions motivate their work. We outline some of these questions here, along with describing the ways they have been addressed throughout the various chapters in the volume. By emphasizing these underlying commonalities, our hope is that the relationships among contrasting perspectives will become more apparent.

THE ISSUES

In seeking contributions to this volume, we asked researchers to consider several questions:

1. What does it mean to know the meaning of a word? How do individuals differ in what they know about word meanings?

2. How does knowledge of word meanings develop? How many word meanings are typically known by individuals at various ages?

3. What is the relationship between vocabulary knowledge and comprehension? What implications does this relationship have for the ways that growth in word knowledge can be promoted?

In what follows, these questions as well as the perspectives on them represented in the volume, are briefly discussed.

Qualitative Aspects of Word Meaning.   General agreement exists among researchers that knowing a word's meaning, in its fullest sense, involves knowing the concept underlying the word. In exploring the implications of this view, William Nagy and Patricia Herman stress that concepts are embedded in larger domains of knowledge. As such, rich ties between the new words that students are learning and what they already know must occur for optimal vocabulary learning.

However, in practice, vocabulary instruction often results in other kinds of knowledge about word meanings. Isabel Beck, Margaret McKeown, and Richard Omanson conceive of these other kinds of knowledge in terms of levels of vocabulary learning, and they discuss the implications these levels have for various verbal performances. In a chapter by Priscilla Drum and Bonnie

Konopak and one by Michael Graves, dimensions of vocabulary knowledge are explored, as well as the kinds of vocabulary learning needed to expand different kinds of word knowledge. Dimensions of vocabulary knowledge are also integral to Edward Kameenui, Robert Dixon, and Douglas Carnine's discussion of the relation between vocabulary assessment tasks and kinds of vocabulary instruction.

Concern with how word meanings should and can be known is complemented in the volume by a focus on individual differences in the way word meanings are known. In her chapter, Mary Beth Curtis links variation in students' vocabulary test performances to differences in the state of their word knowledge and their comprehension performance. Marianne Elshout-Mohr and Maartje van Daalen-Kapteijns, on the other hand, describe differences among individuals in the ability to adapt their processes of vocabulary acquisition to what they know and what is demanded by a task.

Acquisition of Vocabulary Knowledge. Much consideration is given in the volume to the means by which vocabulary is acquired and to the conditions surrounding its acquisition.

Jeanne Chall distinguishes between two kinds of vocabulary necessary for reading — recognition and meaning — and describes how overcoming gaps in each is characteristic of different stages in acquisition of reading ability. Nagy and Herman suggest that context is the means by which most vocabulary is acquired, stressing that this acquisition occurs in small increments. Robert Sternberg also asserts that context is the major source of growth in vocabulary knowledge. In his chapter, he describes the processes, text cues, and variables used to learn vocabulary from context. Related to Sternberg's analysis is a discussion by Drum and Konopak of the sources available to readers for developing knowledge of word meanings through reading.

Michael Pressley, Joel Levin, and Mark McDaniel distinguish between two kinds of vocabulary learning: inferring the meanings of unfamiliar words and remembering the meanings of unknown words. Like Chall, Kameenui et al., Beck et al., and Graves, Pressley and his colleagues suggest that instruction in word meanings can significantly affect acquisition of vocabulary knowledge, particularly for students who may not be proficient at inferring word meanings from context.

Proficiency in acquiring word knowledge is also a focus for Elshout-Mohr and van Daalen-Kapteijns and for Curtis. These authors suggest that a critical factor in determining success in vocabulary learning may be the way that prior knowledge of word meanings affects the cognitive processes used to acquire new word meanings.

Also related to questions about the acquisition of vocabulary knowledge is the issue of vocabulary size. Nagy and Herman suggest that during each year of schooling, students typically encounter tens of thousands of new words, learning the meanings of about 3,000 of them per year. This, they argue, supports the view that most vocabulary is learned incidentally from context. Chall discusses the difficulties in estimating vocabulary size, however, and chooses to focus instead on differences in size between recognition and meaning vocabularies. Beck et al., adopting still another approach, focus on the proportion of words a learner needs to know well (rather than the absolute number of words that are known).

Vocabulary Knowledge and Comprehension.   Virtually all of the authors in the volume emphasize the substantial correlation between vocabulary and comprehension, and view improvement in comprehension as a primary goal of vocabulary instruction. Many different perspectives are presented, however, on why vocabulary and comprehension are related, and on what the implications of this relationship are for vocabulary instruction.

In several chapters, the effects of quantity and quality of vocabulary knowledge on comprehension are stressed. Curtis, for example, discusses how the extent and kind of knowledge individuals have about words can affect comprehension. Beck et al. emphasize that the semantic processes involved in comprehension can require accurate, fluent, and rich, decontextualized knowledge. In a similar vein, Elshout-Mohr and van Daalen-Kapteijns stress that promoting consolidation of available knowledge about word meanings can improve skill in comprehension.

Other authors in the volume view the relationship between vocabulary and comprehension in a different light. Nagy and Herman, for example, suggest that individuals who know many word meanings know much about the world in general. It is this general knowledge base (rather than word meanings per se) that makes these individuals skilled comprehenders, according to Nagy and Herman. Sternberg, on the other hand, argues that comprehension is the ability to learn from context, whereas vocabulary is a byproduct of that ability. Thus, rather than viewing vocabulary as a cause of comprehension difficulty, Sternberg sees it as more of a consequence. Kameenui et al., after reviewing many different explanations for the link between vocabulary and comprehension, choose to focus on a different question: how vocabulary instruction can influence reading comprehension. Identifying factors that can convey word meanings to students in a way that will promote comprehension is their primary interest.

Implications for vocabulary instruction are both widely discussed and a source of spirited disagreement in the volume. Although Pressley et al. recommend instruction in the explicit pairings of new words and their meanings, Curtis suggests that students be provided with opportunities to learn more about word meanings already familiar to them. Elshout-Mohr and van Daalen-Kapteijns outline a program for building knowledge about familiar words, whereas the program described by Beck et al. involves teaching about new word meanings, along with motivating students to use the words outside of class.

Nagy and Herman suggest that students need to encounter large numbers of new words through frequent and regular reading. Drum and Konopak caution, however, that exposure to words in context may not be sufficient for building conceptual knowledge. Sternberg addresses both these points by recommending that students be taught to use context, independently, in all of their reading.

Chall concludes that instruction in both word meanings and contextual learning has value for students. She questions, however, why the strong benefit of direct teaching of word meanings often is not recognized. Kameenui et al. and Graves seem to be in basic agreement with Chall's concern. Kameenui et al. sketch a vocabulary program that includes both individual and contextual word learning. Graves discusses the importance of both kinds of learning as well, but also stresses the need to promote students' desire to acquire word meanings.

ORGANIZATION OF THE VOLUME

Although all of the authors evidence much concern for each of the aforementioned issues, a division of labor did occur in terms of the major emphasis in each chapter. To reflect this, we have organized the volume into two sections. The focus of the first section is on the ways that knowledge of word meanings develop, and on the nature and extent of vocabulary acquisition. Topics in this section include: the learning and teaching of recognition and meaning vocabularies (Chall, chapter 1), the size and nature of the vocabulary learning task (Nagy & Herman, chapter 2), issues in vocabulary testing and variations in vocabulary knowledge (Curtis, chapter 3), individual differences in vocabulary acquisition and their relation to comprehension (Elshout-Mohr & van Daalen-Kapteijns, chapter 4), and factors influencing expansion of vocabulary knowledge through reading (Drum & Konopak, chapter 5).

The focus of the second section is on the ways that knowledge of word meanings can be promoted, and on specific approaches for vocabulary instruction. Topics in this section include: instruction in learning word meanings from context (Sternberg, chapter 6), the keyword method of vocabulary learning (Pressley, Levin, & McDaniel, chapter 7), instruction in individual word meanings, contextual word learning, and content-based vocabulary learning (Kameenui, Dixon, & Carnine, chapter 8), the role of traditional and expanded vocabulary instruction (Beck, McKeown, & Omanson, chapter 9), and instruction in learning words, learning to learn words, and learning about words (Graves, chapter 10).

AUDIENCE FOR THE VOLUME

This volume is intended for those concerned with both theory and practice of vocabulary learning. Researchers and practitioners have long been interested in understanding how knowledge of word meanings is acquired and how vocabulary learning can be promoted. This interest has resulted in an extensive body of research findings that should be invaluable in guiding the design of vocabulary instruction. However, as we noted earlier, results have accumulated in the absence of a framework for interpreting them, making it difficult to make sense out of conflicting recommendations for instruction. Our hope is that this volume brings about a better understanding of the factors that affect vocabulary acquisition as well as the differing perspectives and kinds of evidence from which implications for instruction have been drawn.

REFERENCES

Carroll, J. B. (1971). Development of native language skills beyond the early years. In C. Reed (Ed.), *The learning of language* (pp. 97–156). New York: Appleton-Century-Crofts.

Dale, E., & Razik, T. (1963). *Bibliography of vocabulary studies.* Columbus, OH: Ohio State University Bureau of Educational Research and Service.

I HOW KNOWLEDGE OF WORD MEANINGS DEVELOPS

1 Two Vocabularies for Reading: Recognition and Meaning

Jeanne S. Chall
Harvard University

THE TWO VOCABULARIES

This chapter is concerned with two kinds of vocabulary important for reading—word recognition and word meaning. It treats how they develop over time, how they relate to the reading process, and how they relate to the teaching and learning of reading. It is also concerned with the changes that have taken place over the past several decades with regard to how each is best taught.

I begin with a brief overview of these two vocabularies. One way to view them is in Marshall McLuhan's terms—as the medium or the message. Word recognition may be thought of as the medium in the reading process, the medium that conveys the message, and word meaning as the message itself.

At the preliterate stage, before reading skills have been acquired, knowledge of words and their meanings is considerable. Lorge and Chall (1963) after analyzing the relevant studies on vocabulary size, estimated that 6 year olds, for example, know about 5,000 words. A more recent estimate is that 6 year olds know (i.e., understand and use) about 6,000 different words (Moe, 1974). Still others have claimed that first graders know 24,000 words (Seashore, 1947).

There has been a long controversy in the research literature, as well as in the popular press, as to the number of words known by first graders. Early estimates of the 1920s and 1930s based on samplings from abridged dictionaries, were that about 2,000 or 3,000 words were known by first graders. During the 1940s, based upon Seashore's (Seashore, 1947; Seashore & Eckerson, 1940) test that sampled words from an unabridged dictionary, estimates as high as 24,000 were reported for first graders. The analysis of the past research by Lorge and Chall (1963) found vocabulary sizes ranging from 2,000 to 24,000 for Grade 1. These great differences, they concluded, depended on the size of the dictionary sampled, how the words were tested, and the criterion used for knowing a word — whether common or uncommon meanings were tested. In general, the larger the dictionary sampled, the easier the test of "knowing"; and the more the test asked for common meanings, the larger the estimates. After considering these and other methodological issues in estimating vocabulary size, they concluded that estimates in the tens of thousands were probably too high, and that for first graders, an estimate closer to 5,000 was probably more valid than one of 24,000. The recent estimate of 6,000 by Moe (1974) based on use, gives confirmation to the lower rather than to the higher estimates.

Whether one accepts an estimate of vocabulary knowledge for first graders in the thousands or tens of thousands, the issue with regard to its role in the beginning reading process is essentially the same — those who speak the language in which they learn to read, whether children or adults, are much more advanced in their knowledge of word meanings than in their recognition vocabularies. It is the medium, not the message, that they must learn.

Indeed, it takes the typical child about 3 to 4 years, from Grade 1 to Grade 4, to learn to identify in print the 3,000 words and their derivatives known by about 80% of fourth graders (Dale & Chall, in press) — most of which they could already understand and use in Grade 1. An earlier start and better reading programs may make it possible for most children to recognize more than 3,000 words by the end of Grade 3. But we seem not to have yet found ways for typical 9 year olds to identify accurately, and with fluency, all the words they know from hearing and speaking — perhaps about 10,000. Thus the hurdle of the early years, for most children, is word recognition — the medium, not the message. Most children in the primary grades can understand thousands of words more than they can identify and decode.

For most children, at about Grade 4 or 5, a shift begins to take place. The kind of vocabulary that becomes the greater hurdle is word meaning — the message. Although some children in these grades may still be struggling with the medium (the recognition of words), most begin to struggle more with the message (the meanings of the words and ideas). The shift takes place when they can recognize most common words, and can decode others. But the materials they are required to read, content textbooks, for example, contain an ever greater number of words that are unfamiliar, rare, specialized, abstract, literary, and bookish. The shift also takes place in children's language. Up to age 10, the words they know are mostly concrete, and most of their definitions are concrete. At age 10 and later, they are able to define more abstract words, and their definitions tend to move from the concrete to the more abstract and general (Feifel & Lorge, 1950; Werner & Kaplan, 1952).

Thus, the primary grades may be characterized as overcoming a gap in word recognition, whereas the intermediate grades and beyond may be characterized as overcoming a gap in word meanings.

RECOGNITION VOCABULARIES

At least three positions have been held on the meaning/recognition gap in the primary grades. One position is that there is little or no gap — that words known by the child should create no hurdle in print. Thus, Bettelheim and Zelan (1981) in their book, *On Learning to Read: The Child's Fascination with Meaning,* are critical of American primers and beginning reading textbooks because their vocabularies are limited to the commonest hundreds while children know thousands of words. Others in the field of reading have argued in a similar manner (Goodman & Goodman, 1979; Smith, 1979). Basing their theories of beginning reading on the primary importance of language and meaning, or on motivation, they argue that the extensive meaning vocabularies of children when they first begin to read can and should make it possible for them to read any books containing words they know.

Word recognition, according to this position, is acquired best when it is acquired naturally, as in speech. Word recognition is best accomplished, they claim, with no formal instruction, except perhaps through the modeling by an adult who reads to the child. It is the child's search for meaning that "drives" him or her to recognize the printed words. Thus, word recognition is to be acquired only through context. Indeed, some who hold this position claim that it is the explicit teaching of children to recognize and decode words that leads to serious problems in these areas (Smith, 1979). This position has gone under various labels such as *language-experience* and more recently, *a total language approach.*

A second position is one exemplified in the most widely used basal reading programs published during approximately the 50 years from the early 1920s to the late 1960s. Although the word recognition/word meaning gap in beginning reading was often blurred, as in the earlier position, they did provide explicit instruction in learning to recognize words, mostly as whole words, and somewhat later and less explicitly, through word analysis. To facilitate the recognition of words in print, the number of words taught in the early readers was strictly controlled and they were repeated often. Also similar to the first position, there was strong reliance on meaning for acquiring the printed forms of words, thus the primary importance of context and of using stories with the commonest words in the child's meaning vocabulary. This position has also gone under various labels, including *sight* or *whole word methods,* or *a meaning-emphasis.*

A third position on the meaning/recognition gap is explicit recognition that such a gap exists, and that beginning instruction should be designed to overcome this gap as soon as feasible—usually through systematic teaching of the relationship between letters and sounds (decoding, phonics) along with or preceding the reading of stories.

This approach puts explicit and direct focus on early acquisition of the alphabetic principle (i.e., learning how and why words are spelled and how they are related to speech sounds). In modern versions there also is early reading of stories to facilitate transfer of decoding skills to reading words and stories. This approach is probably the oldest, historically, for teaching alphabetic languages (Matthews, 1966). This approach has been referred to by such labels as *alphabetic–phonic, code-emphasis,* or a *phonics-first method.* (For a fuller account of these three approaches, see Chall, 1967, 1983a.)

One or another of these positions has been used to teach children to read in the United States, as well as in other countries. Some seem to be preferred at some times and others at other times.

What is the research evidence on these three positions? Is one more effective than another? Syntheses of the research on these approaches completed during the late 1960s and subsequently confirmed in the 1980s (Anderson, Hiebert, Scott, & Wilkinson, 1985; Chall, 1967, 1983a; Perfetti, 1985) concluded that an early and explicit emphasis on the medium (on word recognition and decoding) was more effective for reading achievement, not only on tests of word recognition and oral reading, but on silent reading comprehension as well. This research brought changes in practice. Starting about the late 1960s, a greater emphasis was placed on teaching word recognition and decoding through earlier and more intensive decoding programs. This permitted earlier learning of word recognition, which further resulted in the use of more words in the basal readers—a loosening of vocabulary control.

MEANING VOCABULARIES

The study of meaning vocabularies is one of the oldest research interests of psychologists and educational researchers, with research activities on vocabulary very common during the 1920s to the 1950s (Dale, 1956). During the 1960s and 1970s, vocabulary research seemed to go into a decline. Then, in 1980, it began to take on a new excitement (Anderson & Freebody, 1981; Johnson & Pearson, 1984).

The earliest word meaning studies were concerned with the measurement of intelligence. In these, word meaning was found to have the highest correlation with verbal intelligence (Terman, 1916; Wechsler, 1949). The correlations were so high that most psychologists who have limited time to test intelligence use the vocabulary subtest, which consists of defining words of increasing difficulty and abstractness, as a substitute for the total verbal test score.

Studies of the factors in reading comprehension have also found consistently, from the 1920s to the present, that vocabulary meanings are the strongest factor in reading comprehension (Chall & Stahl, 1985; Thorndike, 1973-1974). Indeed, word meaning scores are so highly correlated with reading comprehension scores that a reading vocabulary test (word meaning) may be substituted for a paragraph meaning test.

Research on readability has also found, over the past 60 years, that vocabulary difficulty (as measured either by word familiarity, word frequency, word length in syllables or letters, abstractness of words, or difficulty of concepts) has the highest correlation with comprehension difficulty, more than syntax and other structural and organization factors (Chall, 1958; Dale & Chall, in press; Klare, 1963).

Learning and Teaching Word Meanings

Considerable research is available, also, on the learning and teaching of meaning vocabularies. A classic study by Gray and Holmes (1938) asked a question that is as timely today as it was then — whether wide reading or a program of direct vocabulary instruction was more effective for vocabulary development. They found, for fourth graders, that direct instruction resulted in significantly larger gains on tests of vocabulary and comprehension and in greater "interest and general command of ideas and words in group discussion" (p. 56). The positive effects of direct instruction were especially evident for the children of lower ability.

Subsequent research that tried to test the superiority of one type of direct vocabulary instruction over another began to run into some difficulties. In a review of these studies, Petty, Herold, and Stoll (1968) concluded that although each of several direct teaching methods was effective for teaching vocabulary, none was significantly superior to the others. However, using either one was better than none at all. Thus, although no one direct method of teaching meaning vocabulary was superior to another, some direct vocabulary instruction was superior to no direct vocabulary instruction.

It is interesting to trace how this conclusion has been interpreted in the literature and in practice. Few took it as positive evidence for the direct teaching of vocabulary. Most seemed to interpret it rather pessimistically. Because Petty et al. found that no one method for direct teaching of vocabulary was consistently superior to another, it was interpreted to mean that there was little evidence for teaching direct vocabulary. And yet one could make a strong case, from the research, that direct teaching of vocabulary is effective, and that more than one method works. Determining the most effective way may be important for theory, but it may not be for practice. Indeed, the more ways something can be taught effectively, the better the chance of success, for it permits greater teacher flexibility and choice.

Other kinds of meaning vocabulary studies have been conducted during the past several decades. These include research on vocabulary size (Lorge & Chall, 1963), on which words to teach (Dale & O'Rourke, 1981), on how to teach them (Anderson & Freebody, 1981; Dale & O'Rourke, 1971; Johnson & Pearson, 1984; O'Rourke, 1974; Stahl, 1983; Stotsky, 1976). Essentially, the recent research on meaning vocabularies confirms the earlier, classic research — that knowledge of word meanings is of central importance in the development of reading comprehension and in assessing the readability of texts; that meaning vocabularies can be taught directly, benefitting particularly those of lower ability; and that word meanings are also learned from context, from reading or being read to.

Direct versus Indirect Teaching of Vocabulary

The research evidence on the importance of teaching word meanings both directly and from context was there almost from the start of the empirical research of the 1920s. If that is the case, why was there so little recognition of the value of direct teaching of word meanings? Why does it seem, now, to be such a new idea? And why has there been almost total preference and reliance, even today, on context for the acquisition of word meanings? This is a hard question and I am mindful that more than one hypothesis is possible.

One hypothesis that seems viable is the general preference for a "natural," or "meaningful/contextual," model of learning, particularly in the elementary school. Direct teaching has been seen as less effective and as opposed to natural, and meaningful, learning. This seems to have been the ideal view from the 1920s to the early 1970s in teaching word recognition — and was incorporated in the widely used basal reading programs. Based on the weight of the reserach evidence on direct teaching of phonics, the prevailing view seems to have moved more to direct teaching (Anderson et al., 1985; Chall, 1983a).

For word meanings, the consensus still seems to be stronger for natural, meaningful/contextual learning, although there seems to be a renewed interest in direct learning (Beck, Perfetti, & McKeown, 1982). And yet, the research evidence for teaching word meanings directly has been in existence for over 50 years. It indicated strong benefits from direct teaching, particularly for less able students. Why, then, has the research not been paid attention to, in practice, for so long?

I believe my analysis of the long resistance to a code-emphasis (phonics) (Chall, 1967, 1983a) may be of relevance here, as well, for a resistance to the direct teaching of word meanings. Although I was concerned mainly with the sight/phonic debate in teaching word recognition, the issue is relevant also to the natural, meaningful/context versus direct teaching issue for word meanings.

In *Learning to Read: The Great Debate* (Chall, 1967) I noted that the preference for sight methods in the 1920s and 1930s through the 1960s seemed to be associated with preference for progressive education. Phonics, on the other hand, was associated more with traditional schooling, drill, and hard work. Thus, early proponents of sight methods spoke of its facilitating happy learning and pleasant classrooms, whereas the alphabet and phonics methods, they said, produced drill and drudgery. Even today, proponents of language-experience and total language approaches to reading tend to view them as being in tune with natural language development, cognitive development, and with more open and free classroom environments. Direct phonics, according to these proponents, is rejected because of its structure, presumed lack of fun, and strain in learning.

A common assumption is that the more natural and the more open the procedures, the more they lead to cognitive development and to greater satisfaction with school than the more direct and structured approaches. And yet much of the evidence seems to indicate the contrary, particularly for children below Grade 3 and children from lower income families. The direct programs teach more, give children independence earlier, and the children seem to have better self-concepts than with the natural, open, meaningful programs. (Chall, 1983a, p. 41. See also Rosenshine, 1979; Stallings, 1975.)

The long and still active debate on how best to teach word recognition seems to fit the current discussions on the teaching of word meanings. The long-held preference for teaching word meanings mainly through context rather than by direct teaching, I believe, stems from the same philosophical preferences — preferences for more natural approaches to learning and teaching, and a resistance to structure and system — on the assumption that the natural is better for learning and for the learner's emotional well being.

I should like to make clear that I do not argue against context for learning word meanings. There is considerable evidence that context, as well as direct teaching, is necessary (Dale & O'Rourke, 1971). Further, the thousands of words known by children and adults in different grades and ages would indicate that direct teaching alone cannot accomplish the prodigious task. Nagy and Anderson (1984) have argued that if we only depended on learning words through a direct approach, it would not be possible to learn all the words needed.

Just as there is evidence on the effectiveness of learning word meanings directly, there is evidence for learning word meanings from context and reading. Carol Chomsky (1972) studied the effect of reading to, and the independent reading of, elementary school children on language and reading development. She found that those who were read to most and who read more for their own pleasure, were highest on a reading achievement test (vocabulary and reading comprehension) and on language development (syntax). Further, these results showed that the highest scores in syntactic development and reading achievement were made by those who read or were read to from books on higher readability levels than their own linguistic development. Thus, the reading of books with harder words and more difficult syntax contributed even more to the development of reading vocabulary, comprehension, and language.

The findings were similar when the difficulty of textbooks used was compared to SAT scores of high school students from 1945 to 1975. When students' SAT verbal scores were compared to the various measures of the difficulty of the textbooks, it was found that those students who used the harder textbooks (which contained more difficult words, sentence structure, organization, etc.) had the higher SAT verbal scores (composed of vocabulary and reading comprehension; (Chall, Conard, & Harris, 1977). Thus, the use of harder textbooks that exposed students to more difficult vocabularies, syntax, and so on, also led to higher vocabulary learnings and reading comprehension.

These findings were confirmed recently in a study of children in Grades 2 to 7 from low-income families. Ethnographic observations of classrooms revealed greater gains in reading comprehension and in word meanings for students in classrooms with more varied and challenging materials, including trade books, textbooks, and other reading materials. When reading textbooks were below the students' reading levels, less progress in vocabulary and reading comprehension was made. In addition, significant gains in word meaning were made when word meanings were taught directly (Chall & Snow, 1982).

Thus, gains in word meaning can come from reading (context) and from direct teaching. With regard to learning from context, levels of difficulty seem to be an important factor. If the books are on or below the students' level, i.e., contain few words not known to them, they will probably not gain much in word meanings. As the level of difficulty of textbooks rises in relation to students' abilities, there will probably be a greater gain in vocabulary meanings and a greater need to teach words directly.

Surveys and research studies point to the greater difficulty in acquiring a meaning vocabulary by children of low-income families, minorities, and bilinguals, particularly at Grade 4 and beyond (Chall, 1983b; Coleman, Campbell, Hobson, McPartland, Mood, Weinfeld, & York, 1966). In the study of children of low-income families just referred to, it was found that these children had vocabulary scores similar to the general population at Grades 2 and 3, but they began to decelerate in word meanings in Grade 4. The deceleration was most marked in Grades 5, 6, and 7 (Chall & Snow,

1982). Thus, although the problem of acquiring greater meaning vocabularies exists for all children, the need seems to be greater for minority children, and beginning at about Grade 4.

CONCLUSION

Every study of reading achievement points to the importance of vocabulary knowledge — both word recognition and decoding, and word meaning. Word recognition appears to be the major hurdle during the first three grades; word meaning becomes the major hurdle in Grade 4 and above.

In the teaching of both kinds of vocabularies — indirect procedures seem to have been favored. For more than 60 years major faith seems to have been placed on natural and indirect, contextual methods. And yet, considerable research evidence exists that direct teaching is highly beneficial for both. Considerable evidence also exists on the value of context and wide reading, particularly for learning word meanings. It would seem from the research and from experience that both direct teaching and contextual learning are needed. Students need to learn words through reading, and they need to learn words directly, apart from the context.

REFERENCES

Anderson, R. C., & Freebody, P. (1981). Vocabulary knowledge. In J. T. Guthrie (Ed.), *Comprehension and teaching: Research reviews* (pp. 77–117). Newark, DE: I.R.A.

Anderson, R. C., Hiebert, E. H., Scott, J. A., & Wilkinson, I. A. G. (1985). *Becoming a nation of readers: The report of the Commission on Reading*. Washington, DC: The National Institute of Education.

Beck, I. L., Perfetti, C. A., & McKeown, M. G. (1982). The effects of long-term vocabulary instruction on lexical access and reading comprehension. *Journal of Educational Psychology, 74*, 506–521.

Bettelheim, B., & Zelan, K. (1981). *On learning to read: A child's fascination with meaning*. New York: Knopf.

Chall, J. S. (1958). *Readability: An appraisal of research and application*. Columbus: Ohio University Press.

Chall, J. S. (1967). *Learning to read: The great debate*. New York: McGraw-Hill.

Chall, J. S. (1983a). *Learning to read: The great debate* (updated edition). New York: McGraw-Hill.

Chall, J. S. (1983b). *Stages of reading development*. New York: McGraw-Hill.

Chall, J. S., Conard, S., & Harris, S. (1977, June). *An analysis of textbooks in relation to declining SAT scores*. Prepared for the Advisory Panel on the Scholastic Aptitude Test Score Decline, jointly sponsored by the College Board and Educational Testing Service.

Chall, J. S., & Snow, C. (1982). *Families and literacy: The contribution of out-of-school experiences to children's acquisition of literacy*. A final report to the National Institute of Education.

Chall, J. S., & Stahl, S. A. (1985). Reading comprehension research in the past decade: Implications for educational publishing. *Book Research Quarterly, 1,* 95–102.

Chomsky, C. (1972). Stages in language development and reading exposure. *Harvard Educational Review, 42,* 1.

Coleman, J. S., Campbell, E. Q., Hobson, C. J., McPartland, J., Mood, A. M., Weinfeld, F. D., & York, R. L. (1966). *Equality of educational opportunity.* Washington, DC: U.S. Government Printing Office.

Dale, E. (1956). The problem of vocabulary in reading. *Educational Research Bulletin, XXV,* 113–23.

Dale, E., & Chall, J. S. (in press). *Readability revisited.* New York: McGraw-Hill.

Dale, E., & O'Rourke, J. (1971). *Techniques of teaching vocabulary.* Chicago: Field Enterprises.

Dale, E., & O'Rourke, J. (1981). *The living word vocabulary.* Chicago: World Book-Childcraft.

Feifel, H., & Lorge, I. (1950). Qualitative differences in the vocabulary responses of children. *Journal of Educational Psychology, 41,* 1–18.

Goodman, K., & Goodman, Y. (1979). Learning to read is natural. In L. B. Resnick & P. A. Weaver (Eds.), *Theory and practice of early reading* (Vol. 1, pp. 137–154). Hillsdale, NJ: Lawrence Erlbaum Associates.

Gray, W. S., & Holmes, E. (1938). *The development of meaning vocabulary in reading.* Chicago: Publications of the Laboratory Schools of the University of Chicago.

Johnson, D., & Pearson, P. D. (1984). *Teaching reading vocabulary.* New York: Holt, Rinehart & Winston.

Klare, G. R. (1963). *The measurement of readability.* Ames, IA: Iowa State University Press.

Lorge, I., & Chall, J. S. (1963). Estimating the size of vocabularies of children and adults: An analysis of methodological issues. *Journal of Experimental Education, 32,* 147–157.

Matthews, M. M. (1966). *Teaching to read, historically considered.* Chicago: University of Chicago Press.

Moe, A. J. (1974, April). *A comparative study of vocabulary diversity: The speaking vocabularies of selected first-grade primers, and the vocabularies of selected first-grade trade books.* A paper presented at the Annual Meeting of the American Educational Research Association, Chicago. (ED 090 520)

Nagy, W. E., & Anderson, R. C. (1984). How many words are there in printed school English? *Reading Research Quarterly, 19,* 304–330.

O'Rourke, J. P. (1974). *Toward a science of vocabulary development.* The Hague: Mouton.

Perfetti, C. A. (1985). *Reading ability.* New York: Oxford University Press.

Petty, W., Herold, C., & Stoll, E. (1968). *The state of the knowledge of the teaching of vocabulary* (Cooperative Research Project No. 3128). Champaign, IL: National Council of Teachers of English.

Rosenshine, B. (1979). Content, time, and direct instruction. In P. Peterson & H. Walberg (Eds.), *Research on teaching: Concepts, findings, and implications* (pp. 28–56). Berkeley, CA: McCutchan.

Seashore, R. H. (1947). How many words do children know? *The Packet, II,* 3–17.

Seashore, R. H., & Eckerson, L. D. (1940). The measurement of individual differences in general English vocabularies. *Journal of Educational Psychology, 31* 14–38.

Smith, F. (1979). *Reading without nonsense.* New York: Teachers College Press.

Stahl, S. A. (1983). Differential word knowledge and reading comprehension. *Journal of Reading Behavior, 15,* 33–50.

Stallings, J. (1975). Implementation and child effects of teaching practices in Follow Through classrooms. *Monographs of the Society for Research in Child Development, 40* (163 No. 7–8).

Stotsky, S. (1976). *Toward more systematic development of children's reading vocabulary in developmental reading programs in the middle to upper elementary grades.* Unpublished

Doctoral Dissertation, Harvard University, Graduate School of Education, Cambridge, MA.

Terman, L. M. (1916). *The measurement of intelligence.* Boston: Houghton-Mifflin.

Thorndike, R. L. (1973-1974). Reading as reasoning. *Reading Research Quarterly, 9,* 135-47.

Wechsler, D. (1949). *Manual for the Wechsler Intelligence Scale for Children.* New York: Psychological Corp.

Werner, H., & Kaplan, E. (1952). The acquisition of word meanings: A developmental study. *Monographs for the Society for Research in Child Development, 15,* Serial No. 1.

2

Breadth and Depth of Vocabulary Knowledge: Implications for Acquisition and Instruction

William E. Nagy
University of Illinois at Urbana Champaign

Patricia A. Herman
Kamehameha Schools, Honolulu, Hawaii

Much of the research that has been done on vocabulary acquisition and instruction has been at the microscopic level. Researchers in language acquisition often have looked at the very first words children learn, or at how children acquire words in a tightly restricted domain. Similarly, research on vocabulary instruction has often concentrated on the task of trying to determine which of several methods is the best way to teach the meanings of a relatively small set of words; very few studies have tested competing methods using more than 100 words.

Such a microscopic approach cannot by itself give an accurate picture of vocabulary acquisition, or form the basis for making decisions about the most effective approach to vocabulary instruction. Only a more global perspective on vocabulary, one that takes the overall size and nature of the task into consideration, can assess the relative importance of incidental vocabulary learning and explicit vocabulary instruction properly. Our thesis is that explicit vocabulary instruction, even at its best, cannot produce substantial gains in overall vocabulary size or in reading comprehension. Major progress toward these goals can be attained only be increasing incidental vocabulary learning.

In the first section of this chapter we consider the size of the task—that is, the number of words students would have to learn to make any substantial gains in overall vocabulary size. We feel that the size of the task is almost always either underestimated, or else simply not taken into account. Teaching the meanings of individual words may be effective for a specific reading lesson, but it cannot result in any substantial increase in overall vocabulary size.

In the short run, incidental learning looks ineffective when compared to almost any instructional approach to vocabulary growth. But with even a moderate amount of regular reading, the cumulative benefits of incidental learning far outstrip any gains in vocabulary that could be attained through instruction.

In the second section of the chapter, we consider the nature of the task, that is, the type of word knowledge that is necessary to facilitate reading comprehension. Evidence from a number of studies (cf. Pearson & Gallagher, 1983; Stahl & Fairbanks, in press, for reviews) shows that reliable gains in reading comprehension can be produced through instruction of words from a given passage only if the instruction provides multiple encounters that supply a variety of information about the instructed words. Because vocabulary instruction can supply multiple, rich encounters for only a small number of words (or a small number of encounters for a slightly larger number of words), students must have additional opportunities to encounter large numbers of words repeatedly. Only frequent and regular reading can provide this kind of exposure to words.

VOCABULARY SIZE

The most striking thing about vocabulary, viewed from a global perspective, is the immense volume of information involved.

Number of Words in the Language. It is hardly controversial that there are too many words in the language to be dealt with one at a time in any form of vocabulary instruction. Nagy and Anderson (1984) analyzed the word stock of printed school materials for Grades 3 through 9, based on the word lists and analyses in Carroll, Davies, and Richman's *Word Frequency Book* (1971). They found that printed school English contains about 88,500 distinct word families[1], with upwards of 100,000 distinct meanings. If materials for higher grade levels and for adults were included, these figures would be substantially higher.

Unknown Words Encountered in Reading. What part of this large number of words does a person actually encounter in reading? Unfortunately, there is little information available on the number of unfamiliar words stu-

---

[1] A word family consists of the set of words for which there is a transparent, predictable relationship in both form and meaning. For example, *persecute, persecution,* and *persecutor* would all be considered as constituting a single word family, along with regular inflections such as *persecuted* and *persecutions.* On the other hand, *busy* and *business* would be counted as belonging to two separate families, because the latter word has meanings that are not predictable from the meanings of the former.

dents find in text. However, additional analyses of data reported in part in Anderson and Freebody (1983) indicate that even with relatively little reading (500,000 words a year, or less than 3,000 words per school day), an average student in fifth grade would encounter almost 10,000 different words a year that he or she did not know, even by a lenient criterion of word knowledge. For a student with a smaller-than-average vocabulary, the number of unfamiliar words would be even higher.

Yearly Vocabulary Growth.   Not only do students encounter a large number of words, they seem to learn many of them, judging from estimates of growth in absolute vocabulary size that occurs during the school years.[2]

Published estimates of children's vocabulary size vary widely for several reasons (cf. Lorge & Chall, 1963). One is the estimate used for the total word stock of the language. Tests purporting to give absolute vocabulary size generally adopt a dictionary or some other corpus as representing the word stock of the language, and test children's knowledge of what is intended to be a representative sample. The estimate of the word stock of the language depends both on the size of the dictionary or corpus used, and on the definition of "word" adopted (e.g., whether pairs such as *discern* and *discernment* or *glum* and *glumly* are to be counted as one word or two). The analysis of word-relatedness in Nagy and Anderson (1984) gives a basis for recalibrating some earlier estimates of vocabulary size to correct for this latter source of difference. Recalibrations of some published estimates of average vocabulary size at Grades 3 and 12 are given in Table 2.1. In all but one case, our recalibrated figures are higher than the original estimates, because the methods used to sample English vocabulary underestimated the total word stock of English.

The recalibrated figures in Table 2.1 give good reason to believe that the average high school senior's vocabulary is in the neighborhood of 40,000 words. Such vocabulary size estimates imply a tremendous volume of word learning, around 3,000 words per year during the school years. This astounding rate of vocabulary growth by average children sets a mark against which the contribution of any program of vocabulary instruction must be measured.

---

[2]In this chapter, unless we specify otherwise, the term *vocabulary* is used to refer to *reading* vocabulary, that is, words children can read and understand. In discussions of children's absolute vocabulary size, estimates are almost always based on written tests, and hence reflect reading vocabulary. Also, we see increased reading comprehension as the primary, although not the only, goal of vocabulary instruction.

When we talk about vocabulary *growth,* we are primarily thinking of the learning of new word meanings. At the early stages of reading, increase in reading vocabulary may consist primarily of words already in oral or listening vocabulary entering a child's reading vocabulary as his or her decoding ability expands. However, after Grade 3, we believe that the vast bulk of the average student's vocabulary growth consists of the learning of new word meanings.

TABLE 2.1
Some Estimates of Vocabulary Growth and Vocabulary Size During School Years

Author	Estimated Word Stock of English	Original Figures			Recalibrated Figures*		
		Grade 3	Grade 12	Average Annual Growth	Grade 3	Grade 12	Average Annual Growth
Dupuy (1974)	12,300	2,000	7,800	644	4,016	38,457	3,827
Brandenburg (1918)	28,000	5,429	14,975	1,061	7,705	32,290	2,732
Kirkpatrick (1891, 1907)	28,000	6,620	17,600	1,220	10,004	41,517	3,501
M. K. Smith (1941)	166,247	25,500	47,000	2,389	23,672	40,789	1,902
Cuff (1930)	35,000	7,425	21,840	1,602	9,834	42,685	3,650

*Recalibrated figures for grades 3 and 12 were arrived at by the following formula:

$$R = V * (1 + ((V/N) * ((88,533/N) - 1)))$$

where R is the revised estimate of absolute vocabulary size, V is the author's original estimate of absolute vocabulary size, N the total word stock of the language as represented by the dictionary or corpus used by the original author, and 88,533 is the total number of distinct word families estimated to exist in printed school English by Nagy and Anderson (1984). This formula attempts to capture the fact that the size of the estimated word stock of English (N) becomes more of a limiting factor as the size of a person's vocabulary (V) increases.

Individual Differences.   According to figures reported by M. K. Smith (1941), for Grades 4 through 12 there is about a 6,000-word gap in vocabulary size between a child at the 25th percentile in vocabulary and a child at the 50th percentile. Although Smith's figures for absolute vocabulary size probably are inflated somewhat, it still appears that bringing a low-vocabulary student up to the median often would involve a gain of 4,000–5,000 words or more—not to mention keeping up with the yearly 3,000 word vocabulary growth of the average student.

Implications of the Size of the Task

No matter how one measures the task, then, it is extremely large; most children encounter new words by the tens of thousands per year and learn thousands of them. Given this yardstick, what is the role of vocabulary instruction in children's vocabulary growth? Surveys of classrooms (Durkin, 1979; Roser & Juel, 1982) reveal that very little explicit vocabulary instruction occurs. The number of words covered in such instruction is at best a few hundred a year. Thus, it is evident that most children must be acquiring the vast bulk of their vocabulary knowledge apart from instruction specifically devoted to vocabulary learning. It also follows that children who acquire a larger than average vocabulary—who could easily be learning 1,000 or more words per year over and above those learned by the average student—are not doing so simply through better vocabulary lessons.

Should one take this as an indication of the sorry state of current vocabulary instruction in our schools and call for more time spent teaching words? There is no doubt room for improvement in the area of vocabulary instruction; but the size of the task is such that just teaching more words cannot be seen as the answer. With very few exceptions (cf. Draper & Moeller, 1971), even extremely ambitious vocabulary programs do not cover more than a few hundred words per year (e.g., Beck, Perfetti, & McKeown, 1982). Although there are good reasons for teaching children the meanings of individual words, it is important to recognize the limitations of such instruction. Teaching children specific words will not in itself contribute substantially to the overall size of their vocabulary. Even an ambitious and systematic approach to vocabulary will not cover enough words to bring a low-vocabulary student up to average.

Promoting Large-Scale Vocabulary Growth

Given the size of the task, it is clear that teaching individual word meanings cannot in itself produce large-scale vocabulary growth in school children, or make up for the deficiencies of students with inadequate vocabularies. However, this fact should not lead to a fatalistic or laissez-faire attitude about vocabulary. On the contrary, the size of average annual vocabulary growth shows that most children are capable of learning new words rapidly and effectively. Therefore, it is very important to determine *where* and *how* children are learning so many words, and to determine how maximum use can be made of all these avenues of vocabulary acquisition. It is also important to find out why some children fail to utilize them effectively.

Learning Word Meanings From Context

If only a few hundred of the 3,000 words the average child learns in a year are learned in instruction specifically aimed at vocabulary, where are all the other words learned? A number of sources are possible: The speech of parents and peers, classroom lectures and discussion, school reading, free reading, and television.

Many believe that incidental learning of words from context while reading is, or at least can be, the major mode of vocabulary growth once children have really begun to read (cf. Gray & Holmes, 1938; Thomas & Robinson, 1972). This is our position as well. It is not, however, held universally. There are a number of grounds on which one can question the effectiveness of learning from written context as an avenue of vocabulary growth.

For the most part, arguments for learning from context have been largely "default" arguments (Jenkins & Dixon, 1983). That is, learning from context is assumed to be effective because nobody can figure out where else children could be learning all those words.

Even if one accepts the default argument for learning from context, this does not establish that learning from written context is an effective means of vocabulary acquisition; much of the incidental word learning that makes up the bulk of children's vocabulary growth might be from oral context.

Learning word meanings from oral context is obviously a major mode of vocabulary acquisition, especially in the preschool years. Many, if not most, of the thousands of words that children learn before they enter school are learned without any explicit definition or explanation. However, there is good reason to believe that written context will not be as helpful as oral context in illuminating the meanings of unfamiliar words. When a child learns a word from oral context, there is a rich extralinguistic context — in the easiest case, the object named might be physically present. There are clues from intonation and gesture that can make the context richer. In addition, the speaker will almost always have a sensitivity to gaps in the listener's knowledge that a writer could not. Moreover, the listener can usually ask questions if something isn't understood. Written context will, therefore, generally not be as rich or helpful as oral context in providing information about the meanings of new words.

In fact, some studies have found written context very ineffective at providing information about the meanings of new words (Baldwin & Schatz, 1984;

Sachs, 1943). Written contexts usually supply only limited information about the meaning of unfamiliar words, and are sometimes even misleading (Beck, McKeown, & McCaslin, 1983; Deighton, 1959). Furthermore, experimental studies have often found that inferring meanings from context is less effective than more intensive or explicit forms of instruction (e.g., Margosein, Pascarella, & Pflaum, 1982; Pressley, Levin, & Delaney, 1982); in instruction, a combination of context and definitions is more effective than context alone (Stahl & Fairbanks, in press).

Such results pose a problem for those of us who would like to believe that inferring meanings from written context is an effective means of learning new words. We believe that the discrepancy can be resolved by specifying more precisely how incidental learning of word meanings from written context takes place.

Some recent studies (Herman, Anderson, Pearson, & Nagy, 1985; Nagy, Herman, & Anderson, 1985a, b) have attempted to assess the volume of incidental word learning from context under as natural conditions as possible. Subjects were asked to read silently, without any information about the nature of the experiment. Texts were taken from school materials at the grade level of the subjects and represented narratives and expositions. Word knowledge was assessed after reading (in one study, a week later) without the text present. Target words were real words, selected by teachers as being the most difficult words in the text.

In most learning-from-context experiments, prior knowledge of the target words is controlled for by using either nonsense words or real words for which it can be demonstrated or assumed that subjects have no prior knowledge. In the studies by Herman et al. (1985) and by Nagy et al. (1985a, b), on the other hand, it was assumed that subjects would have at least partial prior knowledge of some of the target words. Degree of prior knowledge was controlled for statistically through pretesting and control groups.

A basic presupposition of these studies was that learning word meanings from context proceeds in small increments. Any single encounter with a word in context is likely to provide only a small gain in knowledge of that word (Deighton, 1959). If one starts with words about which nothing is known, a single encounter in context is not likely to produce a measurable degree of word knowledge, especially if the test of word knowledge used requires a fairly complete knowledge of the meanings of the words tested. This, it is argued, accounts for the failure of some experiments to find a significant amount of learning from context.

Using real words from grade-level text insures that for any given student, there will be target words at various points along a continuum of word knowledge. Even a single encounter with a word in context should move most of these words a little bit higher on the scale of knowledge. For any given criterion of word knowledge, it is likely that some words not previously known to that criterion will be known to that criterion after reading.

The results of the studies by Herman et al. (1985) and by Nagy et al. (1985a, b) indicate that reading grade-level texts does produce a small but statistically reliable increase in word knowledge. This effect was found in all grades tested (3, 5, 7, and 8). Although different texts produced differing amounts of learning from context, there was no indication that the younger or less able readers were not able to learn new word meanings through reading.

The absolute amount of learning found was small; the chance of learning a word to any given criterion from one exposure in text is somewhere around 1 in 20. This low figure shows why learning from natural context appears ineffective when compared to any type of instruction on word meanings.

However, learning from context must be evaluated in terms of its long-term effectiveness. The long-term effectiveness of learning from written context depends on how many unfamiliar words are encountered over a period of time. If students were to spend 25 minutes a day reading at a rate of 200 words per minute for 200 days out of a year, they would read a million words of text annually. According to our estimates, with this amount of reading, children will encounter between 15,000 and 30,000 unfamiliar words. If 1 in 20 of these words is learned, the yearly gain in vocabulary will be between 750 and 1,500 words, or between a quarter and a half of the average child's annual vocabulary growth.

Such a gain is substantial, considering the proportion of yearly vocabulary growth that is covered, and the fact that it would be extremely difficult, if not impossible, for any word-by-word approach to vocabulary instruction to cover the same number of words in the same amount of time. The amount of reading required — 25 minutes per school day — may involve more reading than many students actually do, but hardly could be called excessive.

Incidental learning of word meanings from written context may therefore account for a large proportion of the annual vocabulary growth of those students who do read at all regularly. A period of sustained silent reading could lead to substantial yearly gains in vocabulary, probably much larger than could be achieved by spending the same amount of time on instruction specifically devoted to vocabulary.

Given the size of the task — the number of words children should be learning in a year — an effective approach to vocabulary development has to take advantage of all avenues of word learning. Because the bulk of children's vocabulary growth occurs incidentally, that is, outside of situations specifically devoted to word learning, the single most important goal of vocabulary instruction should be to increase the amount of incidental word learning by students. There are two complementary approaches to increasing incidental word learning: First, increasing children's ability to profit from potential word-learning situations outside of vocabulary instruction, and second, increasing children's opportunities to learn.

There are a number of ways in which children's ability to learn words independently might be increased. Reasonable arguments can be made for teaching affixes, for the use of context clues, and for finding ways of increasing children's motivation to learn new words. All of these are undoubtedly of some value, but we are not aware of any published research demonstrating a successful method for making students into better independent word learners. However, it is clear how children's opportunity to learn words independently can be increased: By increasing the amount of time they spend reading. Incidental learning of words during reading may be the easiest and single most powerful means of promoting large-scale vocabulary growth.

THE NATURE OF THE TASK

So far we have presented evidence that the size of the vocabulary-learning task is larger than is often recognized. The large number of words to be learned shows the limitations of any form of vocabulary instruction taking words one at a time, and shows the need for maximizing students' abilities and opportunities for learning words on their own. Now we want to consider the *nature* of the task — what kind of word knowledge one hopes to produce in students, and how different levels of word knowledge affect comprehension.

Vocabulary Knowledge and Reading Comprehension

Educators and researchers have long known that a strong correlational relationship exists between vocabulary knowledge and reading comprehension: Children who know more words understand text better (Anderson & Freebody, 1981; Davis, 1944, 1968; Thurstone, 1946).

This relationship is the motivation for what is done in vocabulary instruction. There are, of course, other reasons for teaching words — increasing students' speaking or writing vocabularies, improving scores on standardized tests, or teaching specific concepts in content areas. Most of the time, however, words are taught to enable students to understand what they read. Even if the words are taught for another purpose, the instruction would be suspect if it did not enable students to understand sentences containing the instructed words. An appropriate measure of the effectiveness of most vocabulary instruction, then, is its effectiveness in increasing reading comprehension.

Two Hypotheses About the Relationship of Vocabulary Knowledge and Reading Comprehension. The strong correlational relationship between vocabulary knowledge and reading comprehension would seem to imply that there is a direct causal relationship between the two. The simplest model of this relationship, labeled the *instrumentalist hypothesis* by Anderson and Freebody (1983) is that word knowledge enables reading comprehension: Knowing the meanings of the words in a text is the necessary and sufficient condition for understanding that text. This hypothesis predicts that teaching words should increase reading comprehension automatically.

This is not the case, however. Surveys of attempts to increase reading comprehension through vocabulary instruction (Pearson & Gallagher, 1983; Stahl & Fairbanks, in press) reveal that different approaches to vocabulary instruction differ widely in the extent to which they lead to an increase in the comprehension of texts containing the instructed words. Stahl and Fairbanks report that "methods which provided only definitional information about each to-be-learned word did not produce a significant effect on comprehension, nor did methods which gave only one or two exposures to meaningful information about each word." Pearson and Gallagher found that studies that were successful in increasing passage comprehension through pre-teaching vocabulary were the exception rather than the rule.

Where does the instrumentalist hypothesis break down? In several studies (e.g., Bransford & Johnson, 1972; Dooling & Lachman, 1971) texts were constructed containing only familiar words, but were still incomprehensible without additional information. Such texts illustrate the role of something beyond vocabulary knowledge in reading comprehension.

At least some of the correlation between vocabulary knowledge and reading comprehension is due to the relationship each of these has with a third construct, background knowledge. Vocabulary knowledge — knowledge about word meanings — is both a subset of, and highly correlated with, general knowledge; a person who knows more words knows more about the world in general. Knowledge of the subject matter of a text plays an important role in the comprehension of that text, above and beyond the effects of knowing the specific words. This account of the relationship between vocabulary size and reading comprehension has been labeled the *knowledge hypothesis* by Anderson and Freebody (1983).

The knowledge hypothesis is based on a schema-theoretic view of reading comprehension, which posits that knowledge does not consist simply of an unstructured set of individual facts, but rather of organized, interrelated structures or schemata. Knowing where a piece of information fits in is an indispensable part of understanding it. Determining what a word contributes to the overall meaning of a text often depends on information that is not specifically included in the definition of the word — information beyond or between the meanings of individual words. A careful look at even a good dictionary makes it clear how inadequate the information in a definition can be for the task of comprehending text. Consider the following hypothetical example: Suppose that there is a concerned parent worried that his or her child might become prematurely sexually enlightened by reading explicit biological definitions in the school dictionary. Here are some of the relevant definitions, taken from *The American Heritage School Dictionary* (1977):

intercourse: the act of mating, as between male and female mammals

mate: to pair or cause to pair (a male and a female animal) and allow them to breed

breed: 1. to produce or reproduce by giving birth, hatching, etc.; produce
2. to mate so as to produce offspring

reproduce: to generate or give rise to (offspring), as a living thing.

One would search in vain for any practical information on reproduction in this dictionary. These definitions almost seem to be written in a secret code, accessible only to those with the inside knowledge. In some sense they are real-life analogues of the incomprehensible texts used by Bransford and Johnson (1972) or Dooling and Lachman (1971).

Is this just a case of lexigraphic Puritanism? Probably not. This example was chosen because for these particular words adults are very aware that they possess a schema, an organized body of knowledge, not possessed by some children. Hence, it is relatively easy for an adult to see what information is lacking in the definitions. In the case of other definitions, it is simply more difficult for adults to become aware of the gaps in children's knowledge. If one could see other definitions from the perspective of a child missing crucial bits of knowledge, many other equally uninformative definitions would be found.

Is this a failure of the dictionary, then? Only in the sense that every dictionary fails to be an encyclopedia. A dictionary can, and probably should, define all the terms found in a child's content area textbooks; but it would be unrealistic to expect the dictionary to contain all the information in those texts. Defintions simply cannot include all the information about a word or concept that is necessary for the comprehension of text.

The inherent limitation on definitions is one of the reasons why vocabulary instruction often fails to increase reading comprehension. Such instruction often is based on learning definitions, and in fact, often on very abbreviated definitions or synonyms.

Knowledge-Based Approaches to Vocabulary Instruction.   Some vocabulary instruction, however, does increase reading comprehension. Support for the knowledge hypothesis is found in the fact that types of instruction that do increase reading comprehension seem to represent a knowledge-based approach to vocabulary (cf. Pearson & Gallagher, 1983). For example, Swaby (1977) found that instruction emphasizing where a new concept fits into prior knowledge was more effective than an approach based on definitions. Similarly, Kameenui, Carnine, and Freschi (1982) found that a technique integrating word meanings with story context was superior to definition drill. The intensive vocabulary programs of Beck and her colleagues (Beck, Perfetti, & McKeown, 1982; McKeown, Beck, Omanson, & Perfetti, 1983), which succeeded in increasing comprehension of texts containing instructed words, incorporated instructional techniques aimed at developing both a network of semantic relationships among instructed words, and ties between instructed words and prior knowledge.

If vocabulary instruction has the goal of improving reading comprehension, instruction must be knowledge-based. Word learning cannot be equated with memorizing synonyms or short definitions. Rather, words must be treated as labels for concepts that are embedded in larger schemata. Instruction must aim at establishing rich ties between new words and prior knowledge and must present new words and concepts in the context of larger domains of knowledge. This is hardly news to some people; however, it is important to emphasize that such an approach to vocabulary is not just a better way to teach words, but apparently a necessary condition for improving reading comprehension.

The Difficulty of Producing Overall Gains in Reading Comprehension Through Vocabulary Instruction.   Some types of vocabulary instruction have been shown to increase reading comprehension for passages containing the instructed words, although much of current practice does not seem to fall into this category of instruction. But can vocabulary instruction produce overall gains in comprehension, that is, for passages that have not been targeted specifically for instruction?

Stahl and Fairbanks (in press) found that vocabulary instruction did in fact produce significant, although small, gains in general reading comprehension. We find it surprising, not that the gain is small, but that it occurs at all. The number of words in print is so great that even an extensive program of vocabulary instruction is unlikely to cover more than a minute percentage of the words in a text selected at random. The type of knowledge-based vocabulary teaching that is most effective at increasing reading comprehension is usually relatively time-consuming, and hence covers that much fewer words. This adds all the more force to the arguments made early about the limited number of words that can be covered in a program of vocabulary instruction.

Stahl and Fairbanks hypothesize that the general increase in reading comprehension produced by vocabulary instruction may be the result, not of the words specifically covered in the instruction, but an increased incidental learning that the instruction may also produce. That is, vocabulary instruction might lead to a greater general interest in words, which might lead to more learning of non-instructed words, and perhaps more skill at learning new words from context (cf. Beck, Perfetti, & McKeown, 1982).

It is highly unlikely that teaching individual word meanings could ever produce more than a very slight increase in general reading comprehension. Overall improvement in reading comprehension requires improvement in skills and strategies. In fact, explicit training in comprehension strategies generally has produced measurable gains in comprehension (Pearson & Gallagher, 1983).

Reading and Reading Comprehension.   Although hard experimental evidence is not at hand, one can make a well-reasoned argument that reading itself can be an effective way of increasing reading comprehension. First, as we have argued already, wide reading seems to be an effective way of producing truly large-scale vocabulary growth. Furthermore, there is reason to believe that the type of word knowledge gained through wide reading would be the type that is effective at facilitating comprehension,. Wide reading will lead to multiple encounters with words in a variety of meaningful contexts. To the extent that the rest of the text is comprehensible, these encounters will help the reader establish ties between the new word and prior knowledge. Pearson and Gallagher (1983), in reviewing the effects of preteaching vocabulary on passage comprehension, conclude that knowledge acquired gradually over time in whatever manner appears more helpful to comprehension than knowledge acquired in a school-like context for the purpose of aiding specific passage comprehension (p. 328). This description certainly fits the type of knowledge gained through wide reading.

Increased vocabulary knowledge is not the only benefit of wide reading that might increase comprehension. Reading will also produce gains in general knowledge, which in turn enhances comprehension. Crafton (1980, cited in Pearson & Gallagher, 1983) found that reading one article on a topic strongly improved comprehension of a second article on the same topic. In addition, practice in reading would lead to improvement or automatization of a wide range of reading skills that contribute to comprehension.

Improving reading comprehension is certainly an important instructional goal. However, vocabulary instruction as such is of limited usefulness in this regard. Teaching the meanings of individual words appears to be an efficient means of increasing comprehension only with specific passages and with a relatively small number of words. To produce general gains in comprehension, the most profitable use of instructional time would appear to be a focus on comprehension skills and strategies. Time spent simply reading will also increase comprehension through the accumulation of background knowledge and practice in various reading subskills.

The Value of "Superficial" Vocabulary Instruction.   Beck has suggested (personal communication, November 30, 1984) that although a strong case can be made for rich, knowledge-based vocabulary instruction, one should not underestimate the possible benefits of less intensive instruction, even definitional methods that often have been shown not to increase reading comprehension directly. A number of studies have shown that the level of word knowledge required to improve reading comprehension can only be gained by multiple exposures to a word providing a variety of information about that word. Learning definitions alone does not produce this level of word knowledge and, therefore, does not enhance reading comprehension. However, just as we have already argued in the case of learning from written context, one should not underestimate the value of any meaningful encounter with a word, even if the information gained from that one encounter is relatively small.

A single encounter with a word in a definitional approach to vocabulary will not produce very deep word knowledge; but it is very likely to provide more information than a reader's initial encounter with that word in context, which in fact, is likely to be rather uninformative, and at worst, possibly misleading (Baldwin & Schatz, 1984; Beck, McKeown, & McCaslin, 1983). This initial definitional encounter may provide a good foundation for learning from additional exposures to the word in context (cf. Jenkins, Stein, & Wysocki, 1984).

This line of reasoning suggests that less intensive methods of vocabulary instruction (e.g., teaching definitions) might be profitable as one component of a comprehensive approach to vocabulary, even though such methods by themselves cannot reliably increase reading comprehension. Less intensive methods would allow a larger number of words to be covered. However, the value of such methods depends on later multiple exposures to the instructed words in meaningful context. Therefore, such an approach to vocabulary would still require a large volume of reading to produce the depth of word knowledge sufficient to increase subsequent reading comprehension.

CONCLUSION

The purpose of this chapter has been to explore the consequences of taking a more global perspective on vocabulary. Only by considering the overall size and nature of the task facing vocabulary learners can one rightly assess the relative contributions of explicit instruction and incidental learning.

The number of words to be learned is simply too large to be covered by instruction specifically aimed at teaching the meanings of individual words; only a small fraction of the words that must be learned could be covered. Furthermore, the rapid rate of vocabulary growth experienced by most children shows that explicit vocabulary instruction even at its best could account for only a small proportion of the words learned by the average child in a year.

For many children, the speech of parents and peers may be the single most significant source of vocabulary growth. However, this source is not under a teacher's control. However, it is within the teacher's power to promote regular reading, which can lead to greater vocabulary gains than any program of explicit instruction.

Many types of vocabulary instruction have resulted in reliable gains in reading comprehension. Vocabulary instruction that does improve comprehension generally has some of the following characteristics: multiple exposures to instructed words, exposure to words in meaningful contexts, rich or varied information about each word, the establishment of ties between instructed words and students' own experience and prior knowledge, and an active role by students in the word-learning process. However, such programs often are very expensive in terms of time spent per word taught; this reduces further the number of words that can be covered in instruction.

There are other ways to spend the large amount of time that would be required for extensive word-by-word vocabulary instruction (e.g., free reading, learning comprehension strategies) which might lead to greater ultimate gains in vocabulary, as well as to other, possibly more valuable benefits such as increased reading comprehension and general knowledge.

We do not want to overstate our case and imply that classroom time should never be devoted to teaching the meanings of new words. But reports of new, effective methods of vocabulary instruction seldom contain any warnings about their limitations. We feel that methods of vocabulary instruction can be effectively developed and implemented only if their limitations as well as their strengths are clearly understood — the most significant limitation being that no method of vocabulary instruction can cover more than a small fraction of the words that students should be learning.

The ultimate test of a comprehensive approach to vocabulary growth must be whether it results in large and long-term gains in reading vocabulary and reading comprehension. Success in these terms cannot be attained without increasing students' incidental word learning. It is important to determine what types of vocabulary instruction are effective in increasing students' ability to learn independently. Attention must be given to affixes, context clues, awareness of words and their meanings, and motivation to learn them. But any attempt to increase incidental learning substantially must include an increase in the opportunity to learn new words, and this will occur primarily through regular, sustained reading.

REFERENCES

The American Heritage school dictionary. (1977). Boston: Houghton-Mifflin.

Anderson, R. C., & Freebody, P. (1983). Reading comprehension and the assessment and acquisition of word knowledge. In B. Hutson (Ed.), Advances in reading/language research: A research annual (pp.231–256). Greenwich, CT: JAI Press.

Baldwin, R., & Schatz, E. (1984, December). *Are context clues effective with low-frequency words in naturally occurring prose?* Paper presented at the National Reading Conference, St. Petersburg Beach, FL.

Beck, I., McKeown, M., & McCaslin, E. (1983). All contexts are not created equal. *Elementary School Journal, 83,* 177–181.

Beck, I., Perfetti, C., & McKeown, M. (1982). The effects of long-term vocabulary instruction on lexical access and reading comprehension. *Journal of Educational Psychology, 74,* 506–521.

Brandenburg, G. (1918). Psychological aspects of language. *Journal of Educational Psychology, 9,* 313–332.

Bransford, J., & Johnson, M. (1972). Contextual prerequisites for understanding: Some investigations of comprehension and recall. *Journal of Verbal Learning and Verbal Behavior, 11,* 717–726.

Carroll, J., Davies, P., & Richman, B. (1971). *Word frequency book.* New York: American Heritage.

Crafton, L. (1980). *The reading process as a transactional learning experience.* Unpublished doctoral dissertation, Indiana University.

Cuff, N. (1930). Vocabulary tests. *Journal of Educational Psychology, 21,* 212–220.

Davis, F. (1944). Fundamental factors of comprehension in reading. *Pychometrika, 9,* 185–197.

Davis, F. (1968). Research in comprehension in reading. *Reading Research Quarterly, 3,* 499–545.

Deighton, L. (1959). *Vocabulary development in the classroom.* New York: Bureau of Publications, Teacher's College, Columbia University.

Dooling, D., & Lachman, R. (1971). Effects of comprehension of retention of prose. *Journal of Experimental Psychology, 88,* 216–223.

Draper, A., & Moeller, G. (1971). We think with words (therefore, to improve thinking, teach vocabulary). *Phi Delta Kappan, 52,* 482–484.

Dupuy, H. (1974). *The rationale, development and standardization of a basic word vocabulary test.* Washington, DC: U.S. Government Printing Office (DHEW Publication No. HRA 74-1334).

Durkin, D. (1979). What classroom observations reveal about reading comprehension instruction. *Reading Research Quarterly, 14,* 481–533.

Gray, W., & Holmes, E. (1938). *The development of meaning vocabularies in reading.* Chicago: The University of Chicago Press.

Herman, P., Anderson, R. C., Pearson, P. D., & Nagy, W. (1985). *Incidental acquisition of word meanings from expositions that systematically vary text features* (Tech. Rep. No. 364). Urbana: University of Illinois, Center for the Study of Reading.

Jenkins, J., & Dixon, R. (1983). Vocabulary learning. *Contemporary Educational Psychology, 8,* 237–260.

Jenkins, J., Stein, M., & Wysocki, K. (1984). Learning vocabulary through reading. *American Education Research Journal, 21,* 767–788.

Kameenui, E., Carnine, D., & Freschi, R. (1982). Effects of text construction and instructional procedures for teaching word meanings on comprehension and recall. *Reading Research Quarterly, 17,* 367–388.

Kirkpatrick, E. (1891). The number of words in an ordinary vocabulary. *Science, 18,* 107–108.

Kirkpatrick, E. (1907). Vocabulary test. *Popular Science Monthly, 70,* 157–164.

Lorge, I., & Chall, J. (1963). Estimating the size of vocabularies of children and adults: An analysis of methodological issues. *The Journal of Experimental Education, 32,* 147–157.

Margosein, C. M., Pascarella, E. T., & Pflaum, S. W. (1982, April). *The effects of instruction using semantic mapping on vocabulary and comprehension.* Paper presented at annual meeting, American Educational Research Association, New York.

McKeown, M., Beck, I., Omanson, R., & Perfetti, C. (1983). The effects of long-term vocabulary instruction on reading comprehension: A replication. *Journal of Reading Behavior, 15,* 3–18.

Nagy, W., & Anderson, R. (1984). The number of words in printed school English. *Reading Research Quarterly, 19,* 304–330.

Nagy, W., Herman, P., & Anderson, R. (1985a). Learning words from context. *Reading Research Quarterly, 20,* 233–253.

Nagy, W., Herman, P., & Anderson, R. C. (1985b). *Learning word meanings from context: How broadly generalizable?* (Tech. Rep. No. 347). Urbana: University of Illinois, Center for the Study of Reading.

Pearson, P., & Gallagher, M. (1983). The instruction of reading comprehension. *Contemporary Educational Psychology, 8,* 317–344.

Pressley, M., Levin, J., & Delaney, H. (1982). The mnemonic keyword method. *Review of Educational Research, 52,* 61–91.

Roser, N., & Juel, C. (1982). Effects of vocabulary instruction on reading comprehension. In J. Niles & L. Harris (Eds.), *New inquiries in reading research and instruction.* Thirty-first Yearbook of the National Reading Conference (pp. 110–118).

Sachs, H. (1943). The reading method of acquiring vocabulary. *Journal of Educational Research, 36,* 457–464.

Smith, M. (1941). Measurement of the size of general English vocabulary through the elementary grades and high school. *Genetic Psychology Monographs, 24,* 311–345.

Stahl, S., & Fairbanks, M. (in press). The effects of vocabulary instruction: A model-based meta-analysis. *Review of Educational Research.*

Swaby, B. (1977). The effects of advance organizers and vocabulary introduction on the reading comprehension of sixth grade students. *Dissertation Abstracts International, 39,* A115. (University Microfilms No. 78-09, 754).

Thomas, E., & Robinson, H. (1972). *Improving reading in every class.* Boston: Allyn & Bacon.

Thurstone, L. (1946). A note on a reanalysis of Davis' reading tests. *Psychometrika, 11,* 185–188.

3 Vocabulary Testing and Vocabulary Instruction

Mary E. Curtis
Harvard University

Students' knowledge of word meanings is widely agreed upon as a significant factor in their success in comprehension (e.g., Anderson & Freebody, 1981; Carroll, 1971; Davis, 1968; Thorndike, 1974). In spite of the importance assigned to vocabulary knowledge, however, the value of tests designed to measure knowledge of word meanings often has been questioned. In particular, concerns have been raised about the way that vocabulary tests assess word knowledge (e.g., Anderson & Freebody, 1981), the nature of the word knowledge that the tests assess (e.g., Cronbach, 1942), and the reasons why vocabulary measures are so predictive of comprehension performance (e.g., Anderson & Freebody, 1981; Farr, 1969; Thorndike, 1974).

My goal in this chapter is to examine these concerns about vocabulary tests and the value that vocabulary testing has for instruction. In addition to research that analyzes vocabulary tests, I discuss research that focuses on the word knowledge of the students to whom we give these tests. It is my belief that through this kind of approach we may be able to better understand what vocabulary tests tell us about students' knowledge of word meanings and what kinds of vocabulary instruction can improve comprehension.

The initial focus of the chapter is on what standardized multiple-choice reading vocabulary tests measure. Two aspects of the tests are addressed: (a) the nature of the words contained on the tests, and (b) the nature of the knowledge about word meanings that the tests assess. Following this, two issues concerning the relationship between vocabulary testing and instruction are discussed: (a) the diagnostic value of vocabulary tests, and (b) the implications of research on vocabulary testing for instruction that seeks to increase students' knowledge of word meanings.

WHAT DO VOCABULARY TESTS MEASURE?

Because tests are only samples of what students know and can do, the decision about which kinds of items to include on a test is a critical one. From the perspective of test construction, item selection is guided by how difficult the items are and how well the items differentiate among those who take the test (e.g., see Green, 1981). But, from the perspective of test score interpretation, test items must also be representative of a universe of knowledge and/or skill that the test user considers to be important for the test taker to have. Thus, in addressing the question of what vocabulary tests measure, we can begin by examining the universe of words that vocabulary tests sample.

The Nature of the Words on Vocabulary Tests

Various approaches have been used to describe the universe of words represented by the items on vocabulary tests. For example, Dolch and Leeds (1953) examined the relationship between the words on tests and those contained in a dictionary. They did this by comparing the percentages of various parts of speech represented by the words on five vocabulary tests with the percentages contained in a sample of words selected from a dictionary. Dolch and Leeds found fairly close agreement between the tests and their dictionary sample, suggesting that the tests were representative of all of the words contained in a dictionary, at least with regard to form class.

As Lorge and Chall (1963) pointed out, however, several problems can arise in using a "dictionary-sampling" method. Dictionaries differ in the way that they define what a word is, and in the number of words that they contain. Of more significance, however, is the fact that dictionaries can tell us very little about the difficulty of the meanings of the words contained within them.

To address the issue of word difficulty, another approach has been used to examine vocabulary tests, one based on the frequency with which words appear in print (Lorge & Chall, 1963). It has long been assumed that the more frequently a word appears in print, the more likely it is that the word's meaning will be known (e.g., Gates, Bond, & Russell, 1938; Kibby, 1977; Kirkpatrick & Cureton, 1949). Thus, in order to better describe the difficulty of the universe of words of which vocabulary tests are samples, the printed frequencies of the words on tests have been examined.

Using this method, Wesman and Seashore (1949) compared printed frequency counts for the words contained on several vocabulary tests. Their conclusion was that vocabulary tests differed greatly in the way they sampled from the entire range of frequency in print. Whereas some tests were found to include a larger number of low-frequency words than high-frequency words (e.g., the vocabulary sections from intelligence tests), the opposite pattern was found with other tests (e.g., the vocabulary section from a reading test).

Before discussing the implications of Wesman and Seashore's finding, it is important to note that printed frequencies also have been used to estimate the size of the universe of which vocabulary tests are samples. For example, Nagy and Anderson (1984) analyzed a random sample of 7,260 words selected from the 86,741 listed in *The American Heritage Word Frequency Book* (Carroll, Davies, & Richman, 1971). Based on a weighted analysis of the word frequencies in their sample, Nagy and Anderson suggested that there may be as many as 600,000 graphically distinct word types in printed English, about 88,500 of which are morphologically distinct (i.e., knowing the meaning of one word would not be of much help in figuring out the meaning of another). Furthermore, after looking at the way in which the printed frequencies of their sample were distributed, Nagy and Anderson concluded that about one half of the words in the required and recommended texts for students in Grades 3 through 9 occur only one time or less in a billion words of running text!

Thus, analysis of printed frequencies is not only a way to describe the nature of a vocabulary test (i.e., a sample), but it is also a way to estimate the number of words that appear in print (i.e., the universe of which a test is a sample). In order to better understand what vocabulary tests measure, we can examine the relationship between the two.

Table 3.1 illustrates one way to make this comparison. In column 1, a range of frequencies with which words can appear in print is shown, from one time in a thousand words of running text (e.g., the word "object" occurs about this frequently), all the way down to only once in a million words of

TABLE 3.1
Distribution of Words by Printed Frequencies

Frequency of Occurrence Per Million Words of Text	Estimated Grade Level	Percentage Of Words At or Above Frequency In School Texts	Percentage At or Above Frequency On Grade 6 Tests		Percentage At or Above Frequency on Grade 8 Tests	
			G-M	ITBS	G-M	ITBS
100.00	2nd	0%	0%	2%	0%	0%
30.00	3rd	0%	9%	14%	2%	0%
10.00	4th	1%	24%	36%	13%	16%
3.00	6th	2%	60%	60%	38%	41%
1.00	—	4%	71%	83%	62%	64%

Note: Column 2 is based on recommendations made by Johnson, Moe, and Baumann (1983). Column 3 is based on estimates made by Nagy and Anderson (1984). G-M = Gates-MacGinitie Reading Tests (1978), Level D (Form 1) and Level E (Form 1). ITBS = Iowa Tests of Basic Skills (1978), Level 12 (Form 7) and Level 14 (Form 7).

text (e.g., the word "flaw"). To provide a context for this range in frequencies, column 2 lists the grade levels usually associated with the points along the range. Column 3 is based on Nagy and Anderson's estimates. It contains the approximate percentage of all distinct word types (in Grades 3 through 9 texts) that occur at or above each of the frequency levels listed.

In order to compare the frequencies of words in school texts with the words assessed on vocabulary tests, the printed frequencies for items on two standardized reading vocabulary tests (the *Gates-MacGinitie Reading Tests* and the *Iowa Tests of Basic Skills*), at two grade levels (sixth and eighth), were checked. To simplify the analysis, frequencies were recorded only for the stem words (or words to be defined) as distinct word types in the Carroll, Davies, and Richman (1971) corpus. The results are shown in columns 4–7 of Table 3.1.

What can we conclude about what vocabulary tests measure from the information in this table? In agreement with Wesman and Seashore's (1949) results, it seems that the majority of words on these reading vocabulary tests are words that occur frequently in print. That is, about 75% of the words on the sixth-grade tests, and about 60% of the words on the eighth-grade tests, occur at least once in a million words of running text. According to Nagy and Anderson's estimates, only about 6,700 morphologically distinct words, and 24,000 graphically distinct words, occur this frequently in school English. Supporting the conclusion that vocabulary tests are samples of frequently occurring words is the fact that 80% of the words on the sixth-grade tests, and 50% on the eighth-grade tests, are listed among the 9,000 most frequently used words in English (Johnson, Moe, & Baumann, 1983). Thus, although there may be as many as 600,000 words in the universe of school English, reading vocabulary tests appear to be samples of only a small fraction of that universe.

This result raises some interesting possibilities for why vocabulary tests predict comprehension performance, and for how vocabulary testing can be used to inform instruction. For example, the large number of high-frequency words on these tests suggests that knowledge about the meanings of common words may account for individual differences in success in comprehension. Furthermore, although the large number of words that appear in print would make direct instruction on each word's meaning impossible (see Nagy & Anderson, 1984; Nagy & Herman, this volume), it would seem that the number of words within the universe represented by vocabulary tests could be within the reach of direct instruction.

Before we explore these possibilities however, we need to consider further the relationship between the difficulty of a word and its printed frequency. As was noted earlier, the more often a word occurs in print, the more likely it seems that students will be familiar with the word's meaning. And yet, reading vocabulary tests include a large proportion of relatively high-frequency words. To illustrate why this is the case, consider the following stem words from vocabulary items and their synonyms: (1) *last:* end (2) *box:* case (3) *store:* put away (4) *fire:* let go. All four of the stem words in these examples are words that occur very frequently in print. In fact, all four words are words that are recommended for instruction during first grade (Harris & Jacobson, 1972; Johnson, Moe, & Baumann, 1983). However, items (3) and (4) seem to be more difficult than items (1) and (2) because they require knowedge about less common meanings than do the first two items. The performance of two fifth-grade classes on these vocabulary items confirms this intuition — 90% of the students answered the first two items correctly, whereas only 25% were correct on item (3) and 4% on item (4).

This lack of a straightforward relationship between word frequency and word difficulty presents problems in using printed frequencies alone as a way to describe what vocabulary tests are measuring. Although it appears from Table 3.1 that the majority of items on vocabulary tests assess the meanings of words that occur frequently in print, we cannot assume that high-frequency words will always be easy items, because variation can occur in the "commonness" of the meanings being tested.

Dolch and Leeds (1953) attempted to take this into account by consulting a dictionary to see whether the meanings assessed by items on vocabulary tests were the most common ones listed for the words being tested. Subsequent research by Dale and O'Rourke (1981), however, allows us to take a more systematic approach.

In *The Living Word Vocabulary,* Dale and O'Rourke (1981) catalogued the grade levels at which students knew 44,000 meanings for words. As a result, we can use Dale and O'Rourke's findings to better describe what vocabulary tests measure than we were able to do by looking only at the words being tested.

To illustrate, consider again the sixth- and eighth-grade level vocabulary tests from the *Gates-MacGinitie* and the *Iowa Tests of Basic Skills.* Each item on the tests can be classified at the grade level at which the majority of students in *The Living Word Vocabulary* (at least 67%) knew the word meaning being assessed. For example, one of the items on the *Gates-MacGinitie* tests knowledge of *stray,* meaning "wander." The majority of fourth graders in *The Living Word* knew a meaning for *stray* (i.e., 75% of them understood it to mean "a lost animal"). However, it was not until sixth grade that the majority of the students in *The Living Word* (83%) understood that *stray* can also mean "wander." Thus, this item would be classified at the sixth-grade level.

The classification of all the items on the two tests in this way is summarized in Table 3.2. Occasionally, a word meaning being tested was not listed in *The Living Word* (e.g., *pace* meaning "step"). Thus, the cumulative percentage in each column does not total 100%.

TABLE 3.2
Distribution of Meanings by Grade Level

Grade Level At Which Majority Of Students Know Meaning	Percentage of Meanings At or Above Grade Level On Grade 6 Tests		Percentage of Meanings At or Above Grade Level On Grade 8 Tests	
	G-M	ITBS	G-M	ITBS
4	24%	7%	9%	0%
6	64%	55%	27%	23%
8	77%	79%	60%	64%
10	81%	86%	73%	75%
12	83%	91%	91%	84%

Note: Percentages are based on the grade levels at which at least 67% of the students in Dale and O'Rourke (1981) knew the word meanings being tested by the vocabulary items. G-M = Gates-MacGinitie Reading Tests (1978), Level D (Form 1) and Level E (Form 1). ITBS = Iowa Tests of Basic Skills (1978), Level 12 (Form 7) and Level 14 (Form 7).

As can be seen from this table, the majority of items on these standardized reading vocabulary tests appear to assess knowledge of word meanings already familiar to most students taking the tests. That is, word meanings in about 60% of the items on vocabulary tests designed for sixth graders were already known by the majority of students at or below the sixth-grade level in Dale and O'Rourke's sample; word meanings in about 62% of the items on tests designed for eighth graders were already known by most of the students at or below the eighth-grade level.

Thus, shifting our focus from analysis of words to analysis of word meanings suggests the following conclusion: A standardized reading vocabulary test is a sample of the universe of word meanings already known by most students at the grade level for which the test is intended. A question that remains, however, is the following: What is meant by knowing the meaning of a word on a test? This aspect of vocabulary testing is considered in the next section.

The Nature of Word Knowledge Assessed

In assembling *The Living Word Vocabulary*, Dale and O'Rourke (1981) used a format for testing knowledge of word meaning similar to the one used on many standardized vocabulary tests: a multiple-choice item requiring recognition of a synonym or a phrase that means nearly the same as the word being tested. As many researchers have pointed out, however, many possible routes to a correct or incorrect answer can exist with a multiple-choice format (e.g., see Anderson & Freebody, 1981; Dale, 1965; Dolch & Leeds, 1953). As a consequence, analysis of only test items themselves cannot tell us much about the extent of knowledge about words' meanings that the items require.

In order to address this aspect of what vocabulary tests measure, we need to analyze what students know about the meanings of words they correctly and incorrectly recognize on vocabulary tests.

Characterizing students' knowledge about words' meanings can be approached in many ways. One way has been to consider knowledge of a word's meaning as consisting of possible states or "stages." For example, Dale (1965) discussed four such stages:

Stage 1: "I never saw it before."
Stage 2: "I've heard of it, but I don't know what it means."
Stage 3: "I recognize it in context — it has something to do with . . ."
Stage 4: "I know it."

In order to describe what students know about the meanings of words, tasks can be used that allow distinctions to be made among these various stages. For example, to distinguish between Stage 1 and the other stages of word knowledge, students can be asked to identify which words are real words when the real words appear along with nonwords. If a word is in Stage 1, it should not be identified as a real word. To distinguish between Stage 2 and the stages beyond, students can be asked to define the meanings of words. If a word is in Stage 2, students should not be able to define it. Finally, to distinguish between Stage 3 and Stage 4 word knowledge, the kinds of definitions produced by students can be assessed. Words in Stage 3 should be defined in terms of particular contexts, whereas words in Stage 4 should be defined without tying them to particular contexts.

To establish the relationship between these stages of word knowledge and the word knowledge assessed by vocabulary tests, 28 fifth graders were asked to complete the tasks just described for a set of words selected from standardized vocabulary tests. To identify the number of words that were beyond the Stage 1 level, students were asked to place checkmarks next to all the real words on a page containing nonwords also (see Anderson & Freebody, 1981). The students checked an average of 80% of the real words, along with 10% of the nonwords.

To identify the number of words beyond the Stage 2 level, the students were asked to give definitions for the words. Using a very liberal criterion for knowing a word's meaning (i.e., credit was given even if all a student could do was repeat a word in a sentence — for example, "invent means to invent a machine"), the students knew about 70% of the words. Using a more moderate criterion (i.e., students had to at least give an example or some kind of partial explanation — for example, "invent means to make something"), the students knew about 50% of the words.

Finally, to identify the number of words beyond the Stage 3 level, a conservative criterion for knowing a word's meaning was used (i.e., a synonym like "create," or a complete explanation such as "invent means to make something for the first time," had to be given). By this criterion, the students knew only about 20% of the words.

These results were then compared with the students' performance on the words when they appeared in a multiple-choice vocabulary test format. About 50% of the items were answered correctly. Thus, it appears that to answer an item on the vocabulary test correctly, only knowledge beyond the Stage 2 level was required. In other words, exact knowledge of the word's meaning was not necessary (i.e., Stage 4 – "I know it").

The same pattern of results has been found with college students' definitions of words from vocabulary items that are answered correctly and incorrectly (Curtis, 1981). That is, incorrect test responses seem to result from little or no knowledge about the word meaning being assessed, whereas correct responses can occur with only a moderate amount of knowledge about a word's meaning.

Summary

Up to this point, I have discussed two aspects of vocabulary tests: (a) the nature of the words on the tests, and (b) the nature of the knowledge about word meaning assessed by the tests. Analyses of these aspects have suggested the following conclusions.

First, with regard to the words on the tests, the proportion of high-frequency words was much larger than the proportion of low-frequency words on all of the tests examined. Of course, this pattern is not true of all vocabulary tests (e.g., vocabulary portions of aptitude and intelligence tests are often exceptions). But, if the goal of testing is to obtain an estimate of students' knowledge about the word meanings they need to know in order to comprehend, reading vocabulary tests do seem to be representative samples. When the word meanings assessed by tests at two grade levels were analyzed, the tests appeared to be samples of the universe of word meanings already known by students at those same grade levels.

Second, analysis of the kind of word knowledge assessed by standardized reading vocabulary tests suggests that only a moderate amount of information about a word's meaning is required to answer an item correctly. In other words, it seems that the tests make apparent the difference between at least some knowledge about a word's meaning and little or no knowledge. The extent to which at least some knowledge is really complete knowledge, however, is an aspect that the tests do not seem to measure directly (Cronbach, 1942, 1943).

In the sections that follow, two concerns related to what vocabulary tests assess are addressed: (a) the diagnostic value of vocabulary testing and (b) the implications of vocabulary testing for instruction.

THE DIAGNOSTIC VALUE OF VOCABULARY TESTS

As was noted at the beginning of this chapter, the relationship between vocabulary and comprehension is a well established one. Texts that contain many words whose meanings are unknown to students are poorly comprehended (e.g., see Anderson & Freebody, 1981; Dale & Chall, 1948). In fact, the difficulty of the words in a text seems to be the best single predictor of the difficulty that a student will experience in understanding that text. Thus, word difficulty is the most potent factor in all readability measures (e.g., Chall, this volume; Klare, 1963).

Vocabulary tests provide an important index of the likelihood that students will be successful in understanding texts that require knowledge of word meanings at a particular level. One of the concerns that has been raised about their diagnostic value, however, has to do with the qualitative differences in word knowledge that are not assessed by the tests. As Cronbach (1943) pointed out, students can know the meanings of words "more or less well" (p. 528), a distinction that would seem to be important for instruction, but one not made by the items on most vocabulary tests.

The study of qualitative differences in students' knowledge about known words has a long history and has involved a variety of approaches. For example, Feifel and Lorge (1950) classified students' definitions of words into categories such as synonyms, explanations, uses, descriptions, and demonstrations. In doing so, they found a developmental progression in the responses that students gave, moving from the more concrete (e.g., use and description, demonstration) to the more abstract (e.g., synonym and explanation). Similar developmental results have been found when students are presented with multiple-choice vocabulary items in which more than one answer is correct, but answers differ qualitatively from each other (Kruglov, 1953; Russell & Saadeh, 1962).

In classifying the definitions given by students for the words on vocabulary tests, I have found a similar difference between high- and low-vocabulary scorers within the same grade level. Children and adults who are low-vocabulary scorers tend to define words in terms of the contexts in which they can occur, whereas high scorers define these same words in a more abstract, decontextualized manner. What makes this difference so interesting is that it tends to occur on those words that all the students have been able to get correct on the multiple-choice vocabulary test. For example, *surveillance* is a word that college students, whether they are high or low in vocabulary ability, usually answer correctly on a vocabulary test. When asked to define that word, however, high-vocabulary test scorers tend to give a synonym or explanation (e.g., "watch" or "keep an eye on"), whereas low-vocabulary test scorers describe a context (e.g., "surveillance is what the police do in crime situations").

This skill difference in definitions of known words maps onto Dale's (1965, Dale, O'Rourke, & Bamman, 1971) distinction between Stage 3 word knowledge ("I recognize it in context — it has something to do with . . .") and Stage 4 knowledge ("I know it"). And, even though it is a difference that is not made apparent on vocabulary tests — that is, both kinds of definitions result in getting the item correct — it is a difference that is related to vocabulary test scores. Items answered correctly by both high and low test scorers often are less well known by the low scorers.

The correlation between student's Stage 3 and Stage 4 word knowledge may have played a role in the longevity of traditional vocabulary tests. That is, it seems likely that a test that measured Stage 4 knowledge about word meanings would result in a similar classification of high and low scorers as found with a traditional Stage 3 measure. Moreover, it is unlikely that the correlation between a Stage 4 test and comprehension performance could exceed that attained by the traditional tests. Hence, what need would there be for an additional vocabulary test?

First, we might learn more about the role that vocabulary plays in comprehension by focusing on Stage 4 knowledge. Ease of comprehension (as reflected by reading time) and degree of understanding of what is read (as reflected by recall) have both been shown to be affected by the level of completeness of students' knowledge about familiar words in a text (Curtis, Collins, Gitomer, & Glaser, 1983). Thus, an estimate of the state of students' knowledge about familiar word meanings could be helpful in understanding comprehension difficulties that are related to incomplete knowledge about familiar words.

Second, a distinction in vocabulary testing between Stage 3 and Stage 4 knowledge about word meanings might be useful in making decisions about the content of vocabulary instruction. Because traditional vocabulary tests provide us with an estimate of a student's Stage 3 knowledge, test scores and item analyses can be used to identify the universe of word meanings that a student needs to become familiar with in order to comprehend. In addition, however, information about the state of a student's Stage 4 knowledge could be used to make decisions about word meanings that need to be more finely tuned and/or enriched. A striking illustration of the latter is this definition of desist given by a college student: "My high school teacher used to say that — cease and desist — I think it means sit down, shut up, and pay attention" (Curtis & Glaser, 1983). A Stage 4 test could identify such instances of word knowledge — that is, cases where students have sufficient knowledge to answer a traditional test item correctly (the student correctly chose *stop*) but their knowledge needs further refinement in order to better comprehend.

Thus, the possible gains from measuring how well students know the meanings of words that are familiar to them would seem to make testing in this area worthwhile. Traditional vocabulary tests are of value to us because they provide an estimate of the level of a student's familiarity with word meanings they need to know. But, a measure of the level of completeness of that knowledge would seem to have diagnostic value for improving comprehension as well (Cronbach, 1943).

THE IMPLICATIONS FOR VOCABULARY INSTRUCTION

From the analyses of vocabulary tests and students' vocabulary knowledge presented in this chapter, the implications for instruction would seem to be straightforward. In order to become better comprehenders, students need to learn more word meanings, and learn more about the word meanings that they already know. However, as the various chapters in this volume make apparent, little agreement exists about the best way to teach word meanings, or even whether it makes sense to try at all.

To some extent, this lack of agreement stems from demonstrations that vocabulary instruction does not always seem to lead to improved reading comprehension (e.g., see Jenkins, Pany, & Schreck, 1978; Tuinman & Brady, 1974). If students' comprehension is not improved after they learn new word meanings, it may be that we need to question the view that knowing the meanings of words enables comprehension (Anderson & Freebody, 1981). But, it also could be that we need to examine the effectiveness of the vocabulary instruction (see also Chall & Stahl, 1985). Improvement in students' scores on traditional vocabulary tests should be one of the outcomes of good vocabulary instruction. However, it is possible to raise students' vocabulary test scores (e.g., by teaching the kind of knowledge that the tests measure) without affecting other aspects of word knowledge that are related to, but not directly apparent from, vocabulary test performance (e.g., Stage 4 knowledge). Vocabulary instruction that has resulted in improvement in both vocabulary and comprehension performances (e.g., Beck, McKeown, & Omanson, this volume; Gray & Holmes, 1938) confirms that knowledge other than that measured by vocabulary tests must be addressed as well.

A second reason for disagreement about vocabulary instruction may be that attention has been focused on finding the best method without sufficient regard for (a) the level of word knowledge addressed, and (b) the students who are receiving the instruction. Different methods may vary in their effectiveness as a function of the stage of knowledge about the meanings of the words that are being taught. For example, a method that is effective for moving words that are in Stage 1 or Stage 2 to Stage 3 may not be as effective for moving meanings from Stage 3 to Stage 4. Furthermore, methods may vary in their effectiveness for different groups of students. For example, some students who are low-vocabulary scorers do seem able to use information in the text to learn new word meanings without any instruction in how to do so. Other individuals seem to benefit from instruction in how to use context in order to do this (see Sternberg, this volume). But, when students' comprehension skills are not very well developed, more direct instruction in the meaning of words may be the most effective approach. The use of a variety of vocabulary testing techniques could enable us to establish the methods of instruction and the stages of word knowledge that are most appropriate for each student (e.g., see Dale, O'Rourke, & Bamman, 1971).

Finally, confusion about the value of vocabulary instruction also has stemmed from the fact that an individual's knowledge about word meanings is as much a consequence as a cause of his or her ability to comprehend. Comprehension enables acquisition of vocabulary knowledge just as vocabulary knowledge enables understanding of what is read. It is this interconnectedness between vocabulary knowledge and comprehension that can make vocabulary instruction necessary, particularly for those students who do not do well on vocabulary tests. From current theory and research, we have become more aware of the impact that a reader's knowledge base can have on success in comprehension and the ability to learn from what is read (e.g., see Anderson & Pearson, 1984). Vocabulary tests are one of the means we have for measuring that knowledge. With the exception of students who have rich knowledge bases but experience difficulty in word recognition, students with low vocabulary scores are those who are missing information that can affect their comprehension and their ability to use reading as a means for acquiring new knowledge. Vocabulary testing can tell us which students need instruction in the kinds of knowledge they have been unable to acquire on their own.

CONCLUSIONS

As with any tool, the value of vocabulary tests depends on the goals of the user. This chapter has been concerned with the use of vocabulary testing for three different goals: measuring students' word knowledge, predicting students' success in comprehension, and designing vocabulary instruction.

Measurement of Word Knowledge

Reading vocabulary tests are samples of the universe of word meanings that are known by students at particular grade levels in school. Success in answering an item requires that a student have at least some accurate knowledge about the word meaning that is being assessed, although the level of completeness of the student's knowledge is not made apparent by the tests. Thus, if the goal is to obtain an estimate of the "grade appropriateness" of students' familiarity with word meanings, reading vocabulary tests appear to be valid measures. They are not valid for purposes of measuring the absolute size of students' vocabularies (Anderson & Freebody, 1981) or the precision of their knowledge about word meanings (Cronbach, 1942), although individual differences in each of these may well be correlated with vocabulary test scores (Lorge & Chall, 1963).

Prediction of Success in Comprehension

Vocabulary and comprehension test scores are highly correlated. The sources of this relationship seem to include the following. First, knowledge about the meanings of the words in a text is a powerful measure of text difficulty. Because vocabulary tests assess a student's familiarity with the meanings of words, they are also a measure of the level of text that the student will experience difficulty in comprehending. Second, ease of comprehending and degree of understanding what is read seem to be related to the completeness of knowledge that students have about familiar words in a text. Because completeness of word knowledge is related to familiarity with word meanings, vocabulary test scores can predict success in comprehending texts that contain familiar words as well. Finally, the background knowledge that a reader brings to a text has significant influence on success in comprehension. Because vocabulary tests assess a student's familiarity with word meanings, they are one index of the extent of the knowledge that students bring to a reading task.

Design of Vocabulary Instruction

Reading vocabulary tests tell us which students are likely to have the kinds of word knowledge they need in order to understand and learn from what they read. In particular, vocabulary test scores seem to distinguish between students who have little or no knowledge about the meanings of words and students who have at least some knowledge. In addition, test scores also seem to be related to how well students know the meanings of words that are familiar to them. Thus, vocabulary testing is a way of identifying those students who may not succeed in school without the benefit of some vocabulary instruction.

Vocabulary tests are also a way to obtain information about the kinds of words and kinds of word knowledge that should be the target of vocabulary instruction. For example, because the majority of items on vocabulary tests are relatively high-frequency words, instruction that focuses on words that occur frequently in print (as opposed to all of the words that a student may encounter) would seem to be the most beneficial. Furthermore, because most high-frequency words have multiple meanings, instruction should be designed so that it focuses on the word meanings that students need to know (rather than the words per se).

Current as well as classic research on reading vocabulary tests suggests that students who are familiar with the meanings of many words tend to be the same ones who have rich knowledge about the words that they know. Thus, in making decisions about methods of instruction and the kinds of word meanings to instruct, both of these factors — familiarity and completeness of word knowledge — must be considered. Students can have less complete knowledge about word meanings because of difficulty in comprehending, and abstracting from, new contexts. However, less complete knowledge of word meanings can also result from a restriction in the number of different contexts in which students encounter a word. The design and use of vocabulary tests that address aspects of word knowledge beyond familiarity should aid in our ability to make a better match between a student's word knowledge and skills, on one hand, and the kind of instructional approach and materials that will lead to the greatest vocabulary growth, on the other.

ACKNOWLEDGMENT

The work reported in this paper was supported in part by a seed grant from the Spencer Foundation and in part by the Learning Research and Development Center, with funds from the National Institute of Education.

REFERENCES

Anderson, R. C., & Freebody, P. (1981). Vocabulary knowledge. In J. T. Guthrie (Ed.), *Comprehension and teaching: Research reviews* (pp. 77–117). Newark, DE: International Reading Association.

Anderson, R. C., & Pearson, P. D. (1984). A schema-theoretic view of basic processes in reading. In P. D. Pearson (Ed.), *Handbook of reading research* (pp. 255–291). New York: Longman.

Carroll, J. B. (1971). Development of native language skills beyond the early years. In C. Reed (Ed.), *The learning of language* (pp. 97–156). New York: Appleton-Century-Crofts.

Carroll, J. B., Davies, P., & Richman, B. (1971). *The American Heritage word frequency book.* Boston: Houghton-Mifflin.

Chall, J. S., & Stahl, S. A. (1985, spring). Reading comprehension research in the past decade: Implications for educational publishing. *Book Research Quarterly,* 95–102.

Cronbach, L. J. (1942). Analysis of techniques for diagnostic vocabulary testing. *Journal of Educational Research, 36,* 206–217.

Cronbach, L. J. (1943). Measuring knowledge of precise word meaning. *Journal of Educational Research, 36,* 528–534.

Curtis, M. E. (1981). Word knowledge and verbal aptitude.

Curtis, M. E., Collins, J. M., Gitomer, D. H., & Glaser, R. (1983). *Word knowledge influences on comprehension.* Paper presented at the American Educational Research Association (ED 229 747).

Curtis, M. E., & Glaser, R. (1983). Reading theory and the assessment of reading achievement. *Journal of Educational Measurement, 20,* 133–147.

Dale, E. (1965). Vocabulary measurement: Techniques and major findings. *Elementary English, 42*, 895–901; 948.

Dale, E., & Chall, J. S. (1948). A formula for predicting readability. *Educational Research Bulletin, 27*, 11–20; 37–54.

Dale, E., & O'Rourke, J. (1981). *The living word vocabulary.* Chicago: World Book.

Dale, E., O'Rourke, J., & Bamman, H. A. (1971). *Techniques of teaching vocabulary.* Palo Alto, CA: Field Educational Publications.

Davis, F. B. (1968). Research in comprehension in reading. *Reading Research Quarterly, 3*, 499–545.

Dolch, E. W., & Leeds, D. (1953). Vocabulary tests and depth of meaning. *Journal of Educational Research, 47*, 181–189.

Farr, R. (1969). *Reading: What can be measured?* Newark, DE: International Reading Association.

Feifel, H., & Lorge, I. (1950). Qualitative differences in the vocabulary responses of children. *Journal of Educational Psychology, 41*, 1–18.

Gates, A. I., Bond, G. L., & Russell, D. H. (1938). Relative meaning and pronunciation difficulties of the Thorndike 20,000 words. *Journal of Educational Research, 32*, 161–167.

Gray, W., & Holmes, E. (1938). *The development of meaning vocabularies in reading.* Publications of Lab Schools, No. 6. Chicago: University of Chicago.

Green, B. F. (1981). A primer of testing. *American Psychologist, 36*, 1001–1011.

Harris, A. J., & Jacobson, M. D. (1972). *Basic elementary reading vocabularies.* New York: MacMillan.

Jenkins, J. R., Pany, D., & Schreck, J. (1978). *Vocabulary and reading comprehension: Instructional effects* (Tech. Rep. No. 100). Urbana: University of Illinois, Center for the Study of Reading.

Johnson, D. D., Moe, A. J., & Baumann, J. F. (1983). *The Ginn word book for teachers.* Lexington, MA: Ginn.

Kibby, M. W. (1977). A note on the relationship of word difficulty and word frequency. *Psychological Reports, 41*, 12–14.

Kirkpatrick, J. J., & Cureton, E. E. (1949). Vocabulary item difficulty and word frequency. *Journal of Applied Psychology, 33*, 347–351.

Klare, G. R. (1963). *The measurement of readability.* Ames, IA: Iowa State University Press.

Kruglov, L. P. (1953). Qualitative differences in the vocabulary choices of children as revealed in a multiple-choice test. *Journal of Educational Psychology, 44*, 229–243.

Lorge, I., & Chall, J. (1963). Estimating the size of vocabularies of children and adults: An analysis of methodological issues. *Journal of Experimental Education, 32*, 147–157.

Nagy, W. E., & Anderson, R. C. (1984). How many words are there in printed school English *Reading Research Quarterly, 19*, 304–330.

Russell, D. H., & Saadeh, I. Q. (1962). Qualitative levels in children's vocabularies. *Journal of Educational Psychology, 53*, 170–174.

Thorndike, R. L. (1974). Reading as reasoning. *Reading Research Quarterly, 9*, 135–147.

Tuinman, J. J., & Brady, M. E. (1974). How does vocabulary account for variance on reading comprehension tests? A preliminary instructional analysis. In P. Nacke (Ed.), *The twenty-third National Reading Conference Yearbook* (pp. 176–184). Clemson, SC: NRC.

Wesman, A. G., & Seashore, H. G. (1949). Frequency vs. complexity of words in verbal measurement. *Journal of Educational Psychology, 40*, 395–404.

4 Cognitive Processes in Learning Word Meanings

Marianne Elshout-Mohr
Maartje M. van Daalen-Kapteijns
Centre for Educational Research (SCO)
University of Amsterdam

Vocabulary learning is a many sided issue. Word meanings are learned in different situations, to different degrees of completeness, and with diverse learning outcomes. In this chapter we approach vocabulary learning as a central component of verbal comprehension. First, we describe why we view verbal comprehension as a skill. Then a detailed description of learning vocabulary from context is given. Our goal in these sections is to elucidate the intricate relation between vocabulary and comprehension, and to explain how vocabulary knowledge affects the cognitive processes used to acquire new word meanings. Finally we view our theory from an educational perspective, and outline a program for vocabulary instruction. This program implements the two-sided idea that promoting comprehension will facilitate growth in vocabulary knowledge, and that promoting consolidation of available vocabulary knowledge will improve skill in comprehension.

VERBAL COMPREHENSION: AN OUTLINE OF THE SKILL

Various kinds of verbal aptitude tests intercorrelate highly, representing a primary factor or primary mental ability (Thurstone, 1938). Does this mean anything? Is it psychologically relevant, or merely of interest to those concerned with the predictive validity of tests? We agree with Elshout (1978) that verbal comprehension is a psychologically meaningful concept, not just a name for a clustering of item types. According to Elshout, primary factors measure mental skills, "coherent wholes of procedural and propositional knowledge, both reflexive (verbalizable) and prereflexive in kind", skills "geared to a family of problems, bound together by the environment *and* their psychological similarity" (p. 324). Our view of verbal comprehension as a mental skill is central to the research we describe in this chapter. The remainder of this section contains an elaboration of this view.

The theory of Elshout (1976, 1978) brings about a connection between the psychometric approach to the study of intelligence and the conceptual framework of cognitive psychology. Of this theory, two assumptions (not uniquely associated with Elshout) are: (a) individual differences in test performance are only found when a test taxes some capacity that is limited; and (b) a primary factor reflects, at least in part, differences in limitations in the human information processing system. To these assumptions Elshout adds a third, one that provides the link with cognitive psychology: (c) limitations of the information processing system interact with one another. Limitations are not directly perceived by a person, nor do they directly affect performance on the tests. But, in interaction, the limitations of the information processing system create a psychologically meaningful demand. It is this demand to which a person who tackles a task reacts. A person's skill in dealing with this demand eventually determines task performance.

Intercorrelations among test scores result when tasks pose the same psychological demand. Experience and knowledge acquired in solving one member of a family of tasks transfers to other tasks of the same family. The structured coherence of the world we live in cooperates with the laws of transfer to make every individual develop a great number of separate intellectual skills (see also Ferguson, 1956). Thus, verbal comprehension is conceptualized as a skill that is geared to a family of tasks in a psychologically meaningful way.

Essential in Elshout's theory is the idea that psychological similarity finds its basis in a configuration of taxing features. According to Elshout (1978):

> the term "configuration" is chosen here to stress that, in my view, the demands put on our system by the taxing features do not stand side by side, but interact. By interacting they form, so to speak, a knot of problemacity, different for each problem type. These "knots" I have called the characteristic demands of problem types. (p. 324)

So each basic limitation of the information processing system is psychologically multifarious. Disposition of a "limited working memory," for instance, is a feature that is psychologically dependent on the kind of materials that are processed. Although a person might be expert in managing the limitations of working memory while processing symbolic information, the person could, at the same time, be a novice in managing these limitations in processing semantic information. The problems created differ in nature, and the skill required to solve these problems differs accordingly.

Elshout's analysis of various configurations of taxing features takes, as its starting point, the factors distinguished in Guilford's (1967) Structure-of-Intellect model. Verbal comprehension is represented by the factor "cognition of semantic units" (CMU). Based on this theory, we want to argue that the demand characteristic of verbal comprehension tasks results from the interaction of (a) *cognition* as the type of process; (b) the *semantic* modality of the information; and (c) the *unit* in which the relevant information is organized.

In the following section we sketch how interactions occur in concrete verbal comprehension tasks. In doing so, our aim is to come to a deeper understanding of what verbal comprehension is about. This essentially qualitative analysis provides the framework for our research into the verbal comprehension skill.

The Characteristic Demand of Verbal Comprehension

The most salient feature of verbal comprehension tasks is, in our opinion, their *units*. Our assumption is that the demand of verbal comprehension tasks centers around the difficulty, typical for units, that "invariance should be achieved and maintained despite the everchanging appearance of the world" (Elshout, 1978, p. 328). This assumption is intuitively plausible. Although difficult, it is at the same time crucial to conceive of words as meaningful entities that are somehow stable enough to resist breakdown under the stress of contextual variance in meaning. First, knowledge about a word's meaning unites what one knows about the different aspects of meaning conveyed by the word in different contexts. Second, understanding a word in a particular context is sustained by the unit of word meaning one has constructed in the past. Finally, processing the word's meaning in a new context may strengthen the unit or add new information to it.

Take, for example, the word "plain." In "plain whiskey" and "plain girl" different aspects of the meaning of this word are conveyed. Yet it is useful to represent a "plain" unit. Such a unit can help to interpret the meaning of "plain" in, for instance, "plain paper." Coming to grips with the everchanging contextual meaning of words taxes the information processing system. We consider it very plausible that a special skill is required in order to construct stable word meaning units.

In creating word meaning units a person must process *semantic* information. The typical difficulty of semantic information is its inherent ambiguity. People need specific knowledge or a specific skill to decide what a word or sentence means in a given context (see Bransford & Johnson, 1973; Schank & Abelson, 1977). The semantic difficulty is especially clear in the case of abstract concepts like "honesty" or "eschew," because no perceptual or behavioral information may exist to sustain processing the semantic information (see also Elshout-Mohr & van Daalen-Kapteijns, 1979). As a skill, verbal comprehension involves adapting to the particular features of semantic information and developing appropriate word meaning units despite the inherent ambiguity and fuzziness of the semantic world.

There is, in conceptualizing verbal comprehension as a skill, a third aspect to take into account: *cognition*. We assume that the limited capacity of working memory contributes to the difficulty of comprehension task performance. Limited capacity is problematical in general, but in a special way where word meanings are concerned. Because one is dealing with semantic information, the inherent ambiguity is likely to cause an overload. And, at the same time, the diversity of contextual meanings may do the same. The task to figure out a word's meaning from contextual information is complicated and asks for a carefully managed learning process. And, in more complex verbal learning tasks, like studying a textbook, only a small amount of mental energy is available for the processing of word meanings. Verbal comprehension as a skill involves using working memory as efficiently as possible.

The Family of Problems Demanding the Verbal Comprehension Skill

In this section we distinguish three types of tests for verbal comprehension. Our aim is to enforce our argument that verbal comprehension is a skill. Therefore, we discuss how verbal comprehension skill and performance might be related in the various test types.

The first type of verbal comprehension test we want to mention is the classical vocabulary test. These tests typically consist of a list of words, and ask a person to indicate the meaning of each word or to choose which one of a number of possible meanings is the right one. In this way the quantity and some aspects of the quality of a person's vocabulary knowledge are assessed. Verbal comprehension as a skill is called for in a special way. A person is invited to show how skillfully he or she has learned word meanings in the past. If the meaning of a particular word is not known, there is usually no way of finding it out on the spot. Thus, vocabulary tests are exceptionally well fit for predictive purposes, using past performance as a predictor of future performance.

The second type of test requires more cognitive activity to be performed by a person. We call tests of this kind skill-in-action-tasks. Typically they instruct a person to: (a) discover the meaning of an unknown word from a given context, or (b) determine the appropriate meaning of a known word in an uncommon context. Skill-in-action-tasks are usually preferred for diagnostic or instructional purposes. Curtis and Glaser (1983), for example, strongly favor vocabulary assessment that takes into account the phenomenon that word meaning knowledge is not all-or-none.

In comparison with tests that ask for sheer reproduction of knowledge, skill-in-action-tasks indicate the knowledge a person has available and the quality of that knowledge. These tasks take more time to be performed and give people more opportunity to verbalize what they are doing. That is why cognitive psychologists as well as instructional scientists prefer skill-in-action-tasks in their experiments. An additional advantage of tasks of this kind is that skill in comprehension can be assessed. A person could theoretically accumulate a vast vocabulary despite a low verbal ability, but one could never perform well on a skill-in-action-task without the necessary verbal comprehension capacity.

The third type of test we have in mind would measure a person's ability to process word meanings with minimal conscious control. An example of an item would be to instruct a reader to evaluate the logical structure of a text and then test the knowledge that is gained about new words occurring in the text. It is feasible to construct a verbal comprehension test by assembling five or six of such items. We would expect such a test to correlate substantially with current verbal comprehension measures. (Indications for the reality of this expectation can be found in Schmeck, 1983.) The indirect assessment of verbal comprehension by such a complex task might have considerable diagnostic value. We consider the degree of automaticity of verbal comprehension skill an important feature of the skill. Word meanings rarely are the explicit target of processing verbal materials. Therefore, automatic access to stored word meanings as well as encoding of new meanings without conscious control, would be all the more important.

Our qualitative analysis of verbal comprehension as a skill helps in understanding the psychological similarity of the three types of tests. Each test poses different conditions for bringing to the fore one's verbal comprehension skill. Nevertheless, the (intercorrelating) test scores represent basically one specialized subsystem of knowledge and of performance.

Understanding verbal comprehension tests in this way yields information about how to make a verbal comprehension task taxing for the cognitive system. This information is often of practical use in test-designing and in designing psychological experiments as well. Difficulty level can be gradually increased by combined or single use of means to: (a) restrict the opportunity of producing knowledge of task relevant word meaning units; (b) enhance the ambiguity of the semantic context; and (c) affect cognition by overloading the capacity of working memory.

Measures (a) and (c) resemble the general guidelines provided by Sternberg (1984). Sternberg's "two-facet theory" of intelligence states that a task taxes intelligence by being novel or by requiring automaticity. Because we want to measure verbal comprehension rather than intelligence, our guidelines can be more specific.

In the next section we describe how we proceeded to design a skill-in-action test of sufficient difficulty to investigate the cognitive processes involved in learning word meanings.

VERBAL COMPREHENSION: COGNITIVE PROCESSES IN LEARNING VOCABULARY FROM CONTEXT

What cognitive processes are required to build a new word meaning unit? How does a person profit from accumulated verbal comprehension skill? Is it possible to distinguish a "coherent whole of procedural and propositional knowledge, both reflexive (verbalizable) and prereflexive in kind" (Elshout, 1978, p. 324), in the cognitive processes of a subject who acquires a new word meaning? Can we discover how the skilled comprehender uses his or her skill to successfully meet the characteristic demand of the task?

To discuss these issues, we refer to some of our own experiments on learning word meanings from contextual information (van Daalen-Kapteijns & Elshout-Mohr, 1981; Elshout-Mohr & van Daalen-Kapteijns, 1977). In these experiments students were asked to think aloud while performing a fairly taxing verbal comprehension task. Two subgroups were selected for the experiments: one relatively high verbal group, consisting of students who scored at least 0.75 standard deviation above the mean verbal intelligence score for a pool of over 200 psychology students, and one relatively low verbal group, consisting of students who scored at least 0.75 standard deviation below the group's mean score. By following this procedure we ensured a considerable variation in the subjects' verbal comprehension skill. This was important in view of our main research question: In what respects is level of skill relevant for the actual verbal comprehension process?

Before discussing the results of the experiments, we describe the learning materials and the learning task in detail. Both were inspired by the work of Werner and Kaplan (1952). The students' task was to figure out the meaning of a new word from a series of five sentences in which the word occurred. Several of these items were presented successively.

The New Words and Word Meanings

The natural conditions for word meaning acquisition from contextual information were simulated as closely as possible. We made up a number of new words (neologisms) to go with new word meanings. An example is "kolper," which sounds like a normal Dutch word and to which we assigned the following meaning: a window that transmits little light because of something in front of it (at the outside). We assume that people have experienced the existence of such windows, as they are a common inconvenience of students' rooms in the inner city of Amsterdam. Such a conceptual entity, to which (as yet) no existing word refers, has been called a *lexical gap* or *possible lexical item* (MacNamara, 1972; Marshall, 1970). We happened to find a vivid description of this phenomenon in Traver (1958):

> Alas, boy, we have plenty of words of bitter invective and scorn for people, but none to describe [. . .] our own Judge Maitland. It seems that humility and kindness and profound intelligence are so seldom blent in one man that the world — at least the English-speaking world — has never felt compelled to coin a word to describe it. [. . .] to describe this judge of ours I have instead to make a small speech! (p. 371)

Likewise our subjects would have to make a small speech to describe the meaning of "kolper" after having figured it out from the sentences in which the word "kolper" occurred.

Among the word meanings that we used in various experiments were:

"bantel": an apparatus that is out-of-date but still works well.
"osker": a verbal remark intended to change the subject of conversation in a subtle way.
"metel": a woman who is both physically and socioeconomically in a condition to have children, but has decided not to have any.
"krinter": a temporary physical ailment that is medically not serious but causes pain and inconvenience for the one who suffers from it.

The items we used were rather complex compared to new word meanings used in the research of others (like the word "minge" from Nitsch's, 1977, experiments, which means to gang up on a person or thing). We made the items complex because we wanted the learning task to be really taxing for all our subjects. In the next section, the measures that we took to assess verbal comprehension skill are described.

The Learning Task

The new words were imbedded in sentences. For each word five sentences were successively presented. In the first sentence the superordinate was roughly indicated, as in: When you are used to a broad view it is quite depressing when you come to live in a room with one or two *kolpers* fronting a courtyard. (The new word was always underlined.) The second sentence was meant to convey a specification that discriminated the new word from others in the same category, as in: He virtually always studied in the library, as at home he had to work by artificial light all day because of those *kolpers*. In sentence 3, a second specification was suggested: During a heat wave a lot of people all of a sudden want to have *kolpers,* so the sales of sunblinds then reach a peak. In sentences 4 and 5, two counter-examples were given, as in: I was afraid the room might have *kolpers* but when I went and saw it, it turned out that plenty of sunlight came into it, and: In those houses you're stuck with *kolpers* all summer, but fortunately once the leaves have fallen off that isn't so anymore.

The subject's task was to think aloud from the first sentence onwards. Each sentence was printed on a new right hand page of a booklet, and the subject was asked to write down what information was gathered about the new word's meaning from each sentence. He or she knew that the new word was not synonymous with any existing word, so that its meaning had to be constructed, not just discovered. The successive presentation of five sentences made sure that the information given about the new word was insufficient and ambiguous. The subjects were instructed not to look back to earlier sentences. Having to keep track of the various hypotheses and pieces of information gathered ensured the possibility of overloading working memory.

In order to describe the meaning of the new word in one or two sentences, the subject was required to construct a coherent word meaning unit from what was remembered of the information gathered during the learning process. The mean scores achieved on this task showed that it was indeed difficult, but not unduly so.

The Processes of Word Meaning Acquisition

Thorough analysis of the thinking aloud protocols of 16 students in a first experiment revealed three components in the word meaning acquisition process that we thought of special interest:

1. the use of a model;
2. the decontextualization process;
3. assemblage of the word meaning unit.

Each of these three components reflected differences in level of skill among students. The components are discussed in turn, with special attention to the differences in cognitive processes as these emerged from the protocols of high and low verbal subjects. Our discussion is restricted to the main issues (see van Daalen-Kapteijns & Elshout-Mohr, 1981, for more details).

The Use of a Model.   During the processing of the five sentences for one new word, almost all subjects chose, at least once, a familiar word as a model for the new word meaning to be constructed. For example, to find out the meaning of the neologism "kolper," a number of subjects used the word "window" as a model; others tried to use "sunblind" as such. The interesting difference appeared to be the difference between *analytic* and *holistic* use of the model. Analytic model use (which eventually proved to be high verbal behavior) means handling the model as a bundle of separable components of meaning, each of which can be matched independently with further information about the neologism's meaning. An analytically used model can easily incorporate new information. If this information is compatible, it is simply added; if it is incompatible with a component of the model's meaning, this component can be replaced. Holistic model use (which eventually proved to be low verbal behavior) means that, as a rule, new compatible information about the neologism's meaning leads to adjustment of the model by widening or restricting its domain of reference. However, incompatible information cannot be incorporated in this way, and in most cases, causes the subject to reject the original model and to switch to a new model altogether.

Suppose, for example, that a subject has chosen "window" as a model for "kolper." Now in sentence 5 he or she gets the impression that "a kolper has to do with shadow." In analytic model use this can lead to the conclusion that "it is a kind of window alright, but not one that transmits much light" let me see, "has to do with shadow?" "shadow is an inherent problem." In holistic model use the given that "a kolper has to do with shadow" is in general thought to be strictly incompatible with the idea that a kolper is a kind of window: "let me see, has to do with shadow, I thought a kolper was a kind of window but I must have been wrong, it is rather something that causes shadow like a big tree, I would like to look back to the other sentences to see if a shadowing something would fit there."

The Decontextualization Process.   Analysis of the thinking aloud protocols revealed that all students used one of three *levels of decontextualization* in dealing with each sentence. At level 0 the sentence structure was transformed so that the new word came first, but the meaning stayed the same. At level 1, a minor transformation of the sentence content was made. At level 2, a real aspect of meaning was derived from the sentence content.

If we take sentence 3 for "kolper" as an example, the three levels of decontextualization can be represented by:

  level 0: kolpers are much asked for during a heat wave;
  level 1: kolpers in some respects resemble sun-blinds;
  level 2: kolpers have a cooling effect.

It was evident from the protocols that the decontextualization process varies with model use. Analytic model use tends to steer and further the decontextualization process by providing the subject with a plan for encoding the information given in the sentences. The subject works toward a level of decontextualization that results in conventional aspects of meaning — that is, aspects that resemble those of already acquired word meaning units (see Werner & Kaplan, 1952).

Subjects who use models holistically tend to decontextualize at a lower level. Their main purpose is to delimit the domain within which the new word's meaning belongs. Their hypotheses about the word's meaning, derived from the sentences, are often sentence-bound and sometimes idiosyncratic. This lack of conventional aspects of meaning proved to be a disadvantage when they were asked for a description of the meaning of the new word. This last stage of assembling the new word meaning unit is discussed here.

Assemblage of the Word Meaning Unit.   Although the instruction given at the beginning of the learning task explicitly mentions that a definition will be asked for at the end, many subjects were not very well prepared. This was especially true of those who switched models from sentence to sentence, because they had much information to retrieve, to reformulate and to weigh. Subjects who had been working with one model throughout the learning process could simply write down the actual state of the model. The necessity of weighing the relative strength of each hypothesis about the new word's meaning is the price low verbals pay for the superficiality of their decontextualizing activities. High verbals suffer less cognitive strain in having to do the definition task without looking back to the sentences.

Verbal Comprehension Skill

How do high verbal subjects profit from their verbal comprehension skill in a word meaning acquisition task? The central feature of skilled performance in our opinion lies in consistent and methodical use of knowledge about word meanings. The way in which this knowledge is used by a high verbal subject leads us to suppose that for him or her word meanings are unitary organizational structures, in which several components can be operated on separately. It may seem odd that high proficiency should be needed to realize this apparently simple quality. It is, however, less odd if we take into consideration that the simplicity in structure and corresponding procedures is not "artificially" constituted, but results from learning and experience in natural settings over a considerable amount of time. Simple models, developed to deal with complex information, may take the form of a formal definition (as in Feldman & Klausmeier, 1974), of a "cogit" (Hayes-Roth, 1977), or of a "typicality" representation (Cohen & Murphy, 1984). Once constructed, the model fulfills several functions. In the acquisition of word meanings four functions can be distinguished:

1. The model provides a plan for retrieval of knowledge that might be relevant for the acquisition of the new word meaning. If, for instance, "window"

is chosen as a model for "kolper," all aspects of the semantic unit for "window" are readily accessible.

2. The model provides a schematic structure for the word meaning to be acquired. In the case of the semantic unit referred to by "kolper," a "window"-like schema will be activated, one in which certain "slots" have yet to be filled.

3. The conventional aspects of meaning, incorporated in the model, steer the decontextualization process toward conventional aspects of meaning for the new word. For example, one of the "kolper"-sentences conveys the information that "kolpers are much asked for during a heat wave." To transform this piece of information, a subject can think of conventional aspects of "window" like: "is meant to let in light" and "is meant to keep out rain"; subsequently he or she can continue the decontextualization process to arrive at "is meant to keep out heat" as an aspect of the meaning of "kolper."

4. The model provides default information to fill empty slots in the schematically anticipated structure. The subject assumes that a kolper resembles a window in all respects that are not at variance with the content of the sentences. So a kolper "inherits" the features of a prototypical window until further notice.

There is a striking correspondence between these four functions of the analytically used word meaning model and what Thorndyke (1984) calls the *properties of schemata*. This correspondence confirms the assumption that the analytic model is indeed a schema: It is the abstraction of more complex knowledge about states or events in the world and their meaning.

In the cognitive processes of high verbal subjects, the four functions of the model are intricately interwoven. For example, some subjects use one general model as a schematic structure for the meaning of the new word (function 2), while using a different local model in each particular sentence to derive an aspect of meaning by decontextualization (function 3). If this derived aspect is compatible with the general schema, it is filled in; if not, another local model is tried and the resulting aspect evaluated in view of the general model.

The protocols of low verbal subjects reveal cognitive processes in which attempts are made to use a model in one of the ways just described. But, a model used holistically is not efficient as a retrieval plan or as a schematic structure for the new word, and it does not provide guidelines for decontextualization. Therefore, low verbal cognitive processes remain predominantly sentence-bound.

Conclusions

We view verbal comprehension as a pocket of knowledge about word meanings that derives its quality from two sources: (a) the number of word meanings that are known; and (b) the quality of each word meaning in itself. In this view, the proficiency of the high verbal person is directly associated with the availability of a great number of well-structured word meaning units. By using word meaning knowledge as simple schemata, the difficulty of the task and the accompanying cognitive strain can be reduced by a person with sufficient verbal comprehension skill. This finding is wholly in line with the description of the characteristic demand of verbal comprehension tasks, given earlier in this chapter. The "knot of problemacity" (Elshout, 1978, p. 324) arises from (a) the necessity to achieve and maintain invariance in meaning, despite the variety in contextual meanings of a word, (b) the high degree of ambiguity of natural language, and (c) the limited capacity of working memory. This "characteristic demand" can be adequately met if: (a) an individual has a great number of knowledge units, (b) each unit is well-structured and can be used as a schema to decontextualize information, and (c) each unit can be accessed in an efficient way.

From the proposed point of view, the psychological similarity among various verbal comprehension tasks comes out clearly. The same knowledge representations that are used propositionally in a vocabulary test manifest their procedural qualities in a skill-in-action test. The degree of representational simplicity is important in both types of test, and even more so in the third type that we discussed earlier. Processing word meanings in conditions of minimal control is probably only feasible if the relevant word meaning knowledge has a simple, well-structured representation in semantic memory.

Our experiments indicate that a person, by handling word meaning knowledge analytically, can avoid many of the impasses that characterize the learning process resulting from holistic use of such knowledge. This finding suggests that there might be a trade-off between the simplicity of the word meaning representations in semantic memory and the procedural complexity that can be accommodated. Adapting the way that word meanings are processed to the present status of one's word meaning knowledge as well as to the task demands might even be conceived of as the core of verbal comprehension as a skill. It must be kept in mind, however, that proficiency in making these adaptations is based on more fundamental elements of verbal comprehension: the amount of knowledge about word meanings and the quality of its representation. Individual differences in verbal comprehension strategies cannot, in our opinion, be properly understood without reference to the underlying word meaning knowledge. This supposition has many consequences, among other things for study strategy training (for relevant discussions see Elshout-Mohr & van Daalen-Kapteijns, 1985; Harris & Sipay, 1980; Schmeck, 1983).

A puzzling question is why some persons store word meanings more efficiently than others. In our experiments high verbal students used knowledge about simple words (like "window," "remark," etc.) differently from low verbal students. Still, all of them must have been acquainted with those words for many years and must have met them in many contexts. The same phenomenon was found when we asked our subjects to define common, well-known words: the high verbals in comparison with the low ones gave definitions that on the whole were better structured, more accurate and more conventionally worded (van Daalen-Kapteijns, 1980; see also Curtis, this volume). Our interpretation of this finding is that low verbal subjects in defining a common word are required to produce on the spot a selective description of a word meaning unit that is essentially an indivisible whole, whereas high verbals have already solved this problem in the past.

Whether a person will develop well-structured word meaning units is most probably partly determined by innate and developmental features of the system (see Keil, 1981; Keil & Batterman, 1984 for a relevant discussion). The individual's life history is without any doubt important too. One factor is the number and variety of problems of the verbal comprehension type that the person has had to solve in the past. A second factor is the amount of internal and external prompting that he or she has experienced to process verbal comprehension tasks in an efficient way. Setting standards of performance is one way of creating external encouragement. Curtis and Glaser (1983) propose to establish standards of performance for the various components of reading. Such standards can in our opinion play an important part in the development of verbal comprehension as a skill, because it is a common phenomenon that the development of a skill halts at some plateau until new requirements are made and other standards of performance are established.

We certainly do not claim that all differences in verbal comprehension will disappear by better schooling, but we are convinced that verbal comprehension can be much improved by appropriate methods of instruction. Some suggestions in this matter follow rather straightforwardly from our view on verbal comprehension as a skill, and are presented in the next section.

PROMOTING VOCABULARY LEARNING

Learning New Words and Word Meanings

Under natural learning conditions, promotion of vocabulary learning entails promoting verbal comprehension skill. The process of learning word meanings starts from the very first day of a child's life and continues up to old age. Parents and teachers are involved, as well as siblings and peers, and last but not least: all sources of information that the individual learner actively seeks, like books, magazines and other kinds of linguistic materials, radio and television programs, and so on. Three factors affect the learning of word meanings:

1. the *frequency* of occurrence of the words, or the frequency with which the words are presented to the learner;
2. the *variety* of situations or contexts in which the words occur, or are presented;
3. the *standards* of performance that are set.

The frequency and variety of situations in which new words are presented to the learner differ widely across individuals. It takes dedicated parents and teachers to continually provide the young child with small but challenging verbal comprehension tasks that stimulate vocabulary learning. Moreover, dedication alone will not do the trick. The capacities that are required are not to be underestimated. However, once a child starts to read, it becomes much easier to provide sufficient diversity in verbal comprehension tasks and sufficient variety in new words that the child encounters.

In regard to maintaining standards of performance, a first relevant question is whether the learner understands the verbal utterances that he or she is confronted with. Does the child follow an instruction in which a new word was used? Does he or she laugh at the appropriate moments in the story? A second relevant question is whether the learner decontextualizes word meanings. Is the child content when a new word is understood in its verbal or situational context? Or is the learner aware of the fact that a word as such is a distinguishable entity, although its meaning is specified and colored by the context? To check the quality of vocabulary learning processes, one has to ask questions and provide models for answering those. If a parent or teacher consistently provides schematic representations of word meanings, while explaining the meaning of new words, the learner will know what he or she is expected to do. When the child is asked: "Do you know what *miser* means?" he or she may answer: "Yes, a *miser* is a person who is stingy with money," or: "No, not quite, though I know that a *miser* is not a nice person, like in this story . . . he could have helped the other man but he did not." The child who is not used to thinking of word meanings as schematically organized units might be tempted to overestimate his or her knowledge. For instance, the answer might be: "yes, I know what *miser* means . . . it means that the man in the story is not nice at all."

Checking what is learned and setting the models for word meaning knowledge can be a tedious affair. Either it interrupts ongoing activities or it must be done afterwards. In either case, it can only be done selectively for a small sample of words. Therefore, we consider it of utmost importance that children are somehow taught to check word meaning knowledge for themselves. Eventually constructing word meaning units should become a mental routine that is performed with minimal mental effort.

In a special program to learn new word meanings, Beck, Perfetti, and McKeown (1982) stimulate a child's awareness of what it means to know a word's meaning. This program creates a situation in which, for once, full attention is given to the processes involved in acquiring new word meanings. In this situation there is no other task than the learning of the new words. Because knowledge about the new words is the direct goal of the instructional program, standards are established in a relatively unambiguous way. Such a special program successfully avoids one of the pitfalls of natural word meaning learning conditions for low verbal students: while the low verbal person is still fully occupied with comprehending the contextual information conveyed by the words, a high verbal peer may be adding word meaning after word meaning to his or her vocabulary. The disadvantage of being low verbal in this way can be ever increasing, until a moment of definite refusal to take part in verbal activities that demand so much mental strain.

In the next section we sketch an instructional program that we believe can help to minimize the low verbals' disadvantage. The program would be similar to the program of Beck et al. (1982) with the difference that not a single new word would be involved. The goal would be to consolidate existing word meaning knowledge and thereby promote the leaners' proficiency in subsequent independent word meaning acquisition.

Consolidation of Existing Word Meaning Knowledge

Activities of the learner determine what word meaning knowledge is acquired from contextual information. From the experiments discussed earlier in this chapter, we concluded that existing knowledge affects what the learner does. If knowledge about a word provides both a simple schematic representation that can be used as a model and a guideline for decontextualization, the learning process is less strenuous and more successful. That is why we would begin with a check on existing knowledge about words in promoting vocabulary learning.

For elementary school children one could consider consolidating the knowledge about words referring to basic level concepts (Rosch, Mervis, Gray, Johnson, & Boyes-Braem, 1976). Both teachers and pupils may too readily assume that the meaning of words like "window," "bird," and so on are well known. Suppose a teacher asks his or her pupils to tell the meaning of the word "window." The pupils may be surprised at such a question, but if they see it as a serious one they will probably all contribute something to the discussion. Things like: "windows are made of glass," "they are in a wall," "my brother broke one last Friday" may be heard. Some pupils will point at the classroom windows, wondering what can be said about such a familiar thing. How does the teacher evaluate the word meaning knowledge of each child? And how can well-structuredness of that knowledge be promoted?

In designing an instructional program, we value three preconditions. First, we want to respect what the children already know. An instruction that simply presents an appropriate schema for "window" will not do, nor will instruction that starts teaching the meaning of "window" as though it were entirely unknown. As Papert (1980) argues, such instructional procedures would "denature" school learning by failing to recognize and respect children's own models of knowledge. Nussbaum and Novick (1982) stress the importance of eliciting existing knowledge, as this gives a teacher the opportunity to correct possible misconceptions. Second, we want to take into account that high quality knowledge about word meanings is characterized by accuracy, richness (or flexibility), and fluency (Beck et al., 1982). Finally, we want to keep in mind that acquisition of new word meanings is furthered by a schematic representation of word meaning knowledge. That is to say that aspects of word meaning should preferably be verbalizable as separate components of the unitized word meaning.

These three preconditions can be met by designing instruction that guides the pupils in:

1. Distinguishing between idiosyncratic experiences they have had, and more general experiences that must become associated with the word's meaning. *Accuracy* of word meaning knowledge demands representation of "conventional" information (see Werner & Kaplan, 1952).

2. Constraining the *richness* implied in the idiosyncratic experiences by completing the knowledge representation with a limited number of word meaning aspects. In particular, this involves verbalization of both structural and functional features (see Miller & Johnson-Laird, 1976) that are "in common with" and "in distinction of" the meaning of other words.

3. Enhancing *fluency* in accessing word meaning knowledge relevant in a particular verbal comprehension task. Processing word meaning knowledge can be made more efficient by pointing out that a single aspect of a word's meaning is often sufficient to comprehend the word in a sentence or to select the right word to fit a particular context.

Although we have no empirical evidence that such an instructional program is effective in promoting verbal comprehension skill, we have reasons to be optimistic. The effectiveness of the Beck et al. program is explained by the high quality of the word meaning knowledge acquired. Therefore, we would also expect some effects of a program that improves the quality of *existing* word meaning knowledge. A second reason to be optimistic is that transfer is at the centre of the proposed instructional program. Only words that are expected to serve frequently as models or schemas for other words, and thereby as guidelines for decontextualization, must be taught. The special investment that is needed to restructure existing knowledge may be compensated by a parsimonious selection.

There is, however, one reason not to be optimistic about the effects of the aforementioned program. The instructional procedure is time-consuming and requires a dedicated teacher who is enthusiastic and high verbal. This last prerequisite is necessary to keep up the level of interest both for high and low verbal children. It is crucial that the teacher is flexible and fluent in helping the children to translate complex ideas into appropriate word meaning components. These problems could be solved, in part, by developing a computer-assisted instructional program to supplement the teacher's activities. Such a program would make the pupils less dependent on the teacher's time and ability to provide the required instruction. Moreover, low verbal children could spend more time on the computer, giving them the opportunity to keep up with their high verbal peers in a natural and inconspicuous way (see Dirk-zwager, Fokkema, Van der Veer, & Beishuizen, 1984).

Our wish to moderate individual differences in word meaning knowledge is based on the strong belief that the quality of this knowledge is of major importance in the more complex verbal comprehension processes like reading with understanding, comprehending and remembering the details of a story, and figuring out a word's meaning from contextual information. Consolidation of available knowledge about carefully selected basic level words might be one of the means to diminish the consequences of being low verbal by birth or by early environmental conditions. If children are encouraged to spend time in improving the quality of their word meaning knowledge, loss of interest in linguistic materials might be prevented. The endeavor is at least worth trying, because transfer of training is not a hoped for miracle (see Resnick, 1984), but a justified prediction in the proposed program.

ACKNOWLEDGMENTS

We wish to thank the former COWO (now the section Higher Education of the SCO), University of Amsterdam, for allotting us time to write this chapter, and W. van Ommen-Reus for typing the manuscript. The research was supported by the Netherlands Organization for the Advancement of Pure Research (Z.W.O.). Valuable comments on earlier drafts were provided by several colleagues. In particular, we want to thank H. van Oostendorp, M. den Uyl and H. van Daalen. The editors of this volume have been of great help in suggesting specific revisions to deal with the problem of length of the original draft.

REFERENCES

Beck, I. L., Perfetti, C. A., & McKeown, M. G. (1982). Effects of long-term vocabulary instruction on lexical access and reading comprehension. *Journal of Educational Psychology, 74,* 506–521.
Bransford, J. D., & Johnson, M. K. (1973). Consideration of some problems of comprehension In W. G. Chase (Ed.), *Visual information processing* (pp. 383–438). New York: Academic Press.

Cohen, B., & Murphy, G. L. (1984). Models of concepts. *Cognitive Science, 8,* 27–58.

Curtis, M. E., & Glaser, R. (1983). Reading theory and the assessment of reading achievement. *Journal of Educational Measurement, 20*(2), 133–147.

Daalen-Kapteijns, M. M. van. (1980). *Het leren van begrippen en woordbetekenissen.* Hoofdstuk III. ICO.275, intern rapport.

Daalen-Kapteijns, M. M. van, & Elshout-Mohr, M. (1981). The acquisition of word meanings as a cognitive learning process. *Journal of Verbal Learning and Verbal Behavior, 20,* 386–399.

Dirkzwager, A., Fokkema, S. D., Van der Veer, G. C., & Beishuizen, J. J. (red.) (1984). *Leren met computers in het onderwijs.* 's Gravenhage: Stichting voor Onderzoek van het Onderwijs (SVO) (SVO-reeks: 76).

Elshout, J. J. (1976). *Karakteristieke moeilijkheden in het denken.* Academisch proefschrift. Universiteit van Amsterdam.

Elshout, J. J. (1978). The characteristic demands of intellectual problems. In A. M. Lesgold, J. W. Pellegrino, S. D. Fokkema & R. Glaser (Eds.), *Cognitive psychology and instruction* (pp. 321–329). New York: Plenum Press.

Elshout-Mohr, M., & Daalen-Kapteijns, M. M. van. (1977). *Aspekten van cognitief leren: het verwerven van woordbetekenissen.* ICO.235, intern rapport.

Elshout-Mohr, M., & Daalen-Kapteijns, M. M. van. (1979). Het leren van begrippen en woordbetekenissen. *Losbladig Onderwijskundig Lexicon,* PO 4220, 1–17.

Elshout-Mohr, M., & Daalen-Kapteijns, M. M. van. (1985). Het leren van begrippen in het bijzonder in het eerste stadium van het hoger onderwijs. *Pedagogische Studiën, 62*(11), 459–471.

Feldman, K. V., & Klausmeier, H. J. (1974). Effects of two kinds of definition on concept attainment of fourth and eighth graders. *Journal of Educational Research, 67,*(5), 219–223.

Ferguson, G. A. (1956). On transfer and the abilities of man. *Canadian Journal of Psychology,* No. 10, 121–131.

Guilford, J. P. (1967). *The nature of human intelligence.* New York: McGraw-Hill.

Harris, A. J., & Sipay, E. R. (1980). *How to increase reading ability.* New York: Longman.

Hayes-Roth, B. (1977). Evolution of cognitive structures and processes. *Psychological Review, 84,(3),* 260–279.

Keil, F. C. (1981). Constraints on knowledge and cognitive development. *Psychological Review, 88,* 197–227.

Keil, F. C., & Batterman, N. (1984). A characteristic-to-defining shift in the development of word meaning. *Journal of Verbal Learning and Verbal Behavior, 23,* 221–236.

MacNamara, J. (1972). Cognitive basis of language learning in infants. *Psychological Review, 79,* 1–13.

Marshall, J. C. (1970). Introduction – A note on semantic theory. In G. B. Flores d'Arcais & W. J. M. Levelt (Eds.), *Advances in psycholinguistics* (pp. 189–196). Amsterdam: North-Holland.

Miller, G. A., & Johnson-Laird, P. N. (1976). *Language and perception.* Cambridge MA: Belknap Press of Harvard University Press.

Nitsch, K. E. (1977). *Structuring decontextualized forms of knowledge.* Ph.D. dissertation, Vanderbilt University.

Nüssbaum, J., & Novick, S. (1982). Alternative frameworks, conceptual conflict and accommodation: toward a principled teaching strategy. *Instructional Science, 11,* 183–200.

Papert, S. (1980). *Mindstorms: Computers, children and powerful ideas.* New York: Basic Books.

Resnick, L. B. (1984). Comprehending and learning: implications for a cognitive theory of instruction. In H. Mandl, N. L. Stein, & T. Trabasso (Eds.), *Learning and comprehension of text* (pp. 431–443). Hillsdale, NJ: Lawrence Erlbaum Associates.

Rosch, E., Mervis, C. B., Gray, W. D., Johnson, M. D., & Boyes-Braem, P. (1976). Basic objects in natural categories. *Cognitive Psychology, 8,* 382–439.

Schank, R. C., & Abelson, R. P. (1977). *Scripts, plans, goals and understanding.* London: Wiley.

Schmeck, R. R. (1983). Learning styles of college students. In R. F. Dillon & R. R. Schmeck (Eds.), *Individual differences in cognition* (Vol. 1, pp. 233-279). New York: Academic Press.

Sternberg, R. J. (1984). Facets of human intelligence. In J. R. Anderson & S. M. Kosslyn (Eds.), *Tutorials in learning and memory* (pp. 137-165). San Francisco/New York: Freeman.

Thorndyke, P. W. (1984). Application of schema theory in cognitive research. In J. R. Anderson & S. M. Kosslyn (Eds.), *Tutorials in learning and memory* (pp. 167-193). San Francisco/New York: Freeman.

Thurstone, L. L. (1938). Primary mental abilities. *Psychometric Monographs,* No. 1.

Traver, R. (1958). *Anatomy of a murder.* New York: Dell Publishing.

Werner, H., & Kaplan, B. (1952). The acquisition of word meanings: A developmental study. *Monographs of the society for Research in Child Development, 15* (Serial No. 51, No. 1).

5 Learning Word Meanings From Written Context

Priscilla A. Drum
University of California, Santa Barbara

Bonnie C. Konopak
Louisiana State University

A word, an acoustic configuration of speech sounds and a written rendition (more or less) of these sounds, comes or is assigned to refer to things, events, and ideas arbitrarily. There is no inherent connection between a word and its referent; a "tree" could be called a "drink" and vice versa. Once a word and a referential meaning have been accepted or conventionalized by a culture, then the word becomes both a means for communicating knowledge within the culture as well as a sign of the user's knowledge of that culture.

The ease with which a person learns new words and their meanings not only depends on that person's exposure to the words and his or her facility in discerning the meaning but also on the characteristics of the words themselves. Words have two major types of meaning (Lyons, 1977): extension or the things, events, or even the stereotypical responses for abstractions such as *courage, honesty,* and *goodness* that denote the meaning; and intension or how the word is intended to mean, its connotation. Whereas extension refers to the referent for the word, intension depends on the topic situation when the word is used and generally must be inferred by the reader/listener. Words within texts have only intensional meaning as the denotative or real world referents must be imaged; they are not present. If the reader is unfamiliar with the text topic and the concepts underlying the particular lexicon used, this inference task will be difficult.

In addition, many words have numerous meanings, particularly those words that are used most frequently. Does the word "force" in isolation refer to a body of people, physical strength, or "a vector quantity that tends to produce an acceleration of a body in the direction of its application" (Morris,

1981, p. 513)? Despite the inherent ambiguity of the task, people do supply definitions for words in isolation, ostensibly, the meaning or meanings that are most salient for them when confronted with the word.

How, then, do people acquire and subsequently distinguish various meanings for words? The usual answer to the preceding question is they have learned them in context (McCullough, 1943; Thorndike, 1917), suggesting a certain prerequisite level of reasoning ability (Sternberg, Powell, & Kaye, 1983). Indeed, word knowledge is highly correlated with measures of verbal intelligence (Anderson & Freebody, 1981; Carroll, 1976; Jensen, 1980; Miller, 1978a; Sternberg, Powell, & Kaye, 1983). As Jensen (1980) noted, "vocabulary tests are among the best measures of intelligence, because the acquisition of word meanings is highly dependent on the *eduction* of meaning from the contexts in which the words are encountered" (p. 146). The learner must not only hear or read the word in some situation but also must figure out what the word is likely to mean through the language and situational cues provided. The more the learner knows about these other cues, the more closely the meaning for the unknown word will be approximated.

Thus, the more knowledge of the world that an individual has, the more words that person will know (Hunt, 1978). Most people will associate strength with the term *force,* but physicists will also be able to specify the vector definition if requested. Each new area of study, new hobby, new acquaintance, or other new experience offers the opportunity of expanding one's personal lexicon, both horizontally in the number of words for which a meaning is known and vertically in the depth of meanings for a single term. The question we are addressing in this chapter is: What sources are available to readers for expanding word knowledge through written discourse?

SOURCES FOR MEANING

What a word means in a text depends on the string of words within which it is embedded. Miller (1978b) suggests at least four sources for disambiguating a particular word's meaning: the situational context, the discourse context, the individual's knowledge about the discourse topic, and the immediate linguistic context. This chapter is organized by these factors that affect the ability to disambiguate the meaning of a word while reading. In our view of reading, the four sources correspond to (a) the reason a reader has for reading a text (a class assignment or the desired knowledge sought by the reader); (b) the underlying conceptual structure for the topic of the text; (c) the mental representation for the topic that the reader possesses prior to reading the text; and (d) the verbal context in which a particular word is found. The four sources are not distinct, particularly (a) and (c), for desired future knowledge and existing prior knowledge are connected. What one wants to learn somewhat depends on what is already known. Despite the overlap, these four sources are treated separately in organizing our discussion in subsequent sections.

Situational Context

Situation, as used by Miller (1978b), refers to who is speaking to whom in a particular place and time, or the physical conditions for the discourse act. In reading, however, conditions external to a reader do not provide much information. Here, we use the term *situation* to refer to what the reader needs to learn about particular words, the learning goal. Although learning implies a previous condition of not knowing something, complete knowledge or complete ignorance are rare states. Thus, to characterize word learning in terms of situational contexts, what the reader needs to learn about particular words must be specified.

To become an expert in a content area, the depth of word knowledge for domain-specific words should ideally approach "completeness"; that is, the learner should not only know a word as it is used within a particular context, but also should be able to use the word in efficient study and in discussion. Often, however, vocabulary instruction in schools does not specify the degree of word knowledge required; it is an "all or none situation," measured by the exercises the student completes (Petty, 1968). For example, no distinction is made between a child's meaning for atom versus that of a physicist. Because words refer to concepts, the learner should be expected to gain in precision and depth of meaning for the *the same word* as well as different words over the years of schooling. A word is not just known; its use represents varying states of knowledge dependent upon the learner's mental representation for the word.

In a discussion of vocabulary development, Graves (1984) presents six different states of what a student knows about a word. In our view, each state refers to a hypothetical situation—that is, what students can and need to learn about a word. In Table 5.1, we have attempted to elaborate on Graves' knowledge states by providing examples and describing the learning needed to change the states to the desired goal. Here, the situational context varies from a comparatively simple task to increasingly more difficult instructional tasks.

The first conditions (states 1 and 2), learning to decode the word or to produce the word, do not concern us here, although state 1 is the rubric for much vocabulary instruction in elementary schools. Exposure to words in texts and in classes can provide the needed familiarity to encourage use (state 2), but again it is reinforcement rather than learning from context.

Contextual information alone can add new labels for old concepts (state 3) and extend the attributes for a label (state 4). Written context can provide the

TABLE 5.1
Prior Student States for Learning Word Meanings

Student's State	Learning Goals	Example
1. knows word meaning aurally	decoding for reading	can describe an *elephant* accurately but cannot read the word
2. knows word meaning but does not express it	production in writing and speech	can understand *chaos* but not sufficiently familiar to use it
3. knows meaning but no word	new label for old concept	knows the idea of fear and hiding but does not know the word *cringe*
4. knows partial meaning of word	extend the attributes for a label	knows the word *guerrilla* means a soldier but does not know the tactics or the type of soldier connoted
5. knows a different meaning for a word	new concept for old label	knows that *force* means strength but does not know the vector meaning
6. knows neither the concept nor the label	new concept and new label	knows nothing about atomic structure including the term *ion*

conditions for expanding knowledge within states 3 and 4, as exemplified in Konopak (1984), Nagy, Herman, and Anderson (1985), and Jenkins, Stein, and Wysocki (1984). These studies are discussed in a subsequent section.

On the other hand, new conceptual learning (states 5 and 6) will require more than the amorphous aids of passage context. Text differs from other forms of discourse in numerous ways. The physical context for silent reading, the place and the time, generally does not help in discerning the meaning, although in classrooms one would assume the text would have something to do with the course content. The only cues available other than dictionaries are those within the text. The reader brings his or her past store of knowledge to the task and then must rely on the text to indicate what is important information and to clarify the nature of this information. If much of the lexicon within the text is new and/or the conceptual framework for the lexicon is at variance with the reader's past knowledge, the task will be difficult. Either the reader/teacher will have to be very judicious in selecting texts that explain the conceptual structure and the meaning for the terms used (a glossary will not suffice), or some form of organized direct teaching must take place.

Much of our discussion of the situational context for learning words has been speculative because we know of few studies that explore vocabulary learning from this perspective. Instead, most work seems to assume that the student either knows or does not know a word. But for many words, most of us are in a state of partial knowledge. Thus, to characterize word learning in context, what the student needs and is able to learn concerning the target words, (i.e., the situation) must be specified.

Topic Information

As readers want or are required to learn words for new concepts in a particular domain (sailing, atomic structures, carpentry, genetics), the acquisition of word meanings becomes more important. There are two sources for words related to this consideration: the domain itself, (e.g., its structure and its lexicon) and the reader's prior knowledge concerning the topic domain. Prior knowledge is discussed in the next section. Here we explore the cohesion of words in a topic domain.

The selection of content words used by an author usually depends on the topic addressed. Bolinger and Sears (1981) stated, "Whenever a combination of words comes to be used again and again in reference to a particular thing or situation, it develops a kind of connective tissue" (p. 250). It is a collocation for that topic environment, defined as "Such habitual association of words, the characteristic company they keep." (p. 53) Although subsequent text[1] indicates that the authors were referring to phrase structures, it seems reasonable to assume that topics also have characteristic words, semantic fields within which lexical items have preference for expressing the underlying concepts.

Moreover, two statements from Miller (1978b) appear particularly apt to us in discussing this possibility: "The meaning of any word depends on how it works together with other words in the same lexical field to cover or represent the conceptual field. If *that statement sounds vague, then it accurately captures the flavor of most writing on this subject*" (p. 53; Italics added). It may prove difficult to describe a semantic field for a topic domain; cultural views do change and words are slippery elements. And yet, without some attention to this question, the answer to how people learn word meanings from context will be elusive.

Content area texts often represent the conditions for a student's first exposure to a body of knowledge. They are the scripts (Calfee & Drum, 1986) for forming the initial mental representation (Anderson, 1983) of a body of knowledge. Thus, the text not only provides the structure of the semantic domain (Kuczaj, 1982), but also the nodes of the structure that contain the lexicon for that domain.

---

[1]Bolinger and Sears used this term to explain word choices within syntactic structures: why a child will say *throw a ball* rather than *toss a ball,* why we are more likely to say "good works [are] *performed* but cement works are *built* and works of art *produced.*

The words selected for a content area text are determined by their subject matter. These include the technical terminology, words specific to a subject such as *photosynthesis, legislature,* and *noun.* Although infrequent against the language at large, these words can often be frequent within a text on a particular topic (Goodman & Bird, 1984). Writing to a topic makes its own requirements on word selection. It is this knowledge and the use of this terminology that distinguishes the expert from the novice (Calfee & Curley, 1984).

The influence of content domain on vocabulary learning has not been examined closely. Any content area contains certain concepts, labeled by particular words, and organized in a framework or structure. Logical analyses of conceptual frameworks as realized in domain-specific words need to be developed and empirically tested in novice/expert studies. The results could provide reasonable instructional goals for learners at various stages of word knowledge.

We know that students can have difficulties comprehending new subject areas because of a lack in the vocabulary necessary to support this comprehension. Perhaps the underlying conceptual framework is not clarified, leaving any vocabulary learned as isolated units rather than as a nodal network supported by the structure. It is for this kind of learning that SQ3R or SQ4R methods are recommended (Robinson, 1961). However, to make use of these approaches, students need to already know what they do not know and what to do about it. Additional work on the structural representation of domain knowledge, including its vocabulary, may provide us with insight for more efficient teaching of new words.

Prior Reader Knowledge

Some of the early work in vocabulary, prior to 1960, addresses what today would be called a *metacognitive question:* Do children know what words they don't know as they read a text? The answer found by Dolch (1932) is "yes." In his study, subsequent tests substantiated the children's claim to ignorance of the prespecified words.

However, Elivian (1938), in investigating the effects of context on learning unknown words, obtained somewhat different results. Relatively difficult words for fifth and sixth graders were embedded in specially written stories with each word "carefully defined in the context: some by the direct method of definition, some by synonym, and others by repeated use throughout the story, their meaining to be gained by inference" (p. 53).

The children first read the stories and identified the words that they did not know, and then they completed a matching exercise on all the embedded difficult words without using the text. After this procedure, the students received a second copy of the matching exercise and the passages to help them find the meaning of any words they did not know. On the first matching exercise without the passages, the poor readers correctly identified only 29% of the words they said they knew, whereas good readers correctly identified only 48%. On the second matching exercise with the passages available, poor readers were able to find the meanings for an additional 22% of the words they had missed on the first test, whereas good readers correctly matched an additional 52% of the items they had missed. Elivian concluded that these students were not aware of the words they did not know, nor were they particularly adept at using context to locate definitions.

Elivian's study differs from Dolch's in that cues to word meaning were written into the Elivian texts deliberately. Dolch used words in isolation. With text in hand, the children in Elivian's study may have felt they understood the general meaning of the text, and as a result, felt they understood the meanings of the words.

Thus, the way that a child is tested can make a difference not only in their accuracy but also in their feelings of knowing. In addition, the use of the general "yes" (I know the word) versus "no" (I don't know the word) response cannot measure partial knowledge or incremental gains in knowledge. Access to word knowledge cannot be compared to an on/off toggle switch. A more appropriate analogy is the increasing luminescence of a rheostat.

The following qualitative scale (Drum, 1983) was developed in order to provide a more appropriate measure of what a reader knows about a word's meaning. The subjects were asked to indicate whether they knew the words listed or not ("yes" or "no"), and then to define each word or to guess what it meant. Categories were determined by the definitions given by a wide range of students from second through twelfth grade.

The scale contains four major categories of student responses:

A. Perceptual — physically similar words
    1. substituting a look- or sound-alike
       "horse" for *house;* "gorilla" for *guerrilla*
    2. defining a look- or sound-alike
       "buddy" for *pall* (pal); "jewelry" for *penance* (pendant)
B. Syntactic — internal structure or grammatical function of words
    3. defining a morpheme
       impropriety as "not a proprietor"
    4. using the word in a phrase or sentence
       "a person's *reflection*"; "follow a *schedule*"
C. Semantic — general meaning dimensions of a word
    5. giving a general semantic attribute
       serendipity as "a feeling"
    6. giving a more precise attribute
       aberration as "bending the rules"

D. Correct — a specific definition
   7. giving part of a correct meaning
     icon as "a holy picture"
   8. giving a complete correct meaning
     finesse as "elegance or smoothness of manner"

In Drum (1983), use of the scale indicated that fifth-, eighth-, and eleventh-grade average students gave correct definitions (7 & 8 on the scale a) for only 25% of the words that they indicated beforehand that they knew. An average of 9% of the definitions that they gave for words they said they did not know were correct definitions.

Another study, by Carroll and Drum (1983), used the scale as a pre- and posttest measure to explore incremental gains made from no context to written context. High school students ($N = 72$) were asked to define a list of 40 words in isolation prior to reading passages that embedded 20 of these words. The mean definitions for the 20 words in isolation was 3.44 on the scale; with the texts in hand, the mean definitions rose to 7.06. Thus, these students could and did use the text information to refine and elaborate word meaning beyond what they expressed before they read the text.

The quality of the contextual cues within the text was analyzed using the scale just described. With text in hand, the 36 high ability readers' responses to the definitional task were almost isomorphic to the text cues, an r of .97. But this task only requires the ability to isolate the appropriate cues.

Although students can and do use context to identify word meanings, they do not seem to retain much of this learning from a single exposure. Konopak (1984) showed this by using the scale to study students' learning of physics terms over time from formal and informal textual material. Students did learn more from the more precise, formal texts, but much of the information was lost over time. Collapsed over all conditions, the 68 subjects had a pretest mean of 4.24, a with-text mean of 6.61, and a delayed posttest mean of 5.12. Thus, it appears that a reader's prior knowledge about a topic domain remains an important source for learning meanings even when a text contains appropriate meaning cues.

Of course, the accessibility of the domain itself is of importance. In earlier studies, we used general passages; for instance, boy meets girl narratives and commonplace descriptions of such things as airports and restaurants, and asked the readers to identify the cues and to replace pseudo words with real words (Carroll & Drum, 1982; Drum, 1983; Madison, Carroll, & Drum, 1982). The readers could appropriately replace the pseudo words, for they had a prior conceptual understanding of these topics that could guide word selection. These procedures do not address learning of new information.

Two additional studies that examine passage context effects on vocabulary learning are those of Nagy, Herman, and Anderson (1985) and Jenkins,

Stein, and Wysocki (1984). However, in both cases the subjects' prior knowledge was assumed or approximated, so gains cannot be necessarily attributed to the contextual information.

In the Nagy et al. study, a prior knowledge checklist test (a Yes/No choice) was used. An interview after reading did provide a score for partial knowledge. However, whether gains in partial knowledge were the result of reading the text cannot be known because no pretest for partial knowledge was used. In the Jenkins et al. study, a lack of familiarity with the words was assumed because of their low frequency. However, even with no exposure to texts containing the words, fifth graders could supply definitions for 17% of them. The students in both studies knew something about these words before reading. The question is what did they know?

Only when there is a fairly precise indication of prior knowledge of word meaning can the effects of context or instruction be determined. Anderson and Freebody (1981) have suggested just asking the students. Our results and those of Nagy, Herman, and Anderson do corroborate the general accuracy of the Yes/No approach. If the semantic and correct categories are summed, students know something about 50% to 75% of the words they say they know. However, this is only a correct–incorrect determination at a very general level. The specificity of what is known, what needs to be learned, or what is learned cannot be determined from such a measure.

The three preceding sections — what is to be learned, the conceptual structure of the topic, and the reader's prior knowledge of the topic and its lexicon — are primary considerations in contextual influences upon subsequent vocabulary learning. But paradoxically, most research on context effects has examined the immediate verbal context for the target words with an emphasis on recognizing and classifying cues rather than on what is learned. The next section discusses some of this research.

Linguistic Context

The verbal context cues[2] of the text itself do facilitate word comprehension (Aulls, 1971; Dulin, 1970; Emans, 1967). Researchers also have explored specific characteristics of readers and of context cues that influence the extent of learning. On reader traits, older readers are better at using cues than younger readers (Klein, Klein, & Bertino, 1974; Robinson, 1963). Both good and poor readers seem to use cues (Rubeck, 1977; Samuels, Begg, & Chen, 1975), but poor readers use them less effectively (Elivian, 1938; Rankin & Overholser, 1969; Schvaneveldt, Ackerman, & Semlear, 1977). Studies also have been

---

[2]Though cue and clue have been used interchangeably in the literature, we prefer cue as its definition "a guiding hint or suggestion" (Kellerman, 1984, p. 245) connotes the amorphous or fuzzy nature of context for revealing meaning.

concerned with the nature of the cues, both within the text and the word itself. These are discussed in more detail later.

Physical Aspects of Cues.   Physical aspects of cues such as the target word's frequency within a text and the proximity of a cue to the target do affect the likelihood that a word's meaning will be discerned. The more often the target word appears within a cloze text, the more likely it will be named because more cues are available (Finn, 1977–1978; Hoffman, 1980). Similar studies by Werner and Kaplan (1952) and van Daalen-Kaptejins and Elshout-Mohr (1981) have examined the successive definitions of students after each of a series of sentences. These results confirm the reasonable finding that the more cues there are available, the more likely that a correct inference about a word's meaning will be made or an appropriate word will be selected.

A cue that is close to the target word proves more helpful than more distant cues (Aborn & Rubenstein, 1956; Carroll & Drum, 1982; Madison, Carroll, & Drum, 1982; Rubin, 1976). This latter finding probably reflects a least-effort principle, where only the neighboring words are used for clarification of an unknown word. Otherwise the word is just skipped.

Within the Word.   A word itself in a text contains contextual information, such as its morphemic properties, and the syntactic properties designated by its phrase and sentence function and its case role. The morphemic and functional information are not independent of one another, but each can add another cue to the puzzle of figuring out what the unknown word might mean.

Morphemic cues refer to the stem word and any derivational or inflectional affixes (prefixes and suffixes) which might be attached to the word. The reader must know, of course, the appropriate meanings for the affixes. For example, the word "thermoluminescence" has been used by both Carpenter and Just (1981) and Sternberg, Powell, and Kaye (1983) to illustrate morphemic analysis. Students might know that *thermo-* is a prefix that "refers to heat," from the Greek root word *therme,* or that *luminesce* is derived from the Latin root word *lumen* meaning "light." Without knowing Latin and Greek terms, however, few readers are able to use these sources for meaning (Sternberg, Powell, & Kaye, 1983). Even when affix knowledge is available, it must be used judiciously. Some fifth graders define *despot* as "to take out spots" (Drum, 1983); the children know the prefix *de* but not that the analysis does not apply in this case.

Although the effects of sentence function and case grammar attributes on word knowledge have not been investigated directly within texts, both have been studied in concept development in early childhood studies (Anglin, 1977; Litowitz, 1976; Nelson, 1977; Watson, 1982). Occasionally, vocabulary targets have been described as nominals, predicates, or modifiers, but knowing that a word fits one of these slots does not provide much information. The case grammar arguments, such as agent, instrument, beneficiary, and so on, are more informative about general semantic properties of a word, but are not sufficient to distinguish an agent from other agents.

Within the Text.   Other than proper nouns, words have no communicative referent except in context. As Halff, Ortony, and Anderson stated (1976), "words do not have a few discrete, qualitatively different meanings. Instead they act in different contexts to establish boundaries in an underlying continuum of knowledge" (p. 378). Even in limited contexts of a phrase or a sentence, the exact referent can be confusing. For instance, in a demographic survey administered to college freshmen, one question asked the students to provide the *state* of their parents. A number of the students filled in the slot provided with such terms as *married, divorced,* or *widowed. State,* for them, meant marital condition not a geographical location (L. Hubert, personal communication, October, 1984).

Most context studies have examined the effects of other words on clarifying a target word's meaning, focusing on the types of information or cues available. In an examination of context effects on guessing a word, both Ames (1966) and Quealy (1969) used the same 20 texts in which a nonsense word was substituted for every fiftieth content word (noun, verb, adjective, or adverb) in the texts. Participants (graduate students and high school students, respectively) were asked to guess the real word and to explain how they derived their answers. A few categories of explanations are listed here:

1. familiar expressions "let us *heag* (look) . . ." (Ames, 1966, p. 67)
2. modifying phrases or clauses "The trucker admitted that his foot had *thammed* (slipped) off the brake and . . ." (Quealy, 1969, p. 523)
3. definitions or descriptions "One towering worry is the problem of the professional *nodar* (donor). A few who sell blood . . ." (Ames, 1966, p. 70)
4. association clues "The AMA Journal states that brutal physical punishment by a parent is likely to be a 'more frequent cause of death than such well-recognized diseases as leukemia, cystic fibrosis and *fomronan* (muscular) dystrophy.' " (Ames, 1966, p. 76)

Given the topics addressed and the linguistic contexts available, most native speakers would recognize that only particular words (*look, slipped, donor, muscular*) would be likely to fit into these slots if the particular word was available in their personal lexicon. New learning of previously unknown words or of unknown meanings is not required by this task; both are known in advance. In addition, of the 14 types of cues, definitions and synonyms were considered the most useful. However, in two attempts to distinguish between these two cues, Carroll and Drum (1982) could not isolate any systematic cue type effects. Other kinds of cues may provide more semantic information about a word (e.g., see Sternberg, this volume). But the usefulness of any cue depends on the reader's knowledge.

A comparison between a graduate student's response (Ames, 1966) and that of a high school student (Quealy, 1969) to the following text used in both studies illustrates the importance of prior knowledge:

> The most withering insult that can be hurled at a man today is "leftist" — a term almost synonymous [with] "Communist." We *grish* (cringe) as the sensitive ears developed by all minority members pick up such expressions as "left-handed compliment" . . .

> Graduate Student — "*cringe*. A verb of action is needed. Terms such as 'withering insult' and 'sensitive ears' give me the idea of cringe." (Ames, 1966, p. 74)

> High School Student — "It was ah, well. . . . Well, ah, you always ah sort of ah inward reaction to something you don't like." (Quealy, 1969, p. 524)

Both students picked up the negative affect of the pseudo word and that it referred to something that people do, but the high school student apparently did not have the exact word available. If the real word had been mentioned in the passage, perhaps the student would have enlarged his or her personal lexicon. However, the concept behind the target word was already known (state 3) as well as the topic for this brief passage, *insults*.

A word is simply a label for some underlying concept. If the concept is known, then the likelihood of acquiring and using the new label will depend on its efficacy for the individual. Target words that are not important for new domain knowledge or for the immediate culture of the student are not likely to be retained. New words have to be useful and thereby practiced to become part of one's personal lexicon.

Implications

The four sources for disambiguating a particular word meaning have important educational implications. *Situational* considerations indicate the learner's purpose and provide a guide for further instruction to attain some specified goal. The *topic domain* delineates the content structure of a text in that domain as well as the pertinent concepts. Attention to the representation of a domain suggests vocabulary instruction that is presented in a systematic network rather than isolated learning of word lists. *Prior knowledge* factors, tied to situational considerations, indicate a continuum of knowledge, so that repeated exposures to a variety of contexts can produce incremental gains. *Linguistic context* does include cues within the word itself as well as throughout the text as a whole.

As noted in this chapter, researchers have studied various questions in learning vocabulary in context. But each study, for the most part, has only dealt with conditions for some arbitrary list of words and some predetermined correct or incorrect response rather than a graduated accrual of knowledge in some human endeavor. Appropriate word usage within any specialized human activity designates the user as knowledgeable in that activity. He or she apparently has the experience to correctly label events, actions, and principles of that domain. Basically, it is the topic, the subject matter, that provides the context, not the cues available within the written text. Although the within text cues can refine and enrich previous meanings for words, if the reader has no understanding of the topic, then learning will likely be confined to a possible recognition memory for the words. Word knowledge accrues with domain knowledge.

We do know that most word meanings are learned in context; it would be hard to imagine any other way that the vast semantic information we have concerning culturally conventionalized meanings could be acquired. But these meanings are not very precise (Cronbach, 1942), no more precise than the contextual information provided as cues to meaning.

Word meaning can be successfully taught as witnessed by several other chapters in this volume, but it is an arduous task. Experience or getting involved in many different activities probably helps along with wide reading on varied topics, but the folk wisdom is that some educe more learning (vocabulary knowledge) from exposure than others. Just doing something without direction from knowledgeable others (parents, teachers, master craftsmen, experts) who can explain the underlying conceptual structure for meaning is unlikely to help many novices. Context without contextual understanding will not suffice.

REFERENCES

Aborn, M., & Rubenstein, H. (1956). Word class distribution in sentences of fixed length. *Language, 32,* 666–674.

Ames, W. S. (1966). The development of a classification scheme of contextual aids. *Reading Research Quarterly, 2,* 57–82.

Anderson, J. R. (1983). *The architecture of cognition.* Cambridge, MA: Harvard University Press.

Anderson, R., & Freebody, P. (1981). Vocabulary Knowledge. In J. Guthrie (Ed.), *Comprehension and teaching: Research reviews* (pp. 77–117). Newark, DE: IRA Publications.

Anglin, J. M. (1977). *Word, object and conceptual development.* New York: W. W. Norton.

Aulls, M. (1971). Context in reading: How it may be depicted. *Journal of Reading Behavior, 3,* 61–73.

Bolinger, D., & Sears, D. (1981). *Aspects of language* (3rd ed.). New York: Harcourt, Brace, Jovanovich.

Calfee, R. C., & Curley, R. (1984). Structure of prose in content areas. In J. Flood (Ed.), *Understanding reading comprehension* (pp. 161–180). Newark, DE: IRA Publications.

Calfee, R. C., & Drum, P. A. (1986). Research on teaching reading. 804–849. In M. C. Wittrock (Ed.), *Handbook of research on teaching* (3rd ed.). New York: Macmillan.

Carpenter, P. A., & Just, M. A. (1981). Cognitive processes in reading: Models based on readers' eye fixation. In A. M. Lesgold & C. A. Perfetti (Eds.), *Interactive processes in reading* (pp. 177–213). Hillsdale, NJ: Lawrence Erlbaum Associates.

Carroll, B., & Drum, P. A. (1982). Effects of context in facilitating unknown word comprehension. In J. A. Niles & L. A. Harris (Eds.), *New Inquiries in reading* (pp. 89–93). Rochester, NY: National Reading Conference.

Carroll, B., & Drum, P. A. (1983). Definitional gains for explicit and implicit context clues. In J. A. Niles & L. A. Harris (Eds.), *Searches for meaning in reading/language processing and instruction* (pp. 158–163). Rochester, NY: National Reading Conference.

Carroll, J. B. (1976). Psychometric tests as cognitive tasks: A new "structure of intellect." In L. B. Resnick (Ed.), *The nature of intelligence* (pp. 27–56). Hillsdale, NJ: Lawrence Erlbaum Associates.

Cronbach, L. J. (1942). An analysis of techniques for diagnostic testing. *Journal of Educational Research, 36,* 206–217.

Daalen-Kaptejins, M. M. Van, & Elshout-Mohr, M. (1981). The acquisition of word meaning as a cognitive learning process. *Journal of Verbal Learning and Verbal Behavior, 20,* 386–399.

Dolch, E. W. (1932). *Reading and word meanings.* New York: Ginn.

Drum, P. A. (1983). Vocabulary knowledge. In J. A. Niles & L. A. Harris (Eds.), *Searches for meaning in reading/language processes and instruction* (pp. 163–171). Rochester, NY: National Reading Conference.

Dulin, K. (1970). New research on context clues. *Journal of Reading, 12,* 33–38.

Elivian, J. (1938). Word perception and word meaning in student reading in the intermediate grades. *Education, 59,* 51–56.

Emans, R. (1967). Teaching the use of context clues. *Elementary English, 44,* 243–246.

Finn, P. J. (1977–1978). Word frequency, information theory, and cloze performance: A transfer theory of processing in reading. *Reading Research Quarterly, 13,* 508–537.

Goodman, K. S., & Bird, L. B. (1984). On the wording of texts: A study of intra-word frequency. *Research in the Teaching of English, 18,* 119–145.

Graves, M. (1984). *The roles of instruction in fostering vocabulary development.* Paper presented at the meeting of the American Educational Research Association. New Orleans, LA.

Halff, H. M., Ortony, A., & Anderson, R. C. (1976). A context-sensitive representation of word meaning. *Memory and Cognition, 4,* 379–383.

Hoffman, J. V. (1980). Studying contextual build-up during reading through cumulative cloze. *Journal of Reading Behavior, 12,* 337–341.

Hunt, E. J. (1978). Mechanics of verbal ability. *Psychological Review, 85,* 109–130.

Jenkins, J., Stein, M., & Wysocki, K. (1984). Learning vocabulary through reading. *American Educational Research Journal, 21,* 767–787.

Jensen, A. R. (1980). *Bias in mental Testing.* New York: Free Press.

Kellerman, D. K. (1984). *New Webster's dictionary of the English language.* Delair.

Klein, H., Klein, G. A., & Bertino, M. (1974). Utilization of context for word identification in children. *Journal of Experimental Child Psychology, 17,* 79–86.

Konopak, B. C. (1984). *The effects of text characteristics on word meaning from high school physics texts.* Unpublished doctoral dissertation. University of California, Santa Barbara.

Kuczaj, S. A. II. (1982). Acquisition of word meaning in the context of the development of the semantic system. In C. J. Brainerd & M. Pressley (Eds.), *Verbal processes in children* (pp. 95–123). New York: Springer-Verlag.

Litowitz, B. (1976). Learning to make definitions. *Journal of Child Language, 4,* 289–304.

Lyons, J. (1977). *Semantics* (V. 1 & 2). New York: Cambridge University Press.

Madison, J., Carroll, B., & Drum, P. A. (1982). The effect of directionality and proximity of context clues on the comprehension of words. In J. A. Niles & L. A. Harris (Eds.), *New inquiries in reading research and instruction* (pp. 105–109). Rochester, NY: National Reading Conference.

McCullough, C. (1943). Learning to use context clues. *Elementary English Review, 20,* 140–143.

Miller, G. A. (1978a). Lexical meaning. In J. F. Kavanagh & W. Strange (Eds.), *Speech and language in the laboratory, school, and clinic* (pp. 394–436). Cambridge, MA: MIT Press.

Miller, G. A. (1978b). Semantic relations among words. In M. Halle, J. Bresnan, & G. A. Miller (Eds.), *Linguistic theory and psychological reality* (pp. 60–118). Cambridge, MA: MIT Press.

Morris, W. (1981). *The American heritage dictionary of the English language.* Boston: Houghton Mifflin Company.

Nagy, W. E., Herman, P. A., & Anderson, R. C. (1985). Learning words from context. *Reading Research Quarterly, 20,* 233–253.

Nelson, K. (1977). Cognitive development and the acquisition of concepts. In R. C. Anderson, R. J. Spiro, & W. E. Montqague (Eds.), *Schooling and the acquisition of knowledge* (pp. 215–239). Hillsdale, NJ: Lawrence Erlbaum Associates.

Petty, W. T. (1968). *The state of knowledge about the teaching of vocabulary.* Champaign, IL: National Council of Teachers of English.

Quealy, R. J. (1969). Senior high school students' use of context aids in reading. *Reading Research Quarterly, 4,* 512–532.

Rankin, E. F., & Overholser, B. M. (1969). Reaction of intermediate grade children to contextual clues. *Journal of Reading Behavior, 1,* 50–73.

Robinson, A. H. (1963). A study of techniques of word identification. *Reading Teacher, 16,* 238–242.

Robinson, F. P. (1961). *Effective study.* New York: Harper & Row.

Rubeck, P. (1977). Decoding procedures: Pupil self analysis and observed behavior. *Reading Improvement, 14,* 187–192.

Rubin, D. C. (1976). The effectiveness of context before, after, and around a missing word. *Perception and Psychophysics, 19,* 214–216.

Samuels, S. J., Begg, G., & Chen, C. C. (1975). Comparison of word recognition speed and strategies of less skilled and highly skilled readers. *Reading Research Quarterly, 11,* 72–86.

Schvaneveldt, R., Ackerman, B. P., & Semlear, T. (1977). The effect of semantic context on children's word recognition. *Child Development, 48,* 612–616.

Sternberg, R., Powell, J. S., & Kaye, D. B. (1983). The nature of verbal comprehension. In A. C. Wilkinson (Ed.), *Communicating with computers in classrooms: Prospects for applied cognitive science* (pp. 121–143). New York: Academic Press.

Thorndike, E. L. (1917). Reading as reasoning: A study of mistakes in paragraph reading. *Journal of Educational Psychology, 8,* 276–282.

Watson, R. (1982, March). *Definitions: The conventionalization of word meaning.* Paper presented at the meeting of the American Educational Research Association, New York.

Werner, H., & Kaplan, E. (1952). The acquisition of word meanings: A developmental study. *Monographs of the Society for Research in Child Development, 15.*

II HOW KNOWLEDGE OF WORD MEANINGS CAN BE PROMOTED

6 Most Vocabulary is Learned From Context

Robert J. Sternberg
Yale University

The thesis of this chapter is simple: Most vocabulary is learned from context. This chapter documents this claim, and draws out some of its main implications. Of equal importance, I discuss what the claim does not imply. What the claim does imply is that teaching people to learn better from context can be a highly effective way of enhancing vocabulary development. What the claim does not imply is that teaching specific vocabulary using context is the most effective, or even a relatively effective, way of teaching that vocabulary. Unfortunately, many believers in learning from context, as well as their detractors, have drawn the second inference rather than the first. As a result, they are on the verge of throwing out a perfectly clean and healthy baby with its, admittedly, less than sparkling bath water.

My chapter is divided into five basic parts. First, I present what I consider to be three basic facts about vocabulary. Second, I attempt to account for these facts within a single explanatory framework. Third, I discuss the implications of the facts and framework for the teaching and learning of vocabulary. Fourth, I provide an overview of some data we have obtained using these facts and framework as a basis for teaching vocabulary-acquisition skills. Finally, I draw some conclusions.

THREE BASIC FACTS ABOUT VOCABULARY

Let's start with the three basic facts: First, although estimates of adult vocabulary sizes differ, there is no disagreement that the typical adult has in his or her vocabulary tens of thousands of words, and in exceptional cases,

89

adults may have vocabularies in excess of 100,000 words. Second, one's level of vocabulary is highly predictive, if not determinative, of one's level of reading comprehension. Despite the gross surface dissimilarity between vocabulary tasks, which seem primarily to measure acquired knowledge, and reading comprehension tasks, which seem primarily to measure the ability to acquire new knowledge, the correlations between these two types of tests often are almost as high as their reliabilities. Third, vocabulary is probably the best single indicator of a person's overall level of intelligence. Stated in another way, if one wants a quick and not-too-dirty measure of a person's psychometrically measured intelligence, and thus has time to give just one brief test of it, vocabulary is generally the best predictor of overall score on a psychometric IQ test.

These are three basic facts about vocabulary. It would be theoretically elegant, at best, and parsimonious, at worst, if we could account for all three of these facts in terms of a single explanatory mechanism, or theory.

AN EXPLANATORY FRAMEWORK
FOR THE THREE BASIC FACTS

There is a simple explanation to account for all three of these facts. The explanation is that most vocabulary is learned from context. During the course of one's lifespan, one is exposed to innumerable words through seemingly countless sources — textbooks, lectures, newspapers, magazines, friends, enemies, parents, movies, and so on. Even if one learned only a small proportion of the words thus encountered in the contexts in which they are presented, one could plausibly develop a vocabulary of tens of thousands of words, which represents only an infinitesimal proportion of our exposure to words. It is difficult to see any other way in which so many words could be learned. Certainly, no one has sat down and memorized tens of thousands of words, or formed keyword images linking new words, old words, and pictures. Nor are memorization or forming of keywords practical strategies for learning a language as a whole, as opposed to selected words within that language. There is just too much to learn! Context can also help explain the link to reading comprehension: Whereas vocabulary is an indirect measure of ability to learn word meanings in context, reading comprehension is a fairly direct measure of ability to learn concepts in context, where the concepts may be single words, facts, ideas, or whatever. The major difference would then be that reading comprehension tests measure present ability to learn from context, whereas vocabulary tests measure past ability. Except in the cases of old age or mental infirmities, where present ability may be significantly less than past ability, one would expect these two measurements to be highly correlated. The contextual view also explains the high correlations with intelligence test scores. Much of intelligence is, quite simply (as well as complexly!), the ability to learn from context. A better learner of anything, not just of words, is someone who can use context to increase his or her knowledge base, which will later form the basis for expertise in any of a variety of content areas.

Just how does one learn vocabulary from context? Sternberg and Powell (1983) have proposed that learning from context involves three basic ingredients: knowledge-acquisition processes, contextual cues, and moderating variables. Consider, for example, the passage fragment:

> Although for the others the party was a splendid success, the couple there on the blind date was not enjoying the festivities in the least. An *acapnotic,* he disliked her smoking; and when he removed his hat, she, who preferred "ageless" men, eyed his increasing *phalacrosis* and grimaced.

Processes of Knowledge Acquisition

According to our theory (Sternberg & Powell, 1983), three processes are applied to learning new words such as *acapnotic* and *phalacrosis.*

1. *Selective encoding* involves separating relevant from irrelevant information for the purposes of formulating a definition. For example, it is relevant to figuring out the meaning of acapnotic that he disliked her smoking, but it is not relevant that the couple was at a party.

2. *Selective combination* involves combining relevant cues into a workable definition. For example, in figuring out the meaning of phalacrosis, one needs to combine at least four relevant cues—that the woman likes "ageless" men, that the removal of the man's hat led to the conclusion that the man is not ageless, that the man with whom she has the date is showing increasing signs of phalacrosis, and that she grimaced as a result.

3. *Selective comparison* is a process by which new information about a word is related to old information already stored in memory. To figure out the meaning of phalacrosis, for example, one needs to know that among men, baldness often increases with age, and even that baldness becomes visible when one removes one's hat.

Contextual Cues

The three processes of selective encoding, selective combination, and selective comparison do not operate in a vacuum, or at random. Rather, they operate on a relatively stable set of cues provided by the context in which new words occur. These cues include:

1. *Temporal cues*: cues regarding the duration or frequency of X (the unknown word), or when X can occur

2. *Spatial cues*: cues regarding the location of X, or possible locations in which X can sometimes be found

3. *Value cues*: cues regarding the worth or desirability of X, or the kinds of affects X arouses

4. *Stative descriptive cues*: cues regarding properties of X (such as size, shape, color, odor, feel, etc.)

5. *Functional descriptive cues*: cues regarding possible purposes of X, actions X can perform, or potential uses of X

6. *Causal/Enablement cues*: cues regarding possible causes of or enabling conditions for X

7. *Class membership cues*: cues regarding one or more classes to which X belongs, or other members of one or more classes of which X is a member

8. *Equivalence cues*: cues regarding the meaning of X, or contrasts (such as antonymy) to the meaning of X.

Moderating Variables

Because of moderating variables, it is not always equally easy to apply the three knowledge-acquisition processes to the eight context cues. These variables make it either easier or harder to apply the processes to the cues. The moderators include variables like the following:

1. *Number of occurrences of the unknown word*: multiple occurrences of an unknown word increase the number of available cues and can increase the usefulness of individual cues if readers integrate information obtained from cues surrounding the multiple occurrences of the word. For example, the meaning of a given temporal cue may be enhanced by a spatial cue associated with a subsequent appearance of the unknown word, or the temporal cue may gain in usefulness if it appears more than once in conjunction with the unknown word. On the other hand, multiple occurrences of an unfamiliar word can also be detrimental if the reader has difficulty integrating the information gained from cues surrounding separate appearances of the word, or if only peripheral features of the word are reinforced and are therefore incorrectly interpreted as being of central importance to the meaning of the unfamiliar word.

2. *Variability of contexts in which multiple occurrences of the unknown word appear*: different types of contexts, for example, different kinds of subject matter or different writing styles, and even just different contexts of a given type, such as two different illustrations within a given text of how a word can be used, are likely to supply different types of information about the unknown word. Variability of contexts, up to a certain point, increases

the likelihood that a wide range of types of cues will be supplied about a given word, and thus increases the probability that a reader will get a full picture of the scope of a given word's meaning. Although variability of contexts can help, too much variability can overwhelm the reader and interfere with learning the meaning of a new word. If the information is presented in a way that makes it difficult to integrate across appearances of the word, or if a given individual has difficulties in making such integrations, then the variable repetitions may actually obfuscate rather than clarify the word's meaning. In some situations and for some individuals, a stimulus overload may occur, resulting in reduced rather than increased understanding. Mere repetition of a given unknown word in essentially the same context as that in which it previously appeared is unlikely to be as helpful as a variable-context repetition, because few or no really new cues are provided regarding the word's meaning.

3. *Importance of the unknown word to understanding the context in which it is embedded*: if a given unknown word is judged to be necessary for understanding the surrounding material in which it is embedded, the reader's incentive for figuring out the word's meaning is increased. If the word is judged to be unimportant to understanding what one is reading (or hearing), one is unlikely to invest any great effort in figuring out what the word means.

4. *Helpfulness of surrounding context in understanding the meaning of the unknown word*: a given cue can be differentially helpful depending upon the nature of the word whose meaning is to be inferred and upon the location of the cue in the text relative to the word whose meaning is to be inferred. Consider first an example of how the nature of the word can affect cue helpfulness. A temporal cue describing a *diurnal* event would probably be more helpful than a spatial cue in aiding an individual to figure out that diurnal means daily. In contrast, a spatial cue would probably be more helpful than a temporal cue in figuring out that *ing* is a low-lying pasture. It is unrealistic to expect a given kind of cue to be equally helpful in figuring out the meanings of all kinds of words. Consider, for example, how the location of the cue relative to the unknown word can affect cue helpfulness. If a given cue occurs in close proximity to the unknown word, then it is likely that the cue will be recognized as relevant to inferring the unknown word's meaning. If the cue is separated from the unknown word by a substantial portion of text, the relevance of the cue may never be recognized; indeed, the cue may be misinterpreted as relevant to an unknown word to which it is more proximal. The helpfulness of a context cue may also be mediated by whether the cue comes before or after the unknown word.

5. *Density of unknown words*: if a reader is confronted with a high density of previously unknown words, he or she may be overwhelmed and be unwilling or unable to use available cues to best advantage. When the density of unknown words is high, it can be difficult to discern which of the cues that are available apply to which of the words that are unknown. In such a situation,

utilization of a given cue may depend upon figuring out the meaning of some other unknown word, in which case the usefulness of that cue (and very likely of other cues as well) is decreased.

6. *Usefulness of previously known information in cue utilization*: inevitably, the usefulness of a cue will depend on the extent to which past knowledge can be brought to bear upon the cue and its relation to the unknown word. The usefulness of prior information will in large part depend on a given individual's ability to retrieve information, to recognize its relevance, and then to apply it appropriately.

For example, the proximity of the context cues to the words acapnotic and phalacrosis makes these cues easier to apply. The necessity of understanding the meanings of these two words to understanding the passage as a whole (which is about why the blind date failed) increases reader motivation to learn the words' meanings. One's knowledge that some people are vigorous anti-smokers and that some men, myself excluded, go bald with age, facilitates one's decontextualization of the meanings of the two words. . . . And so on. Our data show that it is sometimes easier to learn a new word for a new concept rather than to use an old word that already has another meaning for a new concept. The latter case promotes negative transfer (Tetewsky & Sternberg, 1986).

To summarize, I have claimed in this part of the chapter that three basic facts about vocabulary — its size, its relation to reading comprehension, and its relation to intelligence — can be explained, at least in part, by a tripartite theory of vocabulary learning.

IMPLICATIONS OF THE FACTS AND FRAMEWORK
FOR THE TEACHING AND LEARNING OF
VOCABULARY

What are the implications of the facts and framework for the learning and teaching of vocabulary?

Before discussing these implications, I must make clear one thing that the facts and framework do not imply, namely, that learning from context is the fastest or most efficient way of learning specific vocabulary. The inference does not follow logically, and it is not correct empirically. The naturalness or typical use of a method of learning does not imply its optimality. To the contrary, there may be more efficient ways of learning. During the past several years, Joel Levin, Michael Pressley, and their colleagues have performed a series of studies that have convinced me, at least, that for learning specific vocabulary, the keyword method of vocabulary teaching and learning is faster and more efficient than learning from context (see, e.g., Levin, McCormick, Miller, Berry, & Pressley, 1982; Pressley, Levin, Kuiper, Bryant, & Michener, 1982; Pressley, Levin, & McDaniel, this volume). As far as I can tell, it may be the most effective of the currently available methods. If I have any concerns about that method, they are not with its efficacy, but with the nature and durability of its use. I seek here not to criticize the keyword method, but rather to clarify the conditions of its use.

First, the keyword method, and other methods related to it, require one to know in advance the meaning of the unknown word(s) one wishes to learn. Learning from context does not. If one has definitions available, then learning from context is not so efficient. Why waste a good definition? But during the course of most vocabulary learning, one does not have definitions readily available. Usually, a dictionary is not available. Even if it was, many people are too lazy or busy to look up meanings of the new words they encounter. The point to be made is that during the large majority of word-learning experiences, learning from context is the only feasible method of word learning. If one teaches methods of learning from context, it should be with the goal of teaching vocabulary-building skills, rather than of teaching specific vocabulary.

Second, the keyword method lacks a certain spontaneity. In some respects, the method may be reminiscent of speed reading. Speed reading is often more efficient than normal reading. But how many people continue to use it, well beyond the time they learned to use it? Indications are that the overwhelming majority do not. I could swear that once, after taking the Evelyn Wood Speed Reading Dynamics Course, I read several thousand words a minute. Within a short time, I was back to several hundred. Speed reading requires a great deal of mental effort — more than most people are willing to expend during the extended course of their everyday reading — and it is also, at least for some, uncomfortable. I cannot help but wonder how many people who have learned vocabulary by the keyword method, whether in an experiment or in actual language instruction, will continue diligently to use the method on their own. Thus, my concern in this chapter is not with what people might be able to do, but with what they actually do.

Let me turn now to what the facts and framework do imply. I think they imply that learning from context is central to most everyday vocabulary learning, and that teaching people the processes, cues, and moderating variables of contextual learning can help those people if they do not already use these vocabulary-learning aids spontaneously. In order for these aids to be effective, first, they do have to be used spontaneously. Otherwise, laziness or busyness will intervene to render them as ineffective as other methods of vocabulary building might be in the course of one's everyday life. Second, they have to be used almost automatically. By adulthood, good readers should apply the processes of selective encoding, selective combination, and selective comparison to available cues while being at most minimally aware that they are doing so.

If one is to teach learning from context, then I believe there are three principles one must keep in mind. Without them, I doubt such teaching will be effective.

First, presentation of words in context is not enough: One needs theory-based instruction in how to use context. In typical contextual training programs, including those used in experimental comparisons to other methods of vocabulary teaching, the learning-from-context method consists of presenting words embedded in a series of sentences, either with or without prior definitions. But if children (or adults) do not know the processes, cues, and moderating variables that can be used for contextual learning, they will not benefit optimally from such instruction. In essence, they have to learn how to learn from context before they actually can learn from it.

Second, presentation of the words in context, plus decontextualization knowledge and skills, is not enough either: One needs relevance of the training to students' everyday lives, and the students must be convinced of this relevance. It took an "ignorant" graduate student to teach me this. A visiting potential graduate student indicated to me and to some of my graduate students that he was interested in the possibility of working with me in my research on context effects. I took this to mean that he was interested in the work I was doing relating real-world environmental contexts to intelligence. My graduate students took this to mean that he was interested in the work I was doing on learning vocabulary from context. Eventually, it occurred to me that it was odd that I was studying two kinds of context, but treating them as totally distinct. It had never even occurred to me that I was regularly using the same word, "context," in two contexts that I was perceiving as totally distinct.

The visiting graduate student has led me to question whether they are so distinct. If one presents students or subjects with uninteresting words in uninteresting contexts, whether for experimental credit or for a test the next day, it is perhaps unreasonable to expect strikingly high levels of learning. In most of one's life, one learns because one wants to or because one truly has to, or both. The kinds of training we have given in our experiments or in certain training programs scarcely constitutes such learning. For many students, it will be quite irrelevant to their lives. Why is context so effective in everyday life, if not in the lab, then? Because context, whether verbal or otherwise, forms the milieu in which we live. We need to learn from it to survive, or to survive well. Our laboratory experiments and training programs scarcely reproduce these kinds of conditions, at least for most people. I am reminded of my experience in reading a particularly difficult journal article. When its author sent it to me, I read it and hardly understood a thing. When I received it to review, I read it and understood it quite well. The second exposure may have helped. But what helped more was that I needed to understand it the second time, so I made sure I did. In short, then, the ignorant graduate student may have known more than I did.

Third and finally, it is critical in teaching vocabulary to teach students to teach themselves. No matter how many words we teach them directly, those words will constitute only a small fraction of the words they will need to know, or that they eventually will require. They truly constitute a drop in the vocabulary bucket. It doesn't really matter a whole lot how many of those few words students learn, or how well they learn them. What matters is how well they will go on learning long after they have exited from our lives, as we have exited from theirs. This will be true whether we see them during the course of a 1-hour experiment, or a 1-month training program, or whatever. If, indeed, most vocabulary is learned from context, then what we most need to do is not to teach vocabulary from context, but to teach students to use context to teach themselves.

DATA TESTING THE THEORY OF LEARNING VOCABULARY FROM CONTEXT

We have collected data that test both the theory of learning from context and its application to vocabulary learning. This research is ongoing, so this chapter by no means presents the final story. But I am able to summarize here what progress we have made so far, emphasizing the data on testing the theory as applied to teaching vocabulary decontextualization skills.

Initial Test of the Theory

The theory was first tested (Sternberg & Powell, 1983) by asking 123 high school students to read 32 passages of roughly 125 words in length that contained embedded within them from 1 to 4 extremely low-frequency words. Thirty-seven of the words (all nouns) were used in the passages; each target word could appear from 1 to 4 times, resulting in 71 different presentations altogether. Passages were equally divided among four different writing styles: literary, newspaper, scientific, and historical. An additional sample passage was written in the literary style.

The students' task was to define, as best they could, each of the low-frequency words within each passage (except for multiple occurrences of a single word within a given passage, which required only a single definition). Students were not permitted to look back to earlier passages and definitions in making their current responses.

Qualities of definitions were rated independently by three trained raters. Because mean inter-rater reliability was .92, an average of the three ratings was used as a definition-goodness score for each word for each subject. These averages were then averaged over subjects to obtain a mean goodness-of-definition rating for each word. The main independent variables were ratings of the number or strength of the occurrences of our contextual cues and moderating variables (with the exact nature of the rating depending upon the independent variable) with respect to their roles in helping in the deciphering of the meaning of each low-frequency word in the passages.

Theory testing was done via multiple regression. We used a stepwise multiple-regression procedure in which we allowed only three variables plus a regression intercept to enter into our final models. The decision to limit the number of variables was made on the basis of our judgment of the degree of refinement of our data, and in the hope of minimizing the risks of capitalization upon chance that inhere in stepwise regression. Because of multicollinearity (correlation among) independent variables, it was not possible to make strong inferences regarding the "true" subsets of variables that were differentially relevant from one passage style to the next. Variables that entered into at least one of four regressions were enablement, stative-descriptive, functional-descriptive, and equivalence cues, plus moderating variables of helpfulness and importance. The correlations between predicted and observed goodness ratings were .92 for literary passages, .74 for newspaper passages, .85 for science passages, and .77 for history passages. All of these values differed significantly from zero.

We concluded on the basis of these data that the contextual cues and moderating variables proposed by our subtheories provided good prediction of the goodness-of-definition data, although we certainly do not believe that our model accounted for all of the reliable variance. Indeed, the square roots of the internal-consistency reliability coefficients (based on all possible split halves of subjects) for our four data sets, which place an upper limit on each value of R (the multiple correlation), were all .98 or above, showing that there was considerable reliable variance not accounted for by the fitted model. Nevertheless, fits of the model subsets seemed sufficiently high to merit some optimism regarding our initial attempts to understand differential word difficulty in learning from context. Moreover, performance on the task was successful in distinguishing high from low verbal subjects: Definition goodness ratings for individual subjects correlated .62 with IQ, .56 with vocabulary, and .65 with reading comprehension scores. The data, although extremely limited, are consistent with the notion that the proposed theory of cognitive competence is on the right track, at least in the domain of verbal declarative knowledge.

Instructional Experiments

In a second experiment conducted in collaboration with Elizabeth Neuse, we tested 81 sophomores and juniors in an inner-city high school. The subjects were divided into two basic groups, a training group (59 subjects) and a control (no-training) group (22 subjects). The mean IQ of the subjects was 97, with a standard deviation of 11.

The experimental design in this experiment involved seven independent variables: (a) training group (experimental, control), (b) testing time (pretest, posttest), (c) test format (blank, nonword), (d) cue type (stative descriptive, functional descriptive, class membership), (e) unknown word type (abstract, concrete), (f) restrictiveness of context with respect to the meaning of the unknown word (low, high), and (g) sentence function of the unknown word (subject, predicate). These variables were completely crossed with respect to each other. Treatment group was a between-subjects variable; all other variables were within-subject and were manipulated via a crossed-variables testing arrangement. Two different test forms were used, and half the subjects received the first form as a pretest and the second form as a posttest; the other half of the subjects received the reverse arrangement. Test items, involving either neologisms or blanks (cloze procedure), were each presented in the context of a single sentence. There were 48 items on each test. Scores on the pretest were correlated .74 with an IQ test (Henmon–Nelson) given before training, and .71 with an alternative form of the test given after training. Scores on the posttest were correlated .65 and .64, respectively, with the two administrations of the IQ test.

The training sequence was spread out over six sessions. The seven topics covered were:

1. What is context? Subjects were introduced to the concept of context, and of how context can be used to figure out meanings of words whose meanings are unfamiliar.

2. Using sentence context. Subjects were shown examples of how context can be used in different ways to figure out word meanings, and were invited to try out some examples on their own.

3. 20 questions (spotting cue types). Subjects were motivated to learn about cue types by being given examples of unknown words used in context, and then generating the questions one would want to ask about these words in order to figure out what they meant. In this way, they were informally introduced to the various cue types.

4. Cues I (temporal, spatial, stative-descriptive, equivalence). Subjects were instructed as to four of the kinds of cues, learning what each one is, being given examples of it, and then being asked to use it to figure out meanings of unknown words in context.

5. Using paraphrase to figure out word meanings. Subjects were shown how attempting to paraphrase the meaning of a sentence — saying to oneself what the sentence is trying to communicate — can help one figure out the meanings of unknown words.

6. Cues II (functional-descriptive, causal). Subjects were instructed in two more kinds of cues, learning what each one is, being given examples of it, and then being asked to use it to figure out meanings of unknown words in context.

7. Mystery words (neologisms presented in sentences or paragraphs). Subjects were given fairly lengthy sentences and paragraphs with unknown words, and asked to apply all that they had learned to figure out the meanings of these words.

The six class periods proved ample to cover this range of theory-based material.

In the experimental group, significant main effects were obtained for testing time (posttest higher than pretest), cue type (stative–descriptive hardest, functional–descriptive in-between, category membership easiest), context restrictiveness (higher restrictive more difficult than lower restrictive), and sentence function (predicates harder than subjects). In the control group, significant main effects were obtained for cue type (same ordering of means as previously given) and restrictiveness of context (same ordering of means as previously given). Thus, there was a significant pre- to posttest gain in the trained group, but not in the untrained group. However, the interaction between group and training effect was not statistically significant. In addition, there were a number of statistically significant interactions between independent variables, suggesting that model effects were not wholly independent and additive, but were interactive with each other.

Taken as a whole, these results suggest (a) that subsets of the cues and moderating variables do have additive effects that can be quantified and isolated, (b) that the additive effects are supplemented by interactive ones, and (c) that at least some training of decontextualization skills is possible. The set of results is thus supportive of the ideas in the theory of verbal decontextualization, but emphasizes the need to consider interactions as well as main effects in analyses of model fits.

The greatest disappointment in this experiment was the weakness of the training effects. I believed that enough had been learned from this experiment to make possible the design of an experiment that explicitly looked at training effects, without the "distraction" of also testing other things. The next experiment was therefore directed specifically at obtaining improvements in decontextualization ability through theoretically based training.

In this experiment, 150 New Haven area adults (nonstudents) of roughly average intelligence were divided into one of five conditions. There were three training conditions (with a fourth, combined-procedure condition yet to be run) and two control conditions. Subjects in all three training conditions and one of the control conditions received exactly the same practice words and passages, but differed in the instruction they received (if any) regarding the passages. Passages were similar to those in the first experiment.

The 30 subjects in each of these conditions were given a 25-item pretest and a 25-item posttest measuring skill in figuring out word meanings, as well as other tests. The pretest and posttest were transfer tests, in that they measured skill in figuring out word meanings: They did not merely test recall of words in the practice materials. Our goal was not to train specific vocabulary, but rather to train vocabulary-building skills. All words in the experiment were extremely rare English-language words. The same pretest and posttest words were used in each condition, and training words were the same across conditions. Items were scored on a 0–2 point scale, for a maximum score of 50 points per test. Each training session lasted 45 minutes, exclusive of the various kinds of testing, which brought session length to 2½ hours. The conditions, which were between-subjects, were as follows.

In a *process-training condition,* subjects were taught and given practice using the mental processes (selective encoding, selective combination, selective comparison) alleged by the theory to be involved in figuring out meanings of new words from context.

For example, selective encoding was described as the process of sifting out relevant from irrelevant information. Students were presented with several lines of text that contained a rare word, and were given a detailed explanation of how selective encoding could be used to discover the relevant information about the word's meaning in the text. For example, one of the texts read:

> He first saw a *macropodida* during a trip to Australia. He had just arrived from a business trip to India, and he was exhausted.

Processing of these sentences was described as follows:

> There is much information to weed out. For example, we need not know that the man in the passage was on a business trip. We do not need to know that he had been to India or that his *first* exposure to *macropodida* occurred in Australia. That he saw a *macropodida* in Australia is relevant, but we could care less whether he had seen one a hundred times before in every zoo imaginable. In the first sentence there are two important cues: (1) the man saw a *macropodida,* so *macropodida* must be visible, and (2) *macropodida* can be seen in Australia. The second sentence does not contain any relevant information; the facts of this sentence relate to the man, not to the unknown word.

Practice exercises were then presented in which subjects were asked to underline portions of the text that seemed relevant to the meaning of the unknown word.

In a *contextual-cue training condition,* subjects were taught and given practice using the contextual cues upon which the mental processes operate (e.g., class membership, stative–descriptive).

For example, for Cues I (temporal, spatial, stative–descriptive, and equivalence), setting cues were described as temporal, spatial, and situational information about contexts in which an unknown word may be found. Examples of each type of cue were given. Subjects were told to judge cues by sorting out information specifically relevant to the unknown word. For example, one of the texts began:

> Two ill-dressed people, the one a haggard woman of middle years and the other a lean young man, sat around a fire where the common meal was almost ready. The mother, Tanith, peered at her son through the *oam* of the bubbling stew.

Cues in the text were explained as follows:

> There are three setting cues in the first sentence, and the phrase, 'around a fire where the common meal was almost ready', contains them all. 'Around a fire' is a spatial cue because it tells where the action takes place. The words, 'common meal', provide a situational cue, and 'almost ready' is an important temporal cue.

Subjects were then given practice in identifying setting cues.

In a *moderating-variable training condition,* subjects were taught and given practice using the moderating variables that affect how well the processes can be applied to the cues (e.g., the location of a cue in the passage relative to the unknown word).

For example, for number of occurrences of an unknown word, subjects were told that multiple occurrences signal a word's importance to a text and provide additional information about its meaning, but they also require integration of information from the cues surrounding each appearance.

One of the passages used as an example follows:

> The *flitwite* was only one of the judicial remedies available to the justices of the Court of the King's Bench in the 11th century, but it was perhaps the most important. Its frequent use added enormously to the treasury's coffers, and new royal expenditures were often financed by the issuance of an increased number of *flitwites*. However, even the most impartial of justices must have handed them down in multitudes, for the *flitwite* was as much a part of 11th century society as the civil tort is of our own. Medieval men and women related in direct and personal ways; therefore, conflict was likely to take the form of actual fighting. In our litigious culture, the law must often deal with more subtle forms of conflict.

The word's definition is given at the end of the passage: "a fine for fighting." The information from each occurrence of the word was explained as follows:

> We learn from the first sentence that the *flitwite* was an important judicial remedy in the 11th century. The context of the second occurrence tells us that the *flitwite* was important because it 'added enormously to the treasury's coffers'.

The context of the third use of the term informs us that *flitwites* were an important part of 11th century culture. As we read on, we learn that the flitwite appears to be a penalty for fighting.

Subjects were then given practice passages and asked to define target words.

In a *vocabulary-memorization control condition,* subjects were asked to memorize definitions of 75 extremely rare words (that otherwise did not appear in the experiment), and were tested on their memory for these words.

In a *context-practice control condition,* subjects were given exactly the same practice that was given to subjects in the three training conditions, except that the practice occurred in the absence of training.

The mean pretest–posttest gain scores (out of 50 points possible on each test) were 7.2 for the process condition, 5.2 for the contextual-cue condition, 7.6 for the moderating-variable condition, 1.1 for the word-memorization control condition, and 2.6 for the context-practice condition. The results are clear: The training groups showed significantly greater gains than did the control groups. Two additional features of the means are worthy of note: First, as would be expected, the controls receiving relevant practice showed greater gain than did the controls receiving irrelevant memorization. The practice control condition is actually similar to many contextual training programs, which consist of little more than practice. Second, to the extent that other programs involve any training at all, it is in contextual cues, which provide the least facilitation of all three training conditions.

In sum, theoretically motivated instruction in learning words from context can make a significant and substantial difference in people's ability to learn word meanings from context. In just 45 minutes of training, substantial gains in decontextualization ability were obtained. Of course, the durability of this training has yet to be shown.

CONCLUSIONS

Most vocabulary is acquired from context. If one's goal is to develop vocabulary-learning skills, instruction in aspects of decontextualization of word meanings — and particularly in processes of knowledge acquisition, contextual cues, and moderating variables — is an effective way to foster this development. In our own research with a general adult population, training in any one of the three aspects of decontextualization resulted in significant and substantial gains in subjects' ability to figure out meanings of new words, relative to control groups. Thus, training of decontextualization skills develops the natural tendency to use such skills, and potentially enables the individual to apply these skills in his or her everyday life. But there are some caveats on the use of decontextualization training that have perhaps been ignored in much past research on learning vocabulary from context.

First, teaching students specific vocabulary words through the use of context is probably not going to result in gains that are as rapid or as large as the gains attained through the use of other methods, such as the keyword method or possibly even rote instruction. The learning-from-context method is at its best for teaching learning-to-learn skills, not for teaching specific vocabulary. Thus, the purpose of teaching decontextualization skills is, ideally, not the same as teaching the keyword method or teaching vocabulary by rote. As a result, comparisons among the methods may be somewhat misleading. If a school has a given amount of time for teaching verbal comprehension skills, though, I would argue that teaching decontextualization skills constitutes a better use of that time than does teaching specific vocabulary. At best, the specific vocabulary taught will be only a small drop in a very large bucket. Teaching decontextualization skills will enable the student later to acquire new words on his or her own. Thus, one is equipping the student with a transfer mechanism that cannot be gained simply from learning specific vocabulary. Recall, for example, that the tests in our learning-from-context experiments are actually transfer tests. They do not measure merely whether specific vocabulary was learned from context, but whether generalized skills for acquiring new words were so learned and can be applied.

Second, training decontextualization skills is probably appropriate for secondary-school students and a general adult population, but not for highly verbal adult subjects, for example, bright college students. We initially attempted to apply our decontextualization training program to Yale undergraduates, who are already preselected for verbal ability. The results were disappointing, for two reasons. First, students were already performing at near-ceiling levels on our tests, largely because they already had skills either similar or identical to those we were trying to train. Second, their application of these skills was already automatic, and our bringing them back to a controlled, conscious level interfered with rather than facilitated their use of decontextualization. Once information processing is automatized, training in that or related forms of information processing can actually interfere with rather than enhance performance (Wagner & Sternberg, 1984).

Third, a training program for vocabulary-building skills must motivate the students by showing the relevance of the skills being taught to their everyday lives. Our own experience indicates that unless the program motivates the students, it will not succeed.

Finally, such a training program should be theoretically based. We believe that our final program for training vocabulary-building skills was successful because it motivated students, but also because it was based on a theory of decontextualization, rather than merely teaching students by example. In typical programs training specific vocabulary from context, students are expected already to know how to use context to increase their vocabulary. This expectation is unrealistic for many students. Many students need to be taught how to use context, and what they are taught should be based upon psychological theory rather than upon intuitions that may or may not have any psychological grounding.

To conclude, it has been shown that a psychologically based theory of how people learn vocabulary from context can be useful in training vocabulary-building skills. The validation of the theory stems both from empirical data directly testing the theory and data showing the usefulness of the theory for training vocabulary-building skills. It is tempting, in vocabulary-building programs, to train specific vocabulary, just as it is tempting in mathematics programs to train students in particular mathematical formulas and facts. But ultimately, it is what can be used and transferred that matters most, and my hunch is that decontextualization skills are among the most valuable kinds of knowledge one can have. I am not arguing against training specific vocabulary. But I believe such training ought to be supplemented by training in vocabulary-building skills. In this way, the student can teach him or herself well after any particular course has come to an end.

ACKNOWLEDGMENT

Preparation of this chapter was supported by Contract N0001483K0013 from the Office of Naval Research and Army Research Institute.

REFERENCES

Levin, J. R., McCormick, C. B., Miller, G. E., Berry, J. K., & Pressley, M. (1982). Mnemonic versus nonmnemonic vocabulary-learning strategies for children. American Educational Research Journal, 19, 121.136.

Pressley, M., Levin, J. R., Kuiper, N. A., Bryant, S. L., & Michener, S. (1982). Mnemonic versus nonmnemonic vocabulary-learning strategies: Additional comparisons. *Journal of Educational Psychology, 74,* 693–707.

Sternberg, R. J., & Powell, J. S. (1983). Comprehending verbal comprehension. *American Psychologist, 38,* 878–893.

Tetewsky, S. J., & Sternberg, R. J. (1986). Conceptual and lexical determinants of nonentrenched thinking. *Journal of Memory and Language, 25,* 202–225.

Wagner, R. K., & Sternberg, R. J. (1984). Alternative conceptions of intelligence and their implications for education. *Review of Educational Research, 54,* 179–223.

7

Remembering Versus Inferring What a Word Means: Mnemonic and Contextual Approaches

Michael Pressley
University of Western Ontario

Joel R. Levin
University of Wisconsin

Mark A. McDaniel
University of Notre Dame

From our point of view, vocabulary research, and more generally, the entire field of curriculum and instruction, is at its best when it is an experimental discipline. New procedures are compared to old ones; old techniques are examined to determine if they are all that they are "cracked up to be." The potential for growth of the experimental science of vocabulary acquisition in particular, is great, if for no other reason than the large number of procedures that have been hypothesized to promote the growth of vocabulary (e.g., Johnson & Pearson, 1978). In this chapter we are concerned especially with comparisons of mnemonic and context approaches to vocabulary learning, a problem area that has been explored in depth by experimenters interested in vocabulary acquisition.

A critical distinction in this chapter is between remembering what a defined vocabulary item means given the meaning and inferring the meaning from internal and external contextual cues (Jenkins & Dixon, 1984). Most of our previous work focused on remembering, whereas others have been concerned with inferring (e.g., Sternberg & Powell, 1983; Sternberg, Powell, & Kaye, 1983). The distinction between remembering and inferring is important because we emphasize that effective vocabulary-inferring processes and effective vocabulary-remembering strategies are complementary vocabulary-acquisition components, with one's strength being the other's weakness, and vice versa. In particular, we propose here that learning from context and the use of mnemonic techniques (described in detail shortly) are potentially effective vocabulary-inferring and vocabulary-remembering components, respectively. Learners can derive vocabulary meanings from context, but this process alone does not foster retention of meanings. On the other hand, mnemonic techniques positively affect remembering, but do not permit learners to infer the meanings of undefined vocabulary words. There is one other reason for emphasizing the remembering–inferring distinction: Others have confused these two vocabulary-acquisition components and their associated processes (e.g., Sternberg et al., 1983). This is unfortunate because it is easier to understand the existing research literature on vocabulary learning by emphatically distinguishing these two components. Accordingly, empirical contributions bearing on both inference and remembering are reviewed here, but with the lines between the two types of research clearly drawn. Because experimentation on vocabulary remembering is both more extensive and more refined than experimentation on meaning inference, greater attention is given here to the former than the latter.

INTRODUCTION TO VOCABULARY-REMEMBERING APPROACHES

Much of naturalistic vocabulary instruction involves explicit presentation of vocabulary words and their definitions. That is, vocabulary instruction is aimed at getting children to remember provided meanings rather than getting them to infer meanings. For example, much of vocabulary teaching with young children involves repetitive matching of a name with its referent, such as "ball" with a picture of a ball (Werner & Kaplan, 1952). Labeling of referents is a prominent part of mother–infant interaction during the first 3 years of life (Chapman, 1977; Moerk, 1972; Ninio, 1980, 1983; Ninio & Bruner, 1978). Preschoolers' picture books are filled with objects that parents label for their children. Grade-school reading programs include exercises with vocabulary items and their definitions presented together (e.g., Whyte & Shular, 1974). Lists of words and their meanings are included in most second-language curricula (e.g., O'Brien, Lafrance, Brackfeld, & Churchill, 1970), even when the method of instruction is principally language use in context (e.g., Ray & Lutz, 1969). Many high school English and college-preparation courses include lessons on vocabulary, including texts filled with lists of words and their definitions (e.g., Lewis, 1982). These examples fly in the face of the claim that real world vocabulary acquisition follows principally from people inferring meanings from context (see Sternberg et al., 1983; other chapters in this volume). Instructions involving the explicit pairing of new vocabulary words and their definitions is a prominent approach to vocabulary instruction. Inferring definitions from context is required only some of the time.

Mnemonic Vocabulary-Remembering Strategies

There is convincing evidence that one particular strategy facilitates individuals' acquisition of vocabulary definitions. That strategy is the mnemonic *keyword method*, where mnemonic refers to systematic procedures specifically designed to improve one's memory (see, for example, Bellezza, 1983; Paivio, 1983; Paivio & Desrochers, 1981; Pressley, Levin, & Delaney, 1982). Originally developed as an aid to second-language vocabulary learning (Atkinson, 1975), the method has also proven beneficial as a strategy to enhance memory of *native-language* vocabulary (Levin & Pressley, 1985).

The most common version of the keyword method involves construction of interactive visual images. The learner generates an image of the definition referent interacting with a keyword, which is simply a familiar concrete word that resembles a salient part of the unfamiliar vocabulary word. For example, the English word *carlin* means *old woman*. Using the keyword *car*, a learner might generate an image of an old woman driving a car. When presented *carlin* later, ready retrieval of *car* occurs because of its acoustic similarity to *carlin*, which leads to recall of the linking image containing the *old woman*. An alternative version of the method consists of verbally elaborating (Rohwer, 1973) the keyword and the definition; that is, relating the keyword to the definition in a meaningful sentence, as in "The *car* was driven by an *old woman*" (Pressley, Levin, & McCormick, 1980). An important addendum is that subjects need not generate the pictorial or verbal interactions themselves. Experimenter-provided interactions are always at least equally effective.

One of the most replicable findings in the experimental vocabulary literature is that keyword subjects recall many more definitions than do no-strategy control learners (Levin & Pressley, 1985; Pressley, Levin, & Delaney, 1982). Time and again the mnemonic keyword method has proven to be a potent and versatile vocabulary-remembering strategy.

The Range of Keyword Applicability

The Keyword Method Aids Diverse Populations.   In collaboration with colleagues and students, we have provided ample documentation that keyword mnemonics can be employed with any age child except infants (e.g., Pressley, Samuel, Hershey, Bishop, & Dickinson, 1981), although it is not until the late grade-school years that children can generate keyword images proficiently given vocabulary, keywords, and definitions in verbal form only (Pressley & Levin, 1978). In general, there is always a way to engineer materials so that there can be large keyword-based gains, although the younger the child, the greater the need for the experimenter to provide the keyword and interactive mediators (Pressley & Levin, 1978; see Pressley, 1982, for a detailed account of the development of elaboration and keyword-elaborative skills).

Positive keyword benefits are not limited to normal populations either. The keyword method has promoted the vocabulary learning of poor learners in every test to date — learning-disabled children (e.g., Mastropieri, Scruggs, & Levin, 1985), retarded learners (Scruggs, Mastropieri, & Levin, 1985), and low-ability college students (McDaniel & Pressley, 1984; Pressley, Levin, Nakamura, Hope, Bispo, & Toye, 1980; see Pressley & Levin, in press, for detailed commentary).

The Keyword Method is Useful for Learning of a Variety of Vocabulary Item Types.   The method has proven adaptable to materials possessing diverse characteristics. For instance, children and adults can use the method to learn verbs, abstract, nouns, and adjectives (Levin, McCormick, Miller, Berry & Pressley, 1982; Miller, Levin, & Pressley, 1980; Pressley, Levin Kuiper, Bryant, & Michener, 1982; Pressley, Levin, & Miller, 1981b). The keyword method has proven readily adaptable to the world of naturalistic associations (social studies and science facts, expository prose), with published demonstrations of positive keyword effects for many tasks with an associative component. (See Levin, 1985, for an extensive review of the relevant literature.)

Keyword Method Effects are Robust Across Methods of Presentation and Testing.   There have been many different presentation formats in keyword studies — slides (e.g., Paivio, Clark, Pressley, & Desrochers, 1984), cards (e.g., Pressley & Levin, 1978), booklets (e.g., Levin, Pressley, McCormick, Miller, & Shriberg, 1979), live experimenters (in most studies), and televised models (e.g., McGivern, Levin, Ghatala, & Pressley, 1983). The method works with various methods of pacing (e.g., Pressley, Levin, Digdon, Bryant, & Ray, 1983).

In fact there is only one presentation format variable for which there is any evidence of reduced keyword method effects. Keyword/no-strategy control differences did not transpire among adult subjects instructed in classroom groups in a series of experiments conducted by Levin, Pressley, McCormick, Miller, and Shriberg (1979). The bulk of the relevant data (most generated since 1979) contrast with the outcomes reported by Levin et al. (1979). Pressley, Levin, and Delaney (1982) identified many experiments in which mature subjects benefited enormously from in-class keyword interventions. Additionally, McCormick, Levin, Cykowski, and Danilovics (1984) and Aurentz (1983) provided recent classroom demonstrations of keyword method potency with mature learners. We emphasize, as well, that *all* relevant evidence supports the conclusion that classroom instruction in keyword mnemonics improves the associative learning of children. Levin et al.'s (1979) Experiments 5 and 6 are the best references for readers interested in applying the method in grade-school classrooms.

As far as robustness with respect to testing formats, use of the keyword method increases performance on any task mediated by knowledge of vocabulary-meaning linkages (e.g., using vocabulary in sentences; Levin, Dretzke, Pressley, & McGivern, 1985; Pressley, Levin, & Miller, 1981a).

The Keyword Method is a Mature Strategy That can be Taught to Immature Learners.   Children and adults often are required to learn the meanings of vocabulary as well as other naturalistic associations. The keyword method is a flexible approach for real-world associative learning. In teaching it to people, educators are inculcating a skill used extensively by the best adult learners (e.g., Pressley & Ahmad, 1986; Pressley & Levin, 1977; Pressley, Levin, Digdon, Bryant, & Ray, 1983; Pressley, Levin, Kuiper, Bryant, & Michener, 1982). Even adults who do not use keyword strategies spontaneously prefer elaboration once they are exposed to it (O'Sullivan & Pressley, 1984; Pressley & Ahmad, 1986; Pressley & Dennis-Rounds, 1980; Pressley, Levin, & Ghatala, 1984; See Levin (in press), Levin and Pressley (1983, 1985), and Pressley and Levin (in press) for more complete commentaries on keyword method effects and applications. See Pressley, Borkowski, and O'Sullivan (1984, 1985) for discussion of how to inculcate potent elaboration strategies so that learners apply them across a variety of situations.

MNEMONIC VERSUS CONTEXTUAL VOCABULARY-REMEMBERING STRATEGIES

The keyword method fares well compared to vocabulary-remembering strategies based on semantic-contextual analyses, such as provision of sentences or paragraphs that serve to relate unfamiliar vocabulary items to familiar concepts and experiences based on the learner's existing *word* knowledge and *world* knowledge. Comparisons of mnemonic strategies with contextual strategies are informative for two reasons; (a) they permit an empirical assessment of contextual-based vocabulary-remembering strategies, strategies claimed to be effective in the curriculum and instruction literatures (e.g., Johnson & Pearson, 1978); and (b) they can be used to examine theoretical proposals about the role of contextual analysis in vocabulary acquisition (e.g., Sternberg et al, 1983). We first discuss studies conducted with children, and then proceed to the relevant adult literature.

Studies With Children

In a study with fourth- and fifth-grade children, Levin, Johnson, Pittelman, Hayes, Levin, Shriberg, and Toms-Bronowski (1984) compared the mnemonic keyword method with a contextual-analysis strategy. Contextual analysis required that the students search for clues contained in short paragraphs, clues that enabled inference of the meanings of unfamiliar vocabulary words contained in the paragraphs (i.e., Sternberg et al.'s, 1983, "external" cues). For example, the following passage was used to provide contextual support for the word *angler* (*a person who likes to go fishing*):

> The *angler* carried a lot of things down to the stream. He carried a net and a tackle box, as well as his fishing pole. He hoped to catch a lot of fish that afternoon.

The experimenter pointed out the specific fishing- and fisherman-related words within the paragraph [e.g., *stream, he* (to signify that an angler is a person), *fishing pole*] that could furnish clues for deducing and confirming the word's meaning. The keyword method was implemented with illustrations in which two characters were engaged in a dialogue that related the keyword to the vocabulary definition. For *angler* the central figure in the illustration was an *angel* who was fishing. Students provided with keyword illustrations later remembered about 50% more definitions when cued with the vocabulary words than did students in the contextual-analysis condition. This held for both higher and lower achieving populations.

Pressley, Ross, Levin, and Ghatala (1984) demonstrated mnemonic superiority relative to another contextual approach frequently used in schools. Ten- to 13-year-olds were presented a list of 22 low-frequency English nouns and their definitions. Half of the items were studied via the keyword method, and half were studied by constructing sentence contexts in which the vocabulary word was used appropriately. After one learning trial the keyword method advantage was substantial: Definitions of 51% of the keyword items were recalled in contrast to 8.5% of the context items. Definition recall of keyword items exceeded that of context items for 93% of the children.

Levin, McCormick, Miller, Berry, and Pressley (1982) reported two experiments in which keyword and contextual vocabulary-learning approaches were compared. In one experiment, fourth-grade children learned the definition of verbs representing relatively complex concepts (e.g., *persuade, hesitate, gesture, glisten*). All subjects were shown each vocabulary item and its definition (e.g., for *persuade* the definition was *when you talk someone into doing something*). Keyword subjects were additionally presented dialogued illustrations similar to those in the Levin et al. (1984) study, and context subjects were provided a meaningful sentence in which the vocabulary word was used appropriately. For *persuade* the sentence was *The lady's friend was try-*

ing to persuade her to buy a pocketbook. As in the Levin et al. (1984) study, keyword subjects recalled an average of 50% more definitions that did context subjects.

In Levin et al.'s (1982) second experiment, fourth graders learned a variety of vocabulary items. The new words were presented in one of four ways. The mnemonic picture condition was identical to the keyword condition in the first experiment. In particular, for *surplus* (*having some left over, having more than was needed*) children received the keyword *syrup.* A keyword illustration showed one of two children pouring syrup on some pancakes, with many additional bottles of syrup visible in a cupboard. One of the children asked, Should you use so much *syrup?*, while the other replied, It's OK; we have a *surplus* of it in the cupboard. In a nonmnemonic picture context condition the children viewed illustrations similar to those just described except for changes that replaced the keyword-related objects with something equally appropriate. For the example, *surplus, ketchup* replaced *syrup.* A third condition consisted of presenting the vocabulary words and their meanings accompanied by paragraph contexts illustrating the use of the words. No-strategy control subjects used their own best method of study.

Mnemonic picture subjects remembered far more vocabulary-cued definitions than did subjects in any other condition. Performances in the two naturalistic context conditions were equivalent and no better than in the no-strategy control condition.

Studies with Adults

The case in favor of mnemonic over contextual methods is also strong with adult learners. For instance, Pressley, Levin, and Miller (1982) presented low-frequency English words and their definitions to college students to learn according to either the keyword method or one of three semantic-contextual approaches. Keyword subjects generated their own mnemonic images relating keywords to definitions. In one context condition (sentence provided), the vocabulary items were embedded in sentence contexts (as in Levin et al.'s, 1982, first experiment). In a second context condition (sentence judgment), subjects judged whether vocabulary items were used appropriately in sentences (half were and half were not). In the final context condition (sentence construction), subjects generated their own sentences with the vocabulary items used appropriately (as in the Pressley et al., 1984, study). A no-strategy control condition was also included. The pattern of results mirrored those in the just-discussed Levin et al. (1982) experiment with children. Keyword subjects recalled more than anyone else; and levels of recall were comparable in the three context conditions and not different from control recall.

In Sweeney and Bellezza (1982), college students studied the definitions of low-frequency, abstract English vocabulary words. The keyword method was more effective than a provided-sentence context condition on a 4-day de-layed retention test.

One potential criticism of contextual strategies as operationalized in the re-search discussed so far is that subjects were exposed to only a *single* context for each item. The use of *multiple* contextual exposures for a given vocabu-lary item is usually recommended by curriculum specialists (Johnson & Pearson, 1978). Thus, Pressley, Levin, Kuiper, Bryant, and Michener (1982, Exp. 3) incorporated a variety of operations in their test of semantic-contextual approaches to vocabulary learning. Subjects were shown synonyms of the vocabulary items, provided illustrations and sentence elabo-rations of the definitions, and read sentences with the words used appropri-ately. After one trial of exposure to the English vocabulary, subjects in the multiple-contextual treatment recalled 28% of the definitions in contrast to 62% by subjects generating keyword interactions.

New, Improved Studies With Adults

Sternberg (this volume; Sternberg et al., 1983) has argued that the context treatments that were just described do not capitalize on the inference proces-ses that should be associated with such treatments and that this failure ac-counts for their impotency in promoting vocabulary remembering. This is because the definitions of the vocabulary items were provided, and thus, sub-jects did not have to rely on the context to *figure out* the definition. Although such an argument confuses the vocabulary-remembering versus vocabulary-inferring distinction made at the outset, there are some recent data quite rele-vant to it. In the first place, in four experiments Shaughnessy (personal com-munication, November, 1984) reported that college students who have to infer vocabulary definitions from sentence and paragraph contexts do *not* re-member more of those definitions than do subjects who are just provided with the vocabulary items and their definitions (see also Johnson & Stratton, 1966). Secondly, direct comparisons of vocabulary-inferring context treat-ments with the keyword method cast doubt on inference-laden context strate-gies as an aid to remembering.

McDaniel and Pressley (1984). McDaniel and Pressley included four conditions in their first of two experiments with college students. The to-be-remembered vocabulary items consisted of low-frequency English words (e.g., *loggia balcony*). In the *keyword* condition, subjects were provided with the vocabulary items, definitions, and keywords, along with instructions to use the keyword method to remember the definitions. *Context* subjects were presented a three-sentence paragraph that included the vocabulary word a couple times, but without an accompanying definition. These subjects inferred the vocabulary item's meaning from the contextual cues. For *loggia,* context subjects saw:

> We leaned over the loggia during the play. It was on the second floor of the theater. The loggia was open to the stage below.

Clearly, this type of context manipulation satisfies the Sternberg et al. (1983) criterion for affording learners "external cue" opportunities (i.e., it allows them to extract information from surrounding contextual cues in the service of inferring meanings). In the *combined* condition, subjects were presented the paragraphs used in the context condition, told to infer their meanings from them, and then instructed to use the keyword method (as in the keyword condition). There was also a *no-strategy control* condition.

An obvious bottleneck to remembering the meaning of a vocabulary word presented according to a vocabulary-inferring context format (as in the Shaughnessy and the McDaniel and Pressley studies) is that the word's meaning might not be inferred correctly by the subject. Benefits of the context method could be limited to those instances when the word's correct meaning was discovered. Although this "incorrect inference" problem appears to have been operating in the Shaughnessy experiments, McDaniel and Pressley dealt with it by having context and combined subjects write down what they thought each vocabulary word meant on the basis of the paragraphs presented. Then, McDaniel and Pressley examined both vocabulary-cued definition recall ("simple recall") and the same recall conditionalized on items that were inferred correctly (conditional recall).

The results of McDaniel's and Pressley's first experiment were rather complex, with the pattern of conditions differences varying with verbal ability. For lower ability students (verbal SAT scores less than 560), statistical differences among conditions in simple recall were as follows: keyword > control > combined > context. For higher ability students (verbal SAT scores exceeding 560), the ordered conditions were: keyword control > combined context. When conditional recall was considered, the patterns changed little: Most notably, the context treatment was the *least* effective condition for both higher and lower ability students.

Students' verbal ability was quite highly correlated with recall in the control condition, moderately correlated with recall in the context condition, and not at all correlated in the keyword condition. Such differential correlations suggest aptitude-by-treatment interactions at the general ability level, but also suggest that there were differences in the extent to which control subjects spontaneously applied effective vocabulary-remembering strategies. Given the previously reported association between spontaneous mnemonic-strategy use and level of recall in no-strategy control conditions (e.g., Beuhring, 1981; Levin, Dretzke, McCormick, Scruggs, McGivern, &

Mastropieri, 1983; Pressley & Ahmed, 1985; Pressley et al., 1982), a reasonable hypothesis is that McDaniel's and Pressley's higher ability control subjects spontaneously applied mnemonic strategies whereas their lower ability subjects did not. Unfortunately, direct assessment of spontaneous strategy use was not included in the study.

McDaniel and Pressley replicated their main manipulation with an alternative dependent measure. McDaniel and Pressley reasoned that a vocabulary-inferring context experience might produce more effective use *of vocabulary in sentences,* because context subjects have a better understanding of the contextual constraints for a vocabulary item than do keyword subjects. On both simple and conditional definition recall measures, however, the performance of keyword subjects exceeded that of definition-inferring context subjects. Equally interesting — and compatible with previous data (e.g., Levin, Dretzke, Pressley, & McGivern, 1985; Pressley, Levin, & Miller, 1981a), when subjects later constructed sentences containing the vocabulary items, their performance was predictable from the simple recall data. That is, the keyword versus context difference was apparent even on this sentence-construction measure.

In general, McDaniel and Pressley did not find that provision of vocabulary-inferring contexts facilitates vocabulary remembering, relative either to the mnemonic keyword method or no-strategy control instructions. Of course, the major theme that we are continuing to develop here is that although providing contexts should facilitate meaning *discovery,* there is no reason to expect inference operations to facilitate subsequent meaning *retention.* The case grows ever stronger when McDaniel and Tillman's (1985) data are considered.

McDaniel and Tillman (1985).   It could be argued that in order to make optimal use of a vocabulary-inferring context strategy, subjects must first receive explicit instruction in how to extract meaning from context (see, for example, Sternberg et al., 1983). Also, it might be that the amount of time that McDaniel and Pressley allocated to their context subjects (20 secs per item) was insufficient for them both to extract a well-formulated definition and to study the definition. A third possible criticism of the McDaniel and Pressley study concerns the limited breadth of definitions that were included (see Curtis, this volume). The use of simply defined vocabulary items (e.g., *old woman, balcony*) may have been detrimental to the context subjects, who could have extracted an elaborated concept for each vocabulary item, only to be asked to provide a one- or two-word definition at testing. That is, there could have been an acquisition/testing mismatch for context subjects (e.g., McDaniel, Friedman, & Bourne, 1978; Morris, Bransford, & Franks, 1977).

Contrary to the aforementioned hypotheses is another explanation for the context method's inferiority as a vocabulary-remembering strategy. This explanation is based not on shortcomings associated with McDaniel and Pressley's evaluation of the context method, but on shortcomings associated with the method itself. A critical factor in the vocabulary-remembering process is the establishment of a reliable associative link between the vocabulary word and its definition. The context method does not focus the learner's attention on establishing this link, even though the definition itself may be correctly extracted and thoroughly processed. According to this position, the context method might produce good recall or recognition *of individual item definitions,* but it does not operate on the vocabulary/definition link to enhance *vocabulary-cued* definition recall or recognition. On the other hand, the keyword method does include the associative link needed to enhance vocabulary-cued performance, though ostensibly not memory for isolated definitions per se (see also Pressley, Levin, Hall, Miller, & Berry, 1980; and Pressley et al., 1982).

In order to address these issues, McDaniel and Tillman incorporated the following modifications into McDaniel and Pressley's basic design. First, vocabulary-inferring context subjects were given an overview of Sternberg et al.'s (1983) procedures as an aid to discovering the meaning of an unknown vocabulary item. Specifically, the types and uses of both internal contextual cues (furnished from the vocabulary word per se) and external contextual cues (furnished from the surrounding words) were explained. Second, keyword and no-strategy control subjects were provided with elaborated definitions that were adapted from dictionary entries (e.g., *holm* means a small island, especially one in a river or lake), rather than simple one- or two-word definitions. During the acquisition period for each item, *all* subjects were then required to write a one- or two-word synonym for the vocabulary item. Finally, the presentation rate of the items was varied, half of the 60 items presented at 20-sec per item (i.e., the rate used by McDaniel and Pressley) and half presented at a 30-sec per item rate. These modifications permitted examination of the possibility that the previous poor performance of context subjects was due to inadequate instruction, an acquisition/test incongruency, and/or insufficient processing time.

To assess the associative versus free-recall issue, subjects were instructed to recall as many of the vocabulary words and their definitions as possible, writing these on the same line whenever they believed that the words and definitions were correctly paired. It was emphasized that either individual words or definitions should be written down in cases where the two could not be remembered together. After this free-recall test, the subjects were provided a vocabulary-cued definition recall test ("cued recall").

Keyword subjects significantly outperformed context subjects on the cued-recall test (for both simple and conditional measures), but not on the free-recall test. Increases in memory performance due to increases in presentation rate were not accompanied by significant interactions involving conditions, although a marginally significant interaction for free recall of vocabulary definition pairs indicated that the control subjects tended to benefit most from the additional study time. McDaniel and Tillman (1985) concluded that the superiority of the keyword method, relative to the context method, may be traced to subjects' acquisition of associative links between vocabulary items and their definitions. Increasing study time does not narrow the gap in performance between context and keyword conditions, at least within the time limits used by Tillman and McDaniel. Keyword versus context differences are apparent even when context subjects are given explicit instruction in using internal and external contextual cues to infer meanings, and when keyword subjects are required to construct a one- to two-word synonym from an elaborated definition. The keyword subjects' superiority disappears when a memory task is administered that does not depend on remembering specific vocabulary/definition associations (free recall).

Additional findings, stemming from McDaniel and Tillman's no-strategy control condition, are noteworthy. Control subjects performed at least slightly better than context subjects on every measure taken. On none of the seven measures were control subjects statistically different from keyword subjects, with the direction of the means favoring keyword subjects on the cued-recall measures and favoring control subjects on the free-recall measures. Anticipating that they would replicate McDaniel and Pressley's keyword versus control nondifference, McDaniel and Tillman questioned control subjects at the end of the experimental session regarding the strategies that they had used to learn the vocabulary items. Fifty-three percent of them reported spontaneously using keyword-like strategies. These control subjects proved to be comparable to keyword subjects in their mean level of cued recall, whereas the 47% of the control subjects who did not report keyword-like strategies were substantially worse.

Despite McDaniel and Tillman's results, a final verdict on remembering vocabulary from context should await a study involving *thoroughly* trained context subjects. McDaniel and Tillman did give instruction in the use of internal and external contextual cues, but no extensive hands-on practice was provided. On the other hand, only brief instruction and practice are required to implement the keyword method. Thus, it is fair to conclude that when a comparable amount of training is given to context subjects, the keyword method is a superior vocabulary-remembering strategy. This conclusion is especially striking when accompanied by the highly plausible assumption that late adolescents and adults are very experienced at inferring meanings from context (Sternberg et al., 1983). Should context theorists succeed in devising training procedures that enhance vocabulary remembering at all (e.g., relative to no-strategy controls), then a re-rexamination of the keyword versus context issues would be in order (Sternberg, this volume, offers a description of preliminary data relevant to the training issue).

Closing Comments on Keyword versus Contextual Vocabulary-Remembering Strategies

As scientists who believe that empirical data are necessary to support both theoretical claims and practical recommendations, we are puzzled at the positive regard afforded to students' use of external context cues as a vocabulary-remembering strategy. Quite simply, there are no convincing data to support either theory or recommendations associated with context-based strategies. Meager support for the context method is accepted uncritically.

Gipe's (1979) vocabulary-remembering study is a case in point. Although heavily cited as support for the use of context, the study suffers from serious methodological problems including multiple-treatment confounding; does not implement the contextual strategy in the "vocabulary-inferring" manner that is theoretically prescribed (see our previous discussion); and reports only a very small positive effect due to the contextual strategy, an effect that could not be replicated by Gipe herself on at least two occasions (Gipe, 1981). Regarding the last point is that semantic-context benefits on vocabulary-remembering tasks typically have *not* been found empirically. (In addition to the studies mentioned earlier, see Ahlfors, 1980, Crist & Petrone, 1977, and Hare, 1976.) Even when the contextual treatment is properly operationalized, it has proven either no better or significantly *worse* than no-strategy control instructions (McDaniel & Pressley, 1984; McDaniel & Tillman, 1985).

As we have argued since 1982 (Pressley et al., 1982), there is no good theoretical reason, apart from increased processing time and attention, why externally cued context strategies should be effective for remembering vocabulary-definition linkages. Although there is a large literature documenting that meaningful semantic contexts and associations can enhance individual item recall and recognition (e.g., Craik & Tulving, 1975; Hyde & Jenkins, 1973; McDaniel & Masson, 1977; Nelson & Vining, 1978), vocabulary remembering in an associative task in which the major challenge is to form connections between new, unfamiliar words and their definitions. Most of the context-based strategies proposed to date (sentence reading, sentence constructing, sentence evaluating, reading definition-supporting paragraph, and definition inference from paragraph-provided contextual cues) share the deficit demonstrated by McDaniel and Tillman. They do not operate on the associative link, but rather on the meaning of the word per se. For all of these exercises, learners could perform successfully even if they ignored the vocabulary item itself; that is, a blank could be substituted for the vocabulary word and the subjects could still execute the strategy.

Why are mnemonic techniques so much more powerful vocabulary-remembering strategies than are externally cued context approaches? The keyword method provides a direct link between the vocabulary item and its definition. When cued with the vocabulary word, the learner can proceed directly to the keyword, then to the keyword interaction, and finally to the associated definition. This direct retrieval path is the critical processing difference that favors mnemonic- over context-based strategies (see also Levin & Pressley, 1985).

Until now, our discussion seriously challenges those who advocate the use of *external* contextual cues as a strategy for remembering the definitions of new vocabulary items. In contrast, we are far more optimistic regarding the possibilities for exploiting *internal* contextual cues as an effective vocabulary-remembering strategy. Some preliminary evidence from our laboratory shows how this might be done.

Kaye and Sternberg (cited by Sternberg & Powell, 1983) showed that adults can use their knowledge of suffixes, prefixes, and root words to infer the meanings of unfamiliar vocabulary. Of course, to be proficient at this requires knowledge of a large number of prefixes, suffixes, and root words, and, as Kaye and Sternberg have observed, such knowledge is often lacking even among college students. Pressley, Levin, Woo, Sinclair, and Ahmad (1985) provided college and elementary-school students with mastery-learning instruction (to a 100% criterion) of some root words. Students learned roots such as *dorm* meaning *sleep, chrom* meaning *color,* and *taph* meaning *tomb.* When later asked to remember that *dormeuse* means *a sleeping carriage,* that *chromatosis* means *an unnatural coloring of the skin,* and that *cenotaph* means *a monument to a person buried elsewhere,* these internal-context mastery subjects were far superior to control subjects who were not given the previous internal-context instruction. Such findings suggest that remembering new vocabulary can indeed be facilitated through students' capitalization on previously learned word parts.

Additional research on students' use of internal context as a vocabulary-remembering strategy is underway. The root word approach is especially promising because the learning of roots is a manageable task. There are only 3,000 to 4,000 common roots in English (Smith, 1982), and knowledge of these prefixes, suffixes, and stems provides a good foundation for the tens of thousands of words a good reader knows (Nagy & Anderson, 1984) and should make the acquisition of such a formidable lexicon a much easier task.

VOCABULARY-INFERRING STRATEGIES

With respect to the vocabulary-acquisition goal of remembering the definitions of new words, we have just concluded that mnemonic strategies are consistently effective, externally cued context strategies are consistently ineffective, and internally cued context strategies are promising. With respect to the vocabulary-acquisition goal of inferring the definitions of new words, the available evidence generally supports the use of externally cued contextual strategies.

Research on Students' Use of Context

External Context.   There are ample data to suggest that provision of external context (surrounding sentence and paragraph cues) *does* enhance students' ability to define new words or to comprehend passages (see Drum & Konopak, this volume). Yet, additional controlled studies are needed in which students' ability to infer new word meanings from external context is compared with their ability to infer the same word meanings when no context is provided. Of particular interest are studies that assess the magnitude of context effects over a wide range of subject variables including age, cognitive ability, and the like. Research of the kind already conducted by Drum and Konopak (e.g., Carroll & Drum, 1982, 1983) is useful to the extent that it helps to specify the conditions under which skilled readers make better use of context to infer new word meanings, relative to less skilled readers (see also Jenkins, Stein, & Wysoski, 1984; Quealy, 1969). In addition to the topic, type, and placement variables already studied by those investigators, however, external contexts varying in their proximity to subjects' world knowledge should be experimentally manipulated and their effects on subjects' vocabulary-inferring ability assessed. Component-separating training studies of the kind described by Sternberg (this volume) also are valuable for providing an understanding of how individuals capitalize on context to infer new word meanings. Additional research of this kind is to be encouraged.

Internal Context.   With regard to reliance on internal context (inspection of word parts) for inferring new vocabulary, certainly much more empirical research is needed than studies than include only correlations of vocabulary-inferring ability with measures of intelligence (e.g., Sternberg et al., 1983). Controlled investigations of root-word knowledge and use as a vocabulary-inferring *strategy* must be conducted before it can be claimed that such a strategy is effective. Some research now underway in our laboratory is relevant to this issue, and so we discuss it briefly.

Similar to the approach already described for vocabulary remembering, Levin and Pressley (in collaboration with Russell Carney) are investigating the promise of internal-context instruction as a vocabulary-inferring strategy. In a study now in progress, subjects are given initial mastery-learning instruction on a list of root stems (e.g., *sect, pone, ject*) and on a list of prefixes (e.g., *ex, inter, ad*). They are subsequently presented Kaye's and Sternberg's compound words (e.g., *exsect, interpone, adject*). One question is whether the prior mastery instruction enhances subjects' inferences about the meanings of the compound words. An even more interesting question relates to the form in which such prior instruction is delivered: How well will subjects who are taught the separate word parts mnemonically be able to infer the subsequent compound-word meanings, relative both to subjects who are taught the separate word parts with reference to already established semantic concepts and to those who are allowed to study the word parts and their definitions however they wish? The notion of combining mnemonic- and semantic-strategy approaches has been considered previously (e.g., Levin, 1981, 1982) and, given the vocabulary-remembering versus vocabulary-inferring distinction, seems particularly appealing in the present context.

A Final Caveat: Context Misuse

Balanced against the case for encouraging learners to derive meanings from context is evidence that use of context can cause even very sophisticated students to make blatantly *incorrect* inferences about vocabulary meanings (e.g., Bensoussan & Laufer, 1984; Curtis, personal communication, July 1985; McDaniel & Pressley, 1984). For instance, after reading, "There again we see how *tenuous* the urge of the male to provide for his own children is, for it can be so easily destroyed by different social arrangements," a common error is to think that *tenuous* means strong (Laufer & Sim, in press). Laufer and Sim review in detail the extent of these types of errors. Serious vocabulary and text comprehension errors arising from incorrectly interpreted cues occur often. When this problem is combined with the generally negative results in experimental investigations of context as a vocabulary-remembering strategy, there is good reason for skepticism about the benefits that follow from inferring the meanings of vocabulary from context (but see Sternberg, this volume, for a contrasting point of view). Exploiting context is a strategy with pitfalls, including the possibility of leading the learner completely astray.

FINAL WORDS ON KEYWORD VERSUS CONTEXT

So far in this chapter, we have argued for the criticality of distinguishing between remembering and inferring goals of vocabulary instruction. Consistent with our previous caution that no one strategy represents a panacea for facilitating *all* vocabulary-learning objectives (Levin & Pressley, 1985), we are prepared to offer the following empirically derived conclusions regarding mnemonic- versus contextual-based instructional strategies.

If one's objective is to maximize vocabulary remembering, then a mnemonic approach clearly is the instructional strategy of choice. This recommendation follows directly from a decade of vocabulary-remembering research in which mnemonic strategy instruction has consistently proven superior to numerous strategy competitors. On the other hand, if one's objective is to enhance other aspects of vocabulary acquisition and use (e.g., pronunciation, syntax, spelling, motivational aspects), then alternative instructional strategies should be considered. Note that we are reluctant to include measures of *comprehension* in the domain of "other" vocabulary-learning objectives because it has been found that whenever vocabulary comprehending depends upon vocabulary remembering to some extent, the mnemonic instructional strategies are facilitative as well (Levin & Pressley, 1985).

In specific regard to enhancing students' ability to infer the meanings of unknown words (vocabulary inferring), contextual strategies are promising and should continue to be investigated. In situations where internal or external contextual cues are available to permit correct inferences about new word meanings, students should not just be encouraged to capitalize on them but also instructed how to do so systematically and efficiently (e.g., along the lines of Johnson & Pearson's, 1978, "contextual analysis" strategy). Also included here is the provision of relevant surrounding-word and root-word instruction when needed. Whether specific instructional strategies can be devised to minimize the occurrence of the kind of incorrect inferences illustrated by Laufer and Sim (in press) has yet to be explored (see Sternberg, this volume).

Theoretical analyses indicate that vocabulary remembering and vocabulary inferring involve the operation of quite different cognitive processes on the part of a student. Strategies that maximize one's success in one situation are unlikely to do so in the other. Contextual- and mnemonic-strategy approaches appear to work in complementary ways, and thus, strategy efforts directed toward exploiting this complementarity (either separately or in combination) should yield exciting returns.

In closing, we emphasize the need for comprehensive experimental analyses of the many techniques hypothesized to be powerful aids to various aspects of vocabulary acquisition. Armchair analyses about vocabulary learning are not good enough. Reliable knowledge about instructional interventions does not follow either from superficial inspection of the educational world or from high-level theoretical speculation. Solid knowledge about educational interventions only follows from extensive experimentation.

ACKNOWLEDGMENTS

The writing of this chapter was supported by a grant to the first author from the Natural Sciences and Engineering Research Council of Canada and by a grant to the second author from the National Institute of Education through the Wisconsin Center for Education Research.

REFERENCES

Ahlfors, G. (1980). Learning word meanings: A comparison of three instructional procedures. (Doctoral dissertation, University of Minnesota, 1979) *Dissertation Abstracts International, 40,* 5803-A. University Microfilms No. 80-11754)

Atkinson, R. C. (1975). Mnemotechnics in second-language learning. *American Psychologist, 30,* 821–828.

Aurentz, J. (1983). *Self-instruction and the keyword method: Effects upon vocabulary usage.* Unpublished manuscript, Tallahassee, FL: Department of Educational Research, Development, and Foundations, Florida State University.

Bellezza, F. S. (1983). Mnemonic-device instruction with adults. In M. Pressley & J. R. Levin (Eds.), *Cognitive strategy research: Psychological foundations* (pp. 51–74). New York: Springer-Verlag.

Bensoussan, M., & Laufer, B. (1984). Lexical guessing in context in EFL reading comprehension. *Journal of Research in Reading, 7,* 15–32.

Beuhring, T./ (1981). *Elaboration and associative memory development: The metamemory link.* Unpublished manuscript, Department of Psychology, University of Southern California, Los Angeles.

Carroll, B. A., & Drum, P. A. (1982, March). *The influence of text type and context clue type on the comprehension of unknown words.* Paper presented at the annual meeting of the American Educational Research Association, New York.

Carroll, B. A., & Drum, P. A. (1983, April). *The specificity of context clues in refining word meaning.* Paper presented at the annual meeting of the American Educational Research Association, Montreal.

Chapman, R. (1977). Comprehension strategies in children. In J. Kavanaugh & P. Strange (Eds.), *Language and speech in the laboratory, school, and clinic* (pp. 308–327). Cambridge, MA: MIT Press.

Craik, F. I. M., & Tulving, E. (1975). Depth of processing and the retention of words in episodic memory. *Journal of Experimental Psychology: General, 104,* 268–294.

Crist, R. L., & Petrone, J. M. (1977). Learning concepts from contexts and definitions. *Journal of Reading Behavior, 9,* 301–303.

Gipe, J. (1979). Investigating techniques for teaching word meaning. *Reading Research Quarterly, 14,* 624–644.

Gipe, J. (1981). *Investigation of techniques for teaching new word meanings.* Paper presented at the annual meeting of the American Educational Research Association, Los Angeles.

Hare, S. Z. (1976). An investigation of the effectiveness of three methods of teaching reading vocabulary (Doctoral dissertation, University of South Carolina, 1975). *Dissertation Abstracts International, 36,* 7185-A.

Hyde, T. S., & Jenkins, J. J. (1973). Recall of words as a function of semantic, graphic, and syntactic orienting tasks. *Journal of Verbal Learning and Verbal Behavior, 12,* 471–480.

Jenkins, J. R., & Dixon, R. (1984). Vocabulary learning. *Contemporary Educational Psychology, 8,* 237–260.

Jenkins, J. R., Stein, M. L., & Wysoski, K. (1984). Learning vocabulary through reading. *American Educational Research Journal, 21* 767–788.

Johnson, D. D., & Pearson, P. D. (1978). *Teaching reading vocabulary.* New York: Holt.

Johnson, D. M., & Stratton, R. P. (1966). Evaluation of five methods of teaching concepts. *Journal of Educational Psychology, 57,* 48–53.

Laufer, B., & Sim, D. D. (in press). "Taking the easy way out": Non-use and misuse of clues in EFL reading. *English Teaching Forum.*

Levin, J. R. (1981). The mnemonic '80s: Keywords in the classroom. *Educational Psychologist, 16,* 65–82.

Levin, J. R. (1982). Pictures as prose-learning devices. In A. Flammer & W. Kintsch (Eds.), *Discourse processing* (pp. 412-444). Amsterdam: North-Holland.

Levin, J. R. (1985). Educational applications of mnemonic pictures: Possibilities beyond your wildest imagination. In A. A. Sheikh (Ed.), *Imagery in the educational process* (pp.63-87). Farmingdale, NY: Baywood.

Levin, J. R., Dretzke, B. J., McCormick, C. B., Scruggs, T. E., McGivern, J. E., & Mastropieri, M. A. (1983). *Educational Communication and Technology Journal, 31,* 161-173.

Levin, J. R., Dretzke, B. J., Pressley, M., & McGivern, J. E. (1985). In search of the keyword method/vocabulary comprehension link. *Contemporary Educational Psychology, 10,* 220-227.

Levin, J. R., Johnson, D. D., Pittelman, S. D., Hayes, B. L., Levin, K. M., Shriberg, L. K., & Toms-Bronowski, S. (1984). A comparison of semantic- and mnemonic-based vocabulary-learning strategies. *Reading Psychology, 5,* 1-15.

Levin, J. R., McCormick, C. B., Miller, G. E., Berry, J. K., & Pressley, M. (1982). Mnemonic versus nonmnemonic vocabulary-learning strategies for children. *American Educational Research Journal, 19,* 121-136.

Levin, J. R., & Pressley, M. (1983). Understanding mnemonic imagery effects: A dozen obvious outcomes. In M. L. Fleming & D. W. Hutton (Eds.), *Mental imagery and learning* (pp. 33-52). Englewood Cliffs, NJ: Educational Technology Publications.

Levin, J. R., & Pressley, M. (1985). Mnemonic vocabulary instruction: What's fact, what's fiction. In R. F. Dillon (Ed.), *Individual differences in cognition* (Vol. 2) (pp. 145-172). Orlando, FL: Academic Press.

Levin, J. R., Pressley, M., McCormick, C. B., Miller, G. E., & Shriberg, L. K. (1979) Assessing the classroom potential of the keyword method. *Journal of Educational Psychology, 71,* 583-594.

Lewis, N. (1982). *Rapid vocabulary builder.* New York: Perigee.

Mastropieri, M. A., Scruggs, T. E., & Levin, J. R. (1985). Maximizing what exceptional children can learn: A review of research on the keyword method and related mnemonic techniques. *Remedial and Special Education, 6,* 39-45.

McCormick, C. B., Levin, J. R., Cykowski, F., & Danilovics, P. (1984). Mnemonic-strategy reduction of prose-learning interference. *Educational and Communication Technology Journal, 32,* 145-152.

McDaniel, M. A., Friedman, A., & Bourne, L. E., Jr. (1978). Remembering the levels of information in words. *Memory & Cognition, 6,* 156-164.

McDaniel, M. A., & Masson, M. E. (1977). Long-term retention: When incidental semantic processing fails. *Journal of Experimental Psychology: Human Learning and Memory, 3,* 270-281.

McDaniel M. A., & Pressley, M. (1984). Putting the keyword method in context. *Journal of Educational Psychology, 76,* 598-609.

McDaniel, M. A., & Tillman, V. P. (1985). *The keyword method versus learning from context: Where's the link?* Manuscript submitted for publication, Department of Psychology, University of Notre Dame, South Bend, IN.

McGivern, J. E., & Levin, J. R. (1983). The keyword method and children's vocabulary learning: An interaction with vocabulary knowledge. *Contemporary Educational Psychology, 8,* 46-54.

McGivern, J. E., Levin, J. R. Ghatala, E. S., & Pressley, M. (1983). *Developmental differences in the vicarious acquisition of an effective learning strategy.* Paper presented at the annual meeting of the American Educational Association, Montreal.

Miller, G. E., Levin, J. R., & Pressley, M. (1980). An adaptation of the keyword method to children's learning of foreign verbs. *Journal of Mental Imagery, 4,* 57-61.

Moerk, E. L. (1972). Principles of dyadic interaction in language learning. *Merrill-Palmer Quarterly, 18,* 229-257.

Morris, C. D., Bransford, J. D., & Franks, J. J. (1977). Levels of processing versus transfer appropriate processing. *Journal of Verbal Learning and Verbal Behavior, 16,* 519–533.

Nagy, W. E., & Anderson, R. C. (1984). How many words are there in printed school English? *Reading Research Quarterly, 19,* 304–330.

Nelson, T. O., & Vining, S. K. (1978). Effects of semantic versus structural processing on long-term retention. *Journal of Experimental Psychology: Human Learning and Memory, 4,* 198–209.

Ninio, A. (1980). Picture-book reading in mother-infant dyads belonging to two subgroups in Israel. *Child Development, 51,* 587–590.

Ninio, A. (1983). Joint book reading as a multiple vocabulary acquisition device. *Developmental Psychology, 19,* 445–451.

Ninio, A., & Bruner, J. S. (1978). The achievement and antecedents of labeling. *Journal of Child Learning, 5,* 1–15.

O'Brien, K. L., Lafrance, M. S., Brackfeld, G. I., & Churchill, G. G. (1970). *French I.* Boston: Ginn.

O'Sullivan, J. T., & Pressley, M. (1984). Completeness of instruction and strategy transfer. *Journal of Experimental Child Psychology, 38,* 275–288.

Paivio, A. (1983). Strategies in language learning. In M. Pressley & J.R. Levin (Eds.), *Cognitive strategy research: Educational applications* (pp. 189–210). New York: Springer-Verlag.

Paivio, A., Clark, J. M., Pressley, M., & Desrochers, A. (1984). *Imagery mnemonic and control strategies in second-language vocabulary learning.* Unpublished manuscript, University of Western Ontario, London, Ontario.

Paivio, A., & Desrochers, A. (1981). Mnemonic techniques in second-language learning. *Journal of Educational Psychology, 73,* 780–795.

Pressley, M. (1982). Elaboration and memory development. *Child Development, 53,* 296–309.

Pressley, M., & Ahmad, M. (1986). Transfer of imagery-based mnemonics by adult learners. *Contemporary Educational Psychology, 11,* 150–160.

Pressley, M., Borkowski, J. G., & O'Sullivan, J. T. (1984). Memory strategy instruction is made of this: Metamemory and durable strategy use. *Educational Psychologist, 19,* 94–107.

Pressley, M., Borkowski, J. G., & O'Sullivan, J. T. (1985). Children's metamemory and the teaching of memory strategies. In D. L. Forrest-Pressley, G. E. MacKinnon, & T. G. Waller (Eds.), *Metacognition, cognition, and human performance* (pp. 111–153). New York: Academic Press.

Pressley, M., & Dennis-Rounds, J. (1980). Transfer of a mnemonic keyword strategy at two age levels. *Journal of Educational Psychology, 72,* 575–582.

Pressley, M., & Levin, J. R. (1977). Developmental differences in subjects' associative learning strategies and performance: Assessing a hypothesis. *Journal of Experimental Child Psychology, 24,* 431–439.

Pressley, M., & Levin, J. R. (1978). Developmental constraints associated with children's use of the keyword method of foreign language vocabulary learning. *Journal of Experimental Child Psychology, 26,* 359–372.

Pressley, M., & Levin, J. R. (in press). Elaborative learning strategies for the inefficient learner. In S. J. Ceci (Ed.), *Handbook of cognitive, social, and neuropsychological aspects of learning disabilities* (Vol. 2). Hillsdale, NJ: Lawrence Erlbaum Associates.

Pressley, M., Levin, J. R., & Delaney, H. D. (1982). The mnemonic keyword method. *Review of Educational Research, 52,* 61–92.

Pressley, M., Levin, J. R., Digdon, N., Bryant, S. L., & Ray, K. (1983). Does method of item presentation affect keyword method effectiveness? *Journal of Educational Psychology, 75,* 586–591.

Pressley, M., Levin, J. R., & Ghatala, E. S. (1984). Memory strategy monitoring in adults and children. *Journal of Verbal Learning and Verbal Behavior, 23,* 270–288.

Pressley, M., Levin, J. R., Hall, J. W., Miller, G. E., & Berry, J. K. (1980). The keyword method and foreign word acquisition. *Journal of Experimental Psychology: Human Learning and Memory, 5,* 22–29.

Pressley, M., Levin, J. R., Kuiper, N. A., Bryant, S. L., & Michener, S. (1982). Mnemonic versus nonmnemonic vocabulary-learning strategies: Additional comparisons. *Journal of Educational Psychology, 74,* 693–707.

Pressley, M., Levin, J. R., & McCormick, C. B. (1980). Young children's learning of foreign language vocabulary: A sentence variation of the keyword method. *Contemporary Educational Psychology, 5,* 22–29.

Pressley, M., Levin, J. R., & Miller, G. E. (1981a). How does the keyword method affect vocabulary comprehension and usage? *Reading Research Quarterly, 16,* 213–226.

Pressley, M., Levin, J. R., & Miller, G. E. (1981b). The keyword method and children's learning of foreign vocabulary with abstract meanings. *Canadian Journal of Psychology, 35,* 283–287.

Pressley, M., Levin, J. R., & Miller, G. E. (1982). The keyword method compared to alternative vocabulary learning strategies. *Contemporary Educational Psychology, 7,* 50–60.

Pressley, M., Levin, J. R., Nakamura, G. V., Hope, D. J., Bispo, J. G., & Toye, A. R. (1980). The keyword method of foreign vocabulary learning: An investigation of its generalizability. *Journal of Applied Psychology, 65,* 635–642.

Pressley, M., Levin, J. R., Woo, G., Sinclair, C., & Ahmad, F. (1985). *The effect of root-word mastery on vocabulary learning.* Manuscript submitted for publication. University of Western Ontario, London, Ontario.

Pressley, M., Ross, K. A., Levin, J. R., & Ghatala, E. S. (1984). The role of strategy utility knowledge in children's strategy decision making. *Journal of Experimental Child Psychology, 38,* 491–504.

Pressley, M., Samuel, J., Hershey, M. M., Bishop, S. L., & Dickinson, D. (1981). Use of a mnemonic technique to teach young children foreign language vocabulary. *Contemporary Educational Psychology, 6,* 110–116.

Quealy, R. J. (1969). Senior high school students (sic) use of contextual aids in reading. *Reading Research Quarterly, 4,* 512–533.

Ray, M., & Lutz, K. B. (1969). *A-LM French.* New York: Harcourt Brace Jovanovich.

Rohwer, W. D., Jr. (1973). Elaboration and learning in childhood and adolescence. In H. W. Reese (Ed.), *Advances in child development and behavior* (Vol. 8, pp. 1–57). New York: Academic Press.

Scruggs, T. E., Mastropieri, M. A., & Levin, J. R. (1985). Vocabulary acquisition of retarded students under direct and mnemonic instruction. *American Journal of Mental Deficiency, 89,* 546–551.

Smith, R. W. L. (1982). *Dictionary of English roots.* Totowa, NJ: Littlefield, Adams.

Sternberg, R. J., & Powell, J. S. (1983). Comprehending verbal comprehension. *American Psychologist, 38,* 878–893.

Sternberg, R. J., Powell, J. S., & Kaye, D. B. (1983). Teaching vocabulary-building skills: A contextual approach. In A. C. Wilkinson (Ed.), *Classroom computers and cognitive science.* New York: Academic Press.

Sweeney, C. A., & Bellezza, F. S. (1982). Use of the keyword mnemonic for learning English vocabulary. *Human Learning, 1,* 155–163.

Werner, H., & Kaplan, E. (1952). The acquisition of word meaning: A developmental study. *Monographs of the Society for Research in Child Development, 15,* 3–120.

Whyte, G., & Shular, J. (1974). *Teacher's guidebook for Starting points in reading.* Boston: Ginn.

8 Issues in the Design of Vocabulary Instruction

Edward J. Kameenui
Purdue University

Robert C. Dixon
University of Illinois

Douglas W. Carnine
University of Oregon

In his book *The Double Helix,* the Nobel laureate James D. Watson (1968) recounts the vexations and the high-pitched suspense surrounding the discovery of the structure of deoxyribonucleic acid (DNA). Late in his narrative, Watson notes how the discovery of the aesthetically elegant double helix was perhaps precipitated by an intuition he and his colleagues had "that a structure this pretty just had to exist" (p. 131). Watson's intuition about the elegance of the DNA structure should give pause to educational researchers who have been equally driven in pursuing an intuition about the relationship of vocabulary knowledge and reading comprehension. In unwitting deference to the Watson tradition, Beck, Perfetti, and McKeown (1982), in acknowledging the weak empirical connection between access to word meanings and understanding texts, plaintively note that, "If comprehension depends in part on facile access to word meanings, then vocabulary instruction *ought* to affect comprehension" (p. 156, italics added). Beck and her colleagues' intuition is straight forward: The connection between understanding word meanings and understanding texts is so clear logically and so intimate theoretically, that it ought to exist empirically. Because this intuition is widely shared (Anderson & Freebody, 1981; Mezynski, 1983), it perhaps characterizes the state of affairs, if not the process of scientific inquiry, in vocabulary research — a process that appears tenacious in its intuition but tenuous in its methodology, instrumentation, and focus. As Watson has intimated and as Kuhn (1962) and others have acknowledged, such a state of affairs in scientific inquiry is not only unsettling, but perhaps necessary.

The shared intuition about the relationship between vocabulary learning and reading comprehension made public by Beck et al. (1982) warrants further scrutiny. Many subtle but complex issues in vocabulary learning continue to elude researchers. Some of these issues are derived from this shared intuition (e.g., Is the empirical relationship between understanding word meanings and reading comprehension, in fact, a "weak" one? Or, are our conceptions for what passes as empirical robustness in vocabulary research inappropriate?). Other issues cut at more basic questions (e.g., What is a word? When is a word "known?" What words require knowing?). Still other issues go beyond the concern with knowing word meanings per se to a broader concern for the cognitive processes implied in learning word meanings (see Elshout-Mohr & van Daalen-Kapteijns, this volume). These issues notwithstanding, our concern in this particular chapter is not only with what ought to exist in the research on vocabulary knowledge but also with what indeed does exist, but for various reasons, in the words of Shakespeare's Hamlet, "passes show" and has left researchers of vocabulary learning (including us) with what appears to be "the trappings and the suits of woe."

We have organized this chapter into two major sections. In the first section, we discuss what we see as a new way of thinking about vocabulary learning and reading comprehension within the context of reading instruction. In doing so, we examine the four explanations of the vocabulary knowledge and reading comprehension link reviewed by Mezynski (1983). Following her precedent, we propose a new perspective, one that we elaborate on by examining the dimensions of receptive vocabulary knowledge and the features of tasks designed to assess vocabulary learning. In the second section, we propose a comprehensive instructional program for increasing vocabulary development and reading comprehension. A skeletal outline of this multiple strand instructional program is given.

TOWARD A NEW PERSPECTIVE OF VOCABULARY LEARNING AND READING COMPREHENSION

The shared intuition about the link between vocabulary learning and reading comprehension requires careful consideration. Anderson and Freebody (1981) have suggested that how one goes about framing and answering questions concerned with teaching word meanings to a great extent depends on how one explains the strong correlational relationship between vocabulary knowledge and general linguistic ability. Three explanations, initially drawn by Anderson and Freebody, have recently been reviewed and expanded to four perspectives by Mezynski (1983). The four perspectives include the *aptitude* position, which attributes the correlation between vocabulary and comprehension to a more or less innate mental mechanism; the *instrumental* position, which emphasizes the knowing of individual word meanings as the primary prerequisite to comprehension; the *knowledge* position, which considers word meanings to be representative of multiple word and knowledge structures that are the basis for comprehension; and the *access* position, which views the automaticity of word knowledge through practice as the primary subskill among several trainable subskills that together comprise comprehension processing.

The four different positions provide an initial framework for examining the relationship between vocabulary knowledge and reading comprehension. However, these positions are of limited value to a more complete understanding of this elusive relationship, because they rely on single factor explanations of a complex phenomenon. Each of the four positions is concerned with identifying a feature of primacy to account for the relationship between vocabulary knowledge and reading comprehension. For instance, according to the aptitude position, superior mental agility is viewed as the primary factor determining whether a text will be understood. The instrumental position suggests that the number of words taught (and learned) is the primary factor in text understanding. The knowledge position hypothesizes the interrelationships between word meanings and background knowledge as primary factors in text comprehension, and the access position as formulated by Mezynski (1983) considers practice as the primary factor. Each of these different positions centers and revolves around a single primary feature explanation for the relationship between understanding word meanings and understanding texts.

Although Anderson and Freebody (1981) have stated that "no serious scholar in reading or related fields rigidly adheres to any one of these positions" (p. 16), embracing any of these positions of primacy gives the appearance of ignoring to some extent the complexity of the reading comprehension process, as well as the interrelatedness among all four single factors (i.e., aptitude, access, knowledge, instrumentalist). As Mezynski (1983) has duly noted, "One can certainly argue that all these things are important" (p. 255). The fact that such an argument is even necessary points out the degree to which positions of primacy that rely on single factor explanations diminish consideration of other contributing factors that may be of equal importance.

Anderson and Freebody (1981) suggest that knowing the "most nearly correct" view about vocabulary knowledge is important because the proposed views have "radically different implications for the reading curriculum" (p. 10). However, we believe that researchers concerned with curriculum should be interested in a related but different issue — how vocabulary *instruction* influences reading comprehension. More specifically, what is at issue here is not the aptitude, access, knowledge, or instrumental positions per se, but the criteria for deciding which position is "most nearly correct" for designing reading instruction in general. In order to address this issue more completely, an explanation that accounts for more than merely the connection between word meanings and reading comprehension is necessary. Such an explanation must also take into account in part the use to which the vocabulary will be put, as recommended by Beck, McKeown, and Omanson (this volume), as well as the users of the vocabulary, the consistencies among instructional objectives, tasks and assessment procedures, and the design and schedule of the instruction used. To this end, and in keeping with Mezynski's precedent, we propose a new perspective on the relationship between vocabulary knowledge and reading comprehension but within the broader context of reading instruction in general.

We have chosen to characterize our perspective as the *instructional design* position. The reasoning behind the choice of this label can be explained as follows: First of all, we define instruction as the communication of knowledge. Second, we consider designing the communication of that knowledge to be the "most nearly correct" focus for examining the relationship between the acquisition of vocabulary knowledge and reading comprehension within the broader context of reading instruction. The knowledge in this case refers to the various kinds of vocabulary knowledge (e.g., speaking, writing, listening and reading) acquired through instruction. Analyzing the various dimensions of this knowledge and designing the communication of these dimensions to the learner is at the heart of the instructional design position. The instructional design position is not only concerned with *what* gets communicated (i.e., what words should be taught) and *how* it gets communicated to the learner (i.e., how the words should be taught), but also with how what is taught fits into a broader context of instructional goals, task requirements, and learning outcomes within reading comprehension. This position is unlike the four positions previously described because its primary focus is not with a single factor, but with means by which many important factors may interact in conveying word meaning to the learner in a way that ultimately enhances reading comprehension. We identify and examine several such factors in order to illustrate the extensiveness of the instructional design position, as well as the intricate requirements of vocabulary instruction that aspires to substantively affect reading comprehension.

Dimensions of Vocabulary Knowledge

The understanding we seek of how vocabulary instruction affects reading comprehension is heavily dependent on a clear understanding of the various kinds of vocabulary knowledge that can be acquired through instruction. Nagy and Anderson (1984) have estimated that school English contains about 88,500 distinct words, which we accept as a reliable statement of the quantity of words comprising a written school vocabulary. However, determining how vocabulary instruction affects comprehension depends not only on the quantity of words known, but on the quality (or qualities) of that word knowledge. For instance, it is conceivable that two students might know the same number of words, and possibly, even roughly the same words, but that those students have "different vocabularies," due to differences in the quality, or extensiveness, of their knowledge of particular words.

Beck, Perfetti, and McKeown (1982) suggest differences in the quality of word knowledge when they write of levels of lexical access: unknown, acquainted, and established. A student who is acquainted with the meanings for words in a particular set could be said to have a "different vocabulary" from that of another student who has established knowledge of those same words.

The importance of differences between qualities of word knowledge is more apparent if we return to the fundamental question of how vocabulary knowledge affects reading comprehension: Acquainted knowledge of a word, it seems safe to speculate, might affect reading comprehension differently from established knowledge of that same word.

Other differences in the quality of word knowledge might similarly affect the extent to which that knowledge affects overall comprehension. Dixon and Jenkins (1984) contend that the designation "vocabulary" encompasses a wide range of different qualities, or dimensions of knowledge, each of which has the potential for affecting reading comprehension in different ways. For example, *expressive vocabulary* knowledge is demonstrated when one is able to produce labels for meanings. *Receptive vocabulary* knowledge, in contrast, is demonstrated when one is able to associate meanings with labels that are given, which is also a general way of describing the goal of reading. Although it is undoubtedly true that expressive vocabulary has the potential for affecting reading comprehension in some significant ways, that influence is likely to be different from the more direct impact of receptive vocabulary knowledge.

Other categories in the Dixon and Jenkins' analysis are limited specifically to varieties of receptive vocabulary knowledge. They include the following:

Full concept knowledge, partial concept knowledge, or verbal association knowledge. The oft-stated goal of receptive vocabulary instruction is the attainment of *full concept* knowledge. The most usual indication that such knowledge has been attained is the ability to recognize uninstructed examples of concepts as examples, and to discriminate them from similar examples drawn from other concepts.

Although it could be said that full concept knowledge is always desirable, *partial concept* knowledge may in many instances be adequate for the comprehension of text. For example, the knowledge that gold is a heavy and usually yellowish metal is sufficient for understanding text that only relies upon those features of gold, even though it could not be said that such knowledge of gold constitutes complete knowledge. Several degrees of partial knowledge of a single concept are possible. Most concepts are fully defined by a set of critical features (those common to *all* examples) and variable features (those demonstrated by *some* examples but not all). Partial concept knowledge can comprise any of various combinations of such features.

Although full concept knowledge is always desirable and partial concept knowledge is frequently adequate, instruction can result in another category of knowledge altogether: *verbal association* knowledge. A verbal association is a pairing of labels and their meanings. When someone learns that the Spanish word *gato* means cat, or that *altercations* means fights, a verbal association has been learned. A new label has been learned for a concept that is presumably already known, either completely or partially. If the *only* kind of knowledge a learner can demonstrate involves always pairing one member of an association with another, the impact of that knowledge on reading comprehension is likely to be negligible. On the other hand, if the learner can move beyond such simple pairing and recognize uninstructed examples of the new label, then some form of generalizable concept knowledge is being demonstrated, and the learning of the association in that case becomes an efficient means to a more desirable end.

Derived knowledge, prompted recall, and unprompted recall. A unique feature of receptive vocabulary knowledge is that the given labels appear in a context, which has the potential for prompting the meaning of each label. The extent of the prompting is dependent upon the "richness" or "leanness" of the context for conveying meaning of any particular label, but some level of prompting potential is present in every case, nonetheless.

A reader might encounter a word in context for the first time, figure out enough about the word to facilitate comprehension, and move on in the text, promptly forgetting about the newly encountered word. Circumstances such as this can be characterized as *derived* knowledge (Jenkins & Dixon, 1983; Jenkins, Stein, & Wysocki, 1984). Such knowledge is not "knowing" in the usual sense because not much, if anything, is retained. Such knowledge is more akin to looking up information in a reference book. Derived knowledge is by no means unimportant, however, because it could account in part for how a reader might comprehend text containing many unknown words.

It may be the case that readers don't in fact have to "know" as many of the 88,500 words that occur in printed school English as Nagy and Anderson have estimated if "knowing" in some sense includes the recall of word meaning. The most interesting aspect of derived vocabulary knowledge is that it is not knowledge of *words* at all, but rather knowledge of a strategy for figuring out something *about* words, something that isn't necessarily retained, and something that doesn't necessarily *need* to be retained to facilitate verbal comprehension.

Another situation in which prompting plays a role is *prompted* recall. A reader could come across a vaguely familiar word, one that had been encountered elsewhere but not retained well, and utilize the context to prompt recall of that word at some level. The meaning of that same word would not be recalled in the absence of context, where nothing beyond the label itself is present to prompt the recall. This, too, is a somewhat unique sense of "knowing," one that is peculiar to reading (and listening) situations.

Readers know words at the level of *unprompted* recall when they can identify meanings without reference to context (which is most clearly demonstrated when no context is present). Such knowledge is over-learning with respect to normal reading because the recall requirements upon the reader are greater than those imposed by normal reading, which always involves context to some extent, and therefore, always involves some degree of prompting.

In summary, the dimensions of vocabulary knowledge just described imply dozens of permutations of knowledge types, many of which could have effective and valid application to reading comprehension. For example, full concept knowledge, recalled rapidly and without prompts, is undoubtedly a useful dimension of vocabulary knowledge for most reading situations. Similarly, partial concept knowledge, derived only in the presence of prompts, and not too rapidly, might also be adequate for facilitating comprehension in some situations. However, the instruction that leads to different dimensions of vocabulary knowledge could be expected to differ, and the particular impacts of different dimensions of vocabulary knowledge on reading comprehension could be expected to differ as well.

Attributes of Vocabulary Tasks

We believe that the apparently wide variety of kinds of learning incorporated within the general designation "vocabulary" is a key factor in any consideration of vocabulary instruction and its impact upon reading comprehension. Different types of learning are induced and assessed by different performance events, such as instructional and assessment tasks. Because performance on these different tasks indicates different learning, the most concrete and practical representation of various vocabulary dimensions is in the vocabulary tasks themselves.

We analyzed a variety of vocabulary tasks in the interest of associating vocabulary knowledge features with features of both instructional and assessment tasks. There are two practical applications of such an association. First, existing tasks can be analyzed to determine the kind of learning the tasks are most likely to tap. Such analyses are valuable for evaluating vocabulary research and instruction. In addition, a breakdown of task features can be of value in constructing new instructional and assessment tasks when particular dimensions of knowledge are targeted for instruction, assessment, or experimental investigation.

Because the analysis of instructional tasks revealed task features beyond the scope of this chapter, we limit our illustrations of task features to an analysis of assessment tasks. Assessment tasks, are those that most nearly represent the intended outcomes of instruction and learning. These tasks are usually void of typical instructional features such as prompting, feedback, external motivators, sequencing, and so on.

The analysis of assessment tasks revealed two general categories of task features. The first are those attributes that could be observed by looking directly at the form and content of tasks. A list of those attributes and their variations, as well as examples, is given in Table 8.1. The second category involves those attributes that exist outside of the tasks themselves and require

TABLE 8.1
Attributes of Task Form and Content

Attribute	Variation	Example
1. Direction of task	a. Label to concept	a. "What does *equilateral* mean?"
	b. Concept to label	b. Show an equilateral triangle and ask: "What kind of triangle is this?"
2. Context	a. Present—rich	a. Our three houses formed an almost perfect equilateral triangle, so each of us could walk to the houses of the other two in about the same amount of time. "What does *equilateral* mean?"
	b. Present—lean	b. James painted a large equilateral triangle on his bedroom wall. "What does *equilateral* mean?"
	c. Absent	c. "What does *equilateral* mean?"
3. Elements	a. Label given, verbal equivalent required	a. "What does *equilateral* mean?" (Students say: all sides equal.)
	b. Label given, example required	b. "Draw an *equilateral* triangle."
4. Response mode	a. Choice response	a. "Which triangle is *equilateral*?" (Picture of right triangle.) (Picture of isoceles triangle.) (Picture of equilateral triangle.) (Picture of obtuse triangle.)
	b. Production response	b. "Draw an *equilateral* triangle."
5. Conceptual	a. Partial knowledge required	a. "What are some things a person with a hernia is likely to do?"
	b. Full knowledge required	b. "Describe the unique symptoms of a hernia."

TABLE 8.2
Attributes of Task Conditions

Attribute	Variation	Significance
1. Elements	a. Preinstructed b. Uninstructed	a. Indicates potential for memorization b. Indicates generalization
2. Testing time	a. Immediate b. Delayed	a. Knowledge may not be retained b. Indicates potential for retention
3. Response time	a. Fast b. Slow c. No response	a. Established knowledge (when correct) b. Acquainted knowledge (when correct) c. Indicates no knowledge
4. Number & range of examples	a. Many/wide b. Few/narrow	a. Indicates reduced likelihood of undergeneralized knowledge b. Undergeneralized knowledge likely
5. Negative examples	a. Present b. Absent	a. Discrimination ability likely b. Overgeneralized knowledge likely (Discrimination ability unlikely)

attending to conditions under which the tasks are performed. A list of these attributes, their variations and significance are given in Table 8.2.

Analysis of an Existing Task. The following is a common type of vocabulary assessment task.

The word or phrase closest in meaning to *equilateral* is:

1. all sides the same length
2. equality for all
3. along a line
4. balanced

Anderson and Freebody (1981) have questioned the validity of multiple choice task formats such as this one, on the grounds that the distractors affect performance, and that test-taking strategies are factors in performance on such tasks. We further question the validity of such tasks on the grounds that successful performance indicates next to nothing about dozens of dimensions of vocabulary knowledge, including those most likely to be of interest to reading comprehension.

By attending to the attributes in Table 8.1, we can scrutinize the adequacy of this multiple choice task. Briefly, the task is formatted in the direction of receptive vocabulary, wherein the label is given. This is a positive sign, but one of the few positive signs. Because there is no context, the potential for demonstrating prompted recall or the ability to infer is not assessed. Furthermore, the label must be matched with a verbal equivalent (meaning the task lacks evidence of generalized conceptual knowledge), the response mode involves a choice (introducing an artificial form of prompting not found in natural reading situations), and the degree of conceptual knowledge indicated is unknown.

Conditions under which such tasks may be performed (as noted in Table 8.2) further weaken the amount of information about a learner's vocabulary knowledge. If the target words have been preinstructed, then only the recall of verbal equivalents is indicated. If the assessment immediately follows instruction or any form of intervention, then there is no indication that the little knowledge the task does assess will even be retained. If each item is not timed, then the level of lexical access is unknown. And if, as is typical, only one item per target word is provided (with no minimally different negative examples), then whatever ambiguous conceptual knowledge there is that might be reflected by the verbal equivalent is imprecise with respect to discrimination and the range of generalization.

When these considerations of knowledge dimensions in terms of task form, content, and conditions are added to Anderson and Freebody's concerns, we are tempted to conclude that for most purposes, such multiple choice vocabulary tasks are useless at best and dangerous at worst (but see Curtis, this volume, for a contrasting view). Given the number of conclusions that have been drawn about vocabulary learning, based upon tasks whose form, content, and condition features so closely mirror those of our example, one might question what is really known about vocabulary.

A major implication of evaluating the extent to which a given assessment task is sensitive to dimensions of vocabulary knowledge is that no single task format and no single set of task conditions can possibly be adequate for assessing many different dimensions of vocabulary knowledge. The objective of evaluating assessment tasks is not to determine in the abstract which type of task is "the best," but to determine the extent to which the tasks are consistent with the types of knowledge one is interested in assessing.

Design of New Tasks.   If a particular experimental intervention, for example, aspires to improve upon students' ability to infer partial concept knowledge from lean contexts (to the extent that the knowledge is retained), then assessment tasks should be developed that are consistent with that aspiration. The form and content of one such task might look like this:

> Jamie believed her father wanted her to be more ambitious.
> What are some things ambitious people do?

The task direction is label-to-concept (see Table 8.1), which is consistent with the broader goal of increased receptive vocabulary. Because we aspired to improve inference ability, not merely retention of a particular word, a lean context accompanies the question. Therefore, in designing our new task, examples are required, rather than verbal equivalents. The new task's potential for indicating conceptual knowledge is increased. The task is not confounded by artificial prompts, because the question requires a production response. Finally, the format of the question allows for "correct" responses that are short of full concept knowledge but indicative of partial concept knowledge. In other words, some answers might indicate nearly full concept knowledge, but the task does not require such knowledge for successful performance.

The conditions under which such assessment tasks should be performed, in order to be consistent with the aspiration for the intervention, are as follows: First and foremost, the target words must be uninstructed. The assessment is concerned with measuring improvements in the students' ability to infer, not with the acquisition of any particular words. The assessment should be delayed some period of time beyond the completion of the intervention as an indication that the strategy will be retained. "Rapidity of lexical access" implies access to word knowldge, but a timed test for the example test could be useful for indicating "rapidity of strategy access." Finally, the number and range of examples, as well as the presence of negative examples, is not applicable to the assessment of partial concept knowledge (because the notion of partial knowledge is equivalent to undergeneralized knowledge).

We would not argue that this analysis of the correspondence between task features and dimensions of vocabulary knowledge is exhaustive. However, any further factors that researchers might likely identify would serve to strengthen the instructional design position, which holds that the relationship between vocabulary learning and reading comprehension is dependent on consistencies of objectives, instructional tasks, and assessment tasks within an intricate set of requirements that vary.

This position is strengthened further when instructional design considerations are included among the knowledge factors we have discussed thus far. For example, feedback appropriate for a discrimination task would not be consistent with the objectives of a production task. Similarly, instructional factors such as the extensiveness of prompts, the sequencing of examples, the fading of prompts, and schedules for reviewing previously taught skills would all vary according to the particular dimensions of knowledge one intended to induce.

More than anything else, the apparently wide range of knowledge dimensions encompassed by "vocabulary" implies something more for instruction than a general admixture of eclectic tasks related to word knowledge in sometimes oblique and mystical ways. These vocabulary knowledge dimensions also imply something more for assessment than general, objective, machine-scorable tasks. We believe that attending to varieties of word knowledge, along with other factors that we discuss presently, is an important prerequisite to resolving many of the difficult questions of vocabulary knowledge and reading comprehension.

TOWARD A COMPREHENSIVE VOCABULARY AND
READING COMPREHENSION TRAINING PROGRAM

Before outlining our vocabulary training program, several observations should be made and discussed that lead us to the assumption that vocabulary instruction has a valid role in the classroom: (a) little formal vocabulary instruction actually takes place in American classrooms (Beck, McKeown, McCaslin, & Burkes, 1979; Durkin, 1978–1979; Jenkins & Dixon, 1983); (b) vocabulary learning does occur in the absence of instruction, and the uninstructed growth is impressive (Nagy & Anderson, 1984); and (c) vocabulary can be effectively instructed (Mezynski, 1983). Implied in these observations is a competitive tension between the roles of incidental vocabulary learning and systematic, direct vocabulary instruction (See Nagy & Herman, this volume). This tension is based on the assumption that in order for direct vocabulary instruction to be worthwhile, it must in some sense be competitive with incidental vocabulary learning, either by replacing it or by delivering comparable knowledge in a reasonable amount of time.

This "competitive" assumption may be false on two counts: (a) direct vocabulary instruction could not possibly replace incidental learning of vocabulary, and (b) direct vocabulary instruction might deliver knowledge that is valuable in terms of instructional time only if dimensions of vocabulary knowledge are taken into account.

If dimensions or qualities of word knowledge are considered in conjunction with numbers of words learned, then the role of instruction in vocabulary learning could be significant, especially for those students who do not benefit from incidental learning. These learners might benefit from instruction that initially teaches word meanings to minimal levels of application in reading comprehension, since we know that such levels of partial knowledge are likely over time to expand with subsequent exposures (which are better controlled instructionally than incidentally).

Vocabulary instruction must move beyond the teaching of words directly as a primary activity. Because students derive the meanings of many words incidentally, without instruction, another possible role of instruction is to enhance the strategies readers use when they do in fact learn words incidentally. Directly teaching such strategies holds the promise of helping students become better independent word learners. However, learning from context will rarely result in anything like "complete" word knowledge. Levels of quick lexical access, full concept knowledge, and unprompted recall appear to be achieved (if ever) only over long periods of time. Research does not uniformly confirm substantial results from context-learning instruction, but perhaps such research has had unrealistic expectations for both the amount and quality of learning that can take place in short periods of time.

Given our assumption that there is a role for vocabulary instruction in schools, questions remain as to whom that instruction should be delivered to, who should be responsible for delivering it, what form the delivery of that instruction should take, and what levels of word or general vocabulary knowledge should be targeted. Answers to these questions are likely to hinge on the development of an ambitious, comprehensive and empirically based vocabulary training program. This program must be concerned explicitly with increasing the connection between vocabulary knowledge and reading comprehension, and it must also take into account the covariation between the learner, the type of instruction, the schedule of instruction, the type of conceptual knowledge to be induced, the vocabulary dimensions to be conveyed, and the intended use of the vocabulary to be taught.

We propose a comprehensive instructional program that is composed of three discrete strands of vocabulary instruction that are to be taught concurrently for 180 school days. Because of space limitations, only a sketchy description of this program can be provided. The tenets of this program are rather straightforward: (a) sufficient research has identified successful strategies for vocabulary training, (b) vocabulary instruction is a professional and ethical imperative for at-risk children (i.e., those with significantly deficient vocabularies and for whom incidental learning has proven to be ineffective), (c) no single curricular area has sole responsibility for vocabulary instruction, but all areas share that responsibility, and (d) a viable instructional design technology exists that will enhance the designing of vocabulary and reading comprehension tasks.

Each of the three strands focuses on a different set of learning outcomes and task requirements. Table 8.3 presents the strands to be taught, the unit and type of instruction that would occur within each strand, and selected research studies that serve as the empirical basis for each strand. A specific reference to a selected strategy that exemplifies the type of instruction recommended for each strand is also provided in Table 8.3.

Each strand in the program is designed to target vocabulary instruction at the word, sentence, and text level. At the individual word level, we would select words from upcoming passages to facilitate compehension of those passages. The delayed encounter of those learned words in natural contexts should serve to expand a learner's knowledge of words (e.g., fuller conceptual knowledge, faster accessibility, better recall). Following the lead of Beck and her colleagues, we recommend teaching words in semantically related sets. However, we propose a slight modification of developing word sets around "tight" semantic categories instead of "loose" ones (e.g., the more attributes shared by words in a particular set, the tighter that set is likely to be).

In Strand II of our program, we propose targeting instruction at the text level. The instruction would be directed at teaching students a strategy for

TABLE 8.3
Components of a Comprehensible Vocabulary and Reading Comprehension Training Program

Strand	Unit of Instruction	Type of Instruction	Example Strategy	Selected Research
I.	Individual word learning	*Stage* 1. Word Selection (e.g., semantic networks) 2. Teach Definitions 3. Sentence Discrimination Practice 4. Text-Integration Practice 5. Dictionary & Glossary Use	*Stage* 1. Beck, Perfetti, & McKeown (1982); Dixon & Jenkins (1984) 2–4. Kameenui, Carnine, & Freschi (1982) 5. Carnine & Silbert (1979)	1. Gipe (1979) 2. Pany & Jenkins (1978)
II.	Contextual word learning	*Stage* 1. Teach strategy for identifying context clues 2. Apply strategy; High teacher prompting 3. Apply strategy; Low teacher prompting; independent practice	*Stage* 1–3. Carnine, Kameenui, & Coyle (1984); Dixon & Jenkins (1984)	1. Jenkins, Stein, & Wysocki (1984) 2. Sternberg & Powell (1983)
III.	Content-based vocabulary knowledge learning	*Stage* 1. Preteach critical facts using visual-algorithm, no text 2. Read text, no visual-algorithm used 3. Review text using visual-algorithm	*Stage* 1. Engelmann & Carnine (1982) (see Ch. 14, p. 157–169); Engelmann, Davis, & Davis (1981)	1. Ruddell & Boyle (1984) 2. Darch, Carnine, & Kameenui (in press)
Schedule of Instruction	Firming Cycle Procedures Cumulative Review Procedures: Previously taught information is reviewed			

deriving information about unfamiliar words from the varying types of naturally occurring texts in which the words are embedded. The effectiveness of the instruction would not hinge so much on the application of the strategy itself (see Carnine, Kameenui, & Coyle, 1984, pp. 198–199), but on the selected examples of texts to which the strategy would be applied. Utilizing the strategy with varying types of texts (e.g., texts lean or rich in redundant information about unfamiliar vocabulary words, texts that provide multiple or single exposures of an unknown word) would communicate to the learner when and under what contextual circumstances the strategy would be most beneficial.

The strategies proposed in Strands I and II are likely to aid vocabulary learning in the language arts/reading curricula. However, subject matter texts that emphasize heavy vocabulary acquisition and specialized vocabulary knowledge (e.g., physical science, American history) pose a unique set of concerns and problems. These texts have been characterized as "inconsiderate" (Armbruster, 1984) because of their lack of overall text structure and cohesive ties between sentences. This lack of global and local coherence is in part due to the lists of facts that typically comprise these texts. Strand III of our proposed program is designed to teach students the high density of unfamiliar words that occur in content-area texts within the context of facts specific to a given subject area. Such an approach serves to expand a student's knowledge of individual word meanings and of related facts, if not systems of facts and the relationship of facts to dimensions of vocabulary learning.

A number of strategies and techniques have been devised and investigated as aids for helping students read and understand content textbook passages. One very promising area of inquiry is that concerned with investigating the effectiveness of visual-spatial displays or graphic organizers (Alvermann, 1986; Barron, 1979) in facilitating the acquisition of expository material. These formats for organizing information rely on the use of lines, arrows, geometric shapes, and spatial arrangements that describe the text content, structure, and key conceptual relationships typically found in a content-area text. The organizational structure of the graphic organizer is not unlike the systematic arrangement of ideas that specify the relationships connecting these ideas found in a text. In this case, the teaching of unfamiliar vocabulary words and related facts would take place through the use of a visual–graphic display made up of geometric shapes that contain specific facts or targeted vocabulary terms. All cells in the visual display would be connected to each other and arranged in ways that suggest the superordinate, subordinate, and coordinate relationships between facts. The visual algorithm of vocabulary knowledge would be accompanied by a "teaching script" that specified for the teacher the information to be communicated, the questions to be asked, and necessary review of previously taught facts (see Engelmann & Carnine, 1982, pp. 157–169). The research on visual displays and graphic organizers is a rather fallow but growing area of inquiry (Alverman, 1980, 1981; Barron,

1979; Ruddell & Boyle, 1984). Two specific visual display techniques have been reported in the literature: mapping (Anderson & Armbruster, 1981; Hanf, 1971) and networking (Dansereau et al., 1979; Holly, 1979). Although evidence exists to suggest the power of the visual-display system for teaching complex sets of interrelated facts, more experimental research is needed.

The multiple strand program we have described in abbreviated form represents what we believe ought to be taking place in vocabulary learning. As Beck and her colleagues have demonstrated, nothing short of immersing students, in particular at-risk learners, in a program that increases vocabulary knowledge at the word, sentence, and text level and under varying task conditions, will suffice. But the immersing must be done intelligently and with careful attention to the dimensions of vocabulary knowledge. Attention must also be paid to the manner in which those dimensions are communicated and assessed, as we have described in discussing the instructional design position.

We do offer a last word of caution. Our collective intuitions about this comprehensive instructional program are based on rather tenuous empirical footings, at least for the time being. However, our respect for the Watson tradition compels us to note that such a program seems so elegant, instructionally and logically, that it just has to be effective.

REFERENCES

Alvermann, D. E. (1980). Effects of graphic organizers, textual organization, and reading comprehension level on recall of expository prose. (Doctoral disseration, Syracuse University, 1980). *Dissertation Abstracts International, 41,* 3963A.

Alvermann, D. E. (1981). The compensatory effect of graphic organizers on descriptive text. *Journal of Educational Research, 75,* 44–48.

Alvermann, D. E. (1986). Graphic organizers: Cuing devices for comprehending and remembering main ideas. In J. F. Baumann (Ed.), *Teaching main idea comprehension* (pp. 210–226). Newark, DE: International Reading Association.

Anderson, R. C., & Freebody, P. (1981). Vocabulary knowledge. In J. T. Guthrie (Ed.), *Comprehension and teaching: Research reviews* (pp. 77–117). Newark, DE: International Reading Association.

Anderson, T. H., & Armbruster, B. B. (1981). *Content area textbooks.* Proceedings of the Conference Learning to Read in American Schools: Basal readings and content texts, Tarrytown, New York.

Armbruster, B. B. (1984). The problem of "inconsiderable text." In G. G. Duffy, L. R. Roehler, & J. Mason (Eds.), *Comprehension instruction: Perspectives and suggestions* (pp. 202–217). New York: Longman.

Barron, R. R. (1979). Research for the classroom teacher: Recent developments on the structured overview as an advance organizer. In H. L. Herber & J. D. Riley, (Eds.), *Research in reading in the content areas: The fourth report* (pp. 000–000). Syracuse, NY: Syracuse University Reading and Language Arts Center.

Beck, I. L., Perfetti, C. A., & McKeown, M. G. (1982). The effects of long-term vocabulary instruction on lexical access and reading comprehension. *Journal of Educational Psychology, 74,* 506–521.

Beck, I. L., McKeown, M. G., McCaslin, E. S., & Burkes, A. M. (1979). *Instructional dimensions that may affect reading comprehension: Examples from two commercial reading programs* (LRDC Publication 1979/20). Pittsburgh: University of Pittsburgh, Learning Research and Development Center.

Carnine, D., Kameenui, E., & Coyle, G. (1984). Utilization of contextual information in determining the meaning of unfamiliar words. *Reading Research Quarterly, 19,* 188–204.

Carnine, D. W., & Silbert, J. (1979). *Direct instruction reading.* Columbus: Merrill.

Dansereau, D. F., Long, G. L., McDonald, B. A., Actkinson, T. R., Collins, K. W., Evans, S. H., Ellis, A. M., & William, S. (1979). Evaluation of a learning strategy system. In H. F. O'Neal, Jr. & C. D. Speilserger (Eds.), *Cognitive and affective learning strategies* (pp. 000–000). New York: Academic Press.

Darch, C., Carnine, D., & Kameenui, E. J. (in press). The role of graphic organizers and social structure in content area instruction. *Journal of Reading Behavior, 18*(4).

Dixon, R. C., & Jenkins, J. R. (1984). *An outcome analysis of receptive vocabulary knowledge.* Unpublished manuscript, University of Illinois, Champaign-Urbana.

Durkin, D. (1978–1979). What classroom observations reveal about reading comprehension instruction. *Reading Research Quarterly, 14,* 481–533.

Engelmann, S., & Carnine, D. W. (1982). *Theory of instruction: Principles and applications.* New York: Irvington.

Engelmann, S., Davis, K., & Davis, G. (1981). *Your world of facts I.* Tigard, OR: C.C. Publications.

Gipe, J. (1979). Investigating techniques for teaching word meanings. *Reading Research Quarterly, 14,* 624–644.

Hanf, M. B. (1971). Mapping: A technique for translating reading into thinking. *Journal of Reading, 14,* 225–230.

Holly, C. D. (1979). An evaluation of intact and embedded headings schema cuing devices with non-narrative text (Doctoral dissertation, Texas Christian University, 1979). *Dissertation Abstracts International, 40,* 4491A (University Microfilms No. 80-02, 220).

Jenkins, J. R., & Dixon, R. (1983). Vocabulary learning. *Contemporary Educational Psychology, 8,* 237–260.

Jenkins, J. R., Stein, M. L., & Wysocki, K. (1984). Learning vocabulary through reading. *American Educational Research Journal, 21,* 767–787.

Kameenui, E. J., Carnine, D. W., & Freschi, R. (1982). Effects of text construction and instructional procedures for teaching word meanings on comprehension and recall. *Reading Research Quarterly, 17,* 367–388.

Kuhn, T. S. (1962). *The structure of scientific revolutions.* Chicago: University of Chicago.

Mezynski, K. (1983). Issues concerning the acquisition of knowledge: Effects of vocabulary training on reading comprehension. *Review of Educational Research, 53,* 253–279.

Nagy, W., & Anderson, R. C. (1984). How many words are there in printed school English? *Reading Research Quarterly, 19,* 304–330.

Pany, D., & Jenkins, J. R. (1978). Learning word meanings: A comparison of instructional procedures and effects on measures of reading comprehension with learning disabled students. *Learning Disability Quarterly, 1,* 21–32.

Ruddell, R., & Boyle, O. (1984). *A study of the effects of cognitive mapping on reading comprehension and written protocols.* Paper presented at the annual meeting of the National Reading Conference, St. Petersburg Beach, FL.

Sternberg, R., & Powell, J. S. (1983). Comprehending verbal comprehension. *American Psychologist, 38*(8), 878–893.

Watson, J. D. (1968). *The double helix.* New York: Signet.

9 The Effects and Uses of Diverse Vocabulary Instructional Techniques

Isabel L. Beck
Margaret G. McKeown
Richard C. Omanson
University of Pittsburgh

Over the past several years, the authors have been involved in an iterative program of vocabulary research. The purpose of this chapter is to synthesize the findings from a series of experiments in which we engaged. Then, on the basis of our findings, we describe the vocabulary program that we would design were we back in the intermediate grade classroom. To the extent that we need to go beyond our findings, we take off our researchers' hats and call on our teacher intuitions.

THE RELATIONSHIP BETWEEN VOCABULARY AND READING COMPREHENSION

We begin with a discussion of the kind of thinking that led to the initiation of our studies. Our greatest interest was with the relationship between vocabulary knowledge and reading comprehension. That there is a very strong relationship is well established in the literature as are the problematic aspects of that relationship. Numerous factor analytic studies have shown that vocabulary knowledge is a major predictor of reading comprehension (Davis, 1944, 1968; Singer, 1965; Thurstone, 1946). But factor analysis is correlational, and correlational evidence is not causal. The causal links between vocabulary knowledge and reading comprehension are not well understood. For instance, are people good comprehenders because they know a lot of words, or do people know a lot of words because they are good comprehenders and in the course of comprehending text, learn a lot of words, or is there some combination of directionality?

One of the places to look for discerning the relationship is to training studies that attempt to improve comprehension through vocabulary instruction. As it turns out, there are not a lot of studies of this nature, but there are some. At a very general level, there are three findings from these studies. First, virtually all vocabulary training studies succeed in boosting vocabulary knowledge (Draper & Moeller, 1971; Jenkins, Pany, & Schreck, 1978; Kameenui, Carnine, & Freschi, 1982; Tuinman & Brady, 1974). That is, children who are taught words learn words, at least to the point of being able to pass a simple objective test on their definitions. The second finding is that some of the studies do not show improved comprehension (Jenkins et al., 1978; Tuinman & Brady, 1974). The third finding is that some of the studies do show improved comprehension (Draper & Moeller, 1971; Kameenui et al., 1982).

The conflicting findings need to be discussed within the context of two important notions. First, there are various levels of word knowledge, and, second, that given the complexity of processes involved in comprehending text, a high level of word knowledge may be needed. Let us provide some examples of these different levels of word knowledge. A reader might meet the word *quaich* in a text, and have no knowledge of its meaning; one might have some general information about a word, such as understanding that *altruism* has a positive connotation, but knowing nothing about its specific nature; one might have a specific but narrow and context-bound knowledge of a word, such as knowing that a "*benevolent* dictator" is a ruler who does not mistreat people, but being unable to understand how *benevolent* applies to other situations and types of behavior; one might hear the word *bucolic* used, and need to pause momentarily before remembering that it describes something pastoral, or typical of rural life; finally, one might have full, rich decontextualized knowledge of a word, such as knowing not only that *miser* is someone who saves money and lives as if poor, but being able to give examples of miserly behavior, consequences of acting like a miser and able to use the word beyond typical contexts, for example by extending the concept to describe people who are stingy with other things besides money.

Regarding the relationship between vocabulary knowledge and reading comprehension, it would seem that the semantic processes involved in reading comprehension not only require accuracy of word knowledge, but also fluency of access to meanings in memory, and rich decontextualized knowledge of words. The conflicting findings of vocabulary studies might then be understood in that those studies that did not yield gains in reading comprehension failed to consider the full range of semantic processes needed for comprehension, but affected only accuracy of word knowledge. If this is the case, it would seem that, in order to influence reading comprehension and other complex verbal functions, instruction needs to be arranged to affect all three of these processing components.

DESIGN OF A VOCABULARY PROGRAM

Given the instructional goal of producing word knowledge that is rich and proficient enough to facilitate complex verbal tasks such as reading, we then established the instructional features that would be needed in a vocabulary program in order to meet this goal. Although the instruction would need to include associating words with definitions, it would need to go well beyond that. Instructional conditions should be arranged to provide opportunities for a maximum amount of processing of the words. Students should be required to manipulate words in varied and rich ways, for example, by describing how they relate to other words and to their own familiar experiences. To promote and reinforce deep processing, activities should include much discussion of the words and require students to create justifications for the relationships and associations that they discover. This feature we labeled *rich instruction*.

Another feature is that the words should be encountered with great frequency, not just two or three times. Relatedly, reinforcement of the words over time was also to be featured. The final feature is that instruction should set up conditions to encourage students to use the new words outside of the vocabulary lessons. In this way, words might more likely become a permanent part of students' vocabularies. A description of the implementation of these features in an instructional program follows.

Words were presented in semantic groups of 8 to 10 words. For example, one labeled *Moods* included such words as *jovial, indignant,* and *enthusiastic.* Richness of instruction was incorporated into the design as follows. Each set of words was taught over about a week's time, in which the activities required more involvement with the words and deeper processing on each subsequent day. The instruction included a range of task requirements that began with associating words with their meanings. The sequence of instruction then moved beyond relating words to their meanings, for instance by requiring children to associate new words with contexts that did not contain definition elements, but presented consequences, examples or typical actions associated with the taught words. For example, children were to recognize the following context as containing an example of *ridicule:*

> Maria decided she didn't want to play with Terry anymore. Terry was always being nasty about other people. She'd make a big joke out of the way other people looked or talked. What did Terry do to other people?

Further along the sequence, children were sometimes asked to create contexts for words, such as discuss what a *hermit* might have a nightmare about, or describe when they had *consoled* someone. Toward the end of the sequence, attention was given to the relationships among words. In this regard, activities involved comparing and contrasting words to discover relationships, such as answering, "Would you *berate* someone who *inspired* you?" "Would you want to *baffle* someone who tried to *snare* you?" or "Could a *miser* be a *tyrant*?"

A constant aspect of the activities was to encourage children to make their thinking explicit. The activities were mostly whole class, and provided for a great deal of discussion and interaction around the words. Another aspect found throughout the program concerns teacher-modeling. For the activities in which children were asked to construct scenarios, the teacher initially provided a model of a possible response such as suggesting "a hemit might have a nightmare that a big apartment building was built right next to his hideaway."

Another characteristic of the instruction to implement richness was that children were most often asked to give reasons for their answers. Even offbeat answers were encouraged as long as the children could give reasons for them. These justifications were requested to help the children reinforce their processing by making it explicit.

A second design feature was high frequency of encounters with taught words. Each word introduced in the program received at least 10 exposures. In addition, we included a condition to test for differential frequency. For this condition, systematic review activities were provided for a subset of the 104 words taught. These words, designated *many* words, received between 24 and 40 exposures. The other words, designated *some* words, received between 10 and 18 exposures.

The final design feature was to set up conditions to motivate the children to carry their vocabulary learning beyond the classroom. The implementation of this was an activity, called *Word Wizard,* in which children could earn points toward becoming a word wizard by reporting the context in which they had seen, heard, or used an instructed word outside of class. The purpose of the word wizard activity was to provide extrinsic motivation for children to extend their learning of the words presented in the program to nonschool activities.

RESULTS OF IMPLEMENTING THE PROGRAM

An initial study and a replication study were conducted based on the implementation of this program in fourth-grade classrooms (Beck, Perfetti, & McKeown, 1982; McKeown, Beck, Omanson, & Perfetti, 1983). For both of these studies we focused on the assessment of three aspects of verbal skill: a) accurate knowledge of word meanings, b) accessibility of word meanings during semantic processing, and c) reading comprehension. Two control conditions were included in both studies. One was a set of uninstructed words, and the other was a group of children who did not receive instruction.

In the two studies, we found, first, that children gained an accurate knowledge of the meanings of the words taught as measured by multiple choice tests. On tests given at the completion of each week's instruction, the children knew about 95% of the instructed words. On a posttest given 3 weeks after all instruction had been completed, they still knew 80% of the words. There was a difference among words in that children knew significantly more of the *many* words, those words seen most often in the program. Knowledge of the uninstructed words, and of all words by children who did not receive the instruction was approximately at chance level.

Second, as a result of the instruction, the children were able to access meanings of instructed words faster than uninstructed words. Their performance was also better than children who had not received this instruction. The accessibility of word meanings was measured by children's reaction time on word categorization tasks. That is, children were shown a word on a screen and asked to press a *yes* or *no* button to indicate if the word was, for example, "a person." This result suggests that the words were learned well enough to be readily available for complex processing tasks.

Third, reading comprehension was measured by recall of stories containing instructed words. In the initial study, comprehension of a story containing *many* words was slightly better than that of a story containing uninstructed words, and than that of children who had not received instruction. However, comprehension of a story containing the *some* words was no better than that of a story containing uninstructed words and of uninstructed children.

Subsequent analysis of the *some* story revealed that it had a more complex structure than the other stories. This story was revised for the replication study. The recall task was also changed from a probed to a free recall so as not to prompt the children with structural cues from the stories. In addition, a set of multiple choice questions about each story was added. The results of the comprehension task for the replication study were that recall of the *many* and *some* stories was superior to that of the story with uninstructed words and of children who had not received the instruction. The amount of recall did not differ between the *many* and *some* stories for the instructed children. Performance on the questions for the *many* and *some* stories showed the same pattern as that of recall in comparison to the uninstructed words story and children who had not received the instruction. However, for instructed children, more questions were correctly answered for the *many* than for the *some* story. From these two studies we concluded that instruction that improved accurate word knowledge and speed of semantic access could also influence reading comprehension.

A STUDY TO COMPARE TYPE AND FREQUENCY OF INSTRUCTION

As previously noted, the three major features incorporated into the design of the instruction were frequency of encounters, richness of instruction, and extension of word use beyond the classroom. A third study was designed to investigate the role of each of these aspects in bringing about the effects we found (McKeown, Beck, Omanson, & Pople, 1985).

Three types of instruction were used in the study. Two types of instruction, designated *rich* and *extended rich,* were based on the instruction used in our first two studies. The only difference between these two types was that *extended rich* instruction included the Word Wizard activity, which extended learning beyond the classroom. The third type was a more *traditional* instruction, which presented only associations between words and definitions as the content of instruction.

The rich and traditional instruction differed in the critical aspect of content. In rich instruction, the content began with association of words and meanings, but went on to include a variety of rich verbal contexts and elaborations of word meanings. Traditional instruction consisted only of associations between words and meanings. However, other aspects of instruction were held constant between the two types. The format of the rich and traditional activities was the same, in that both sets of instruction began with introduction of definitions and children were given "log sheets" on which to complete the definitions and sample sentences; the mode of responding was kept constant so that both kinds of instruction presented equal opportunities for oral responses and written responses. A few illustrations serve to demonstrate how format remained constant while the content varied between traditional and rich instruction. For example, a word association activity was included in each case. For the traditional instruction, the associations were based on definitions, such as "beginner" for *novice,* and "gives money" for *philanthropist.* In the rich instruction, the associations were based on examples or typical actions, such as "kindergartener," for *novice,* and "gift to build a new hospital" for *philanthropist.*

Each type of instruction included a sentence completion activity, which, for the traditional instruction, was cloze sentences whose content stayed close to the definition: "The (sleuth) became well known as a person who looks for ways to solve mysteries." In the rich instruction, students had to generate an ending to a sentence, and thus had to either create or respond to a context for the word: "A sleuth helped the police by _____."

To test the effect of frequency of encounters with words, the frequency was varied within each type of instruction. Half of the words presented in each condition received four exposures, whereas the other half received 12 exposures. The higher frequency level was determined based on the results of our earlier studies. Although those results do show advantage for the *many* (24–40 exposures) versus the *some* (10–18 exposures) condition for the knowledge and fluency measures, the advantage was not particularly large, and for comprehension as measured by recall, the *some* condition was as good as the *many*. We concluded the *many* exposures did not warrant the extra time needed, as the *some* exposures gave very good results. Thus, for our high number of exposures we chose 12, which was within the range of the *some* condition in our earlier studies. The lower number of exposures was established because of the concern for limited classroom time. Even our *some* condition represents much more time than is ordinarily alloted for vocabulary instruction. Our choice of four encounters reflected an amount that can be found in basal reading lessons, albeit our exposure is still a high estimate of this (Beck, McKeown, McCaslin, & Burkes, 1979).

To assess the results of this instruction, we again measured accuracy of word knowledge, fluency of semantic access, and comprehension of stories containing instructed words. In addition, for this study we also developed a measure to assess context interpretation, an aspect of verbal proficiency that is not easily revealed through recall of text. This aspect involves a problem that young learners sometimes exhibit in being unable to incorporate a word's meaning into the surrounding context to develop an appropriate representation of the context as a whole (McKeown, 1985). A similar notion, "passage integration," described as the ability to integrate a word's meaning within a context, has been discussed as important to comprehension by Jenkins et al. (1978) and Kameenui et al. (1982). Kameenui et al. showed that training in this aspect of verbal processing improved children's comprehension.

The problem of context interpretation is particularly apparent when the surrounding context does not strongly call to mind the target word. For example, consider the following scenario containing the instructed word *commend:* "When father heard that Lisa had ripped up the letter from Steve, father commended her for it." One does not usually think of being commended for destroying something in anger.

The task we presented consisted of scenarios such as the *commend* one, followed by a question that required an understanding of the implications of the target word within the context. The question for the *commend* scenario was "What do you think father thought of Steve?" To answer this question, one must infer that father approved of Lisa's action, and, therefore, must not think much of Steve.

The results of the three types of instruction and two frequency conditions were as follows. For accuracy of knowledge as measured by a multiple choice test, all types and frequencies of instruction showed advantage over no instruction. High encounter words were better known than low encounter words, but for this measure, the type of instruction did not make a difference.

For the fluency of access task, the extended/rich instruction yielded faster access for both high and low encounter words than did the rich and traditional instruction. There was no difference for the extended/rich instruction between high and low encounter words, both of which were responded to as fast as common words selected from high frequency word lists, such as *friend, grandfather,* and *follow.* For the rich and traditional instruction, high encounter words were accessed faster than low encounter words.

For the comprehension task, the only significant result was that the rich and extended/rich instruction produced greater recall for the high encounter story in comparison to the recall of children who had received no instruction. Although there was a similar difference between the rich and extended/rich instruction groups' recall of the story with high encounter words and of a story containing unfamiliar words that had not been taught, the difference was not significant.

For the context interpretation task, rich and extended/rich instruction better enabled children to respond to the questions that followed the context than did traditional instruction. For all types of instruction the words that had been encountered more often produced greater results. One tendency for children who received the traditional instruction was to react by defining the target word rather than responding to the situation presented. This suggests they did not have readily available a network of associations for the target word that they could draw upon in establishing an interpretation of the situation.

Several conclusions can be drawn from this study about the effects of various aspects of instruction. First of all, even a few, in this case four, encounters with a word within rather narrow instructional activities will produce some, albeit limited, results. Second, a greater number of encounters with words is generally more helpful toward a variety of vocabulary learning goals. One exception to this was that even a higher number of encounters with traditional instruction did not enhance reading comprehension. Only rich instruction, and only in the high encounter condition, was powerful enough to affect comprehension. Finally, extending instruction beyond the classroom held advantage in making knowledge about the words more readily available for processing. This could be important when processing capacity limitations threaten a breakdown of comprehension.

THE ROLE OF RICH INSTRUCTION

To discuss the success of instruction that offers a high number of encounters with rich activities and extends learning beyond the classroom is not to say that this type of instruction is appropriate for all vocabulary learning situations. Let us present what we view as the role of this type of instruction. First, this type of instruction is not suited to all types of words. To elaborate, consider a mature, literate individual's vocabulary as comprising three tiers. The first tier consists of the most basic words — *cat, mother, go, red, talk, chocolate,* and so on. It would be difficult to argue that any direct instruction be devoted to the meanings of these words in school. The third tier consists of words whose frequency of use is quite low, or that apply to specific domains. This tier might include words such as *divertimento, nebula, resistivity, nonrestrictive,* and *tidal pool.* In general, a rich conceptual knowledge of such words would not be of high utility for most learners. These words are probably best learned when a specific need arises, such as presenting *nebula* during a lesson or discussion of the solar system.

Now, to return to the second tier. It is this tier that contains words of high frequency for mature language users. They are also words of general utility, not limited to a specific domain. Some examples might be *unique, convenient, retort, influence, ponder,* and *procrastinate.* It is words of this type toward which the most productive instructional efforts can be directed. Because of the role they play in a language user's verbal repertoire, rich knowledge of words in this second tier can have a significant impact on verbal functioning.

We have made an initial attempt to estimate the percentage of a vocabulary repertoire that would be included in this second tier, using data from Nagy and Anderson's (1984) analysis of words in printed school English for grades 3 to 9. Nagy and Anderson estimate that good readers of this age range may read a million words of text a year. They also estimate that about half of the 88,500 word families they calculate to exist in printed school English are so rare that they may be encountered no more than once in an avid reader's lifetime. With these figures in mind, it seems reasonable to consider words — or, rather, word families — that would be encountered once in 10 years, namely those that occur once or more in 10 million running words of text, as comprising tiers one and two. That translates into about 15,000 word families. A stab at estimating tier one, those most familiar words that need no instruction, would be 8,000 word families. We have chosen this figure because Nagy and Anderson state that it may be reasonable to assume that a third grader already knows 8,000 words. That gives us about 7,000 word families for tier two, which we want to focus on. Based on our third study, which lowered the frequency of the words taught, we estimate that it would not be unreasonable to suggest that about 400 words could be taught per school year. Teaching 400 words per year over Grades 3–9, would provide rich knowledge for 40% of the word families that make up tier two.

This estimate must be presented with a cautionary note; it is only an attempt to get a handle on a possible figure for the words that this type of instruction would focus on. No degree of precision can be assumed. Yet, it is useful for making two important points. First, nowhere near all the words that are available in print or oral contexts would be candidates for this kind of rich instruction. Second, providing rich conceptual networks for a portion of words that would be good candidates — approximately 40% of them — is a significant contribution to the verbal functioning of an individual.

The contribution is particularly significant for those children in the lower half of the distribution in both reading skill and socioeconomic status (SES). For example, in our original vocabulary study, the subjects were fourth graders from a city school, and 79% of them were below the 50th percentile on standardized pretests in reading comprehension and vocabulary. It is this type of child who is less likely to acquire, and become proficient in using, rich conceptual networks of tier two words independently. We base this statement on two sets of evidence, and a conjecture.

The first set of evidence about richness of vocabulary knowledge comes from work by Curtis (this volume). She found that students of lower ability knew not only fewer words, but had more narrow knowledge of words with which they were familiar.

The other evidence and the conjecture are concerned with the issue of how the acquisition and proficient use of rich vocabulary knowledge might develop without specific in-school instruction. One way is through extensive reading, where familiar words are encountered in new and varied contexts and each new context is a potential new facet of that word's network. However, the children we are talking about are less able readers. Not only are these children less likely to read extensively, but evidence shows that they are not particularly facile in deriving word meaning information from context (McKeown, 1985; Quealy, 1969; Rankin & Overholser, 1969; Sternberg, Powell, & Kaye, 1983). Specifically, McKeown found that less skilled fifth graders were less able to identify concepts from context that constrained the meaning of an unfamiliar word, less able to evaluate the meaning of a word even when correct constraints were identified, less able to take advantage of multiple contexts that used the unknown word, and less able to identify the meaning of the word after a series of context clues had been presented. In addition, even after the meaning of a word was identified or presented, less-skilled children were less able to identify correct use of the word in subsequent contexts. Thus, the power of increasing vocabulary through reading is significantly diminished for less able readers.

In addition to extensive reading, another way rich networks are likely to develop is through exposure to a verbal environment in which words unfamiliar to the child are used regularly. Characteristic of such an environment is an extensive and sophisticated vocabulary, with words often used in reflective, playful, or novel ways. Our conjecture is that this kind of environment is not a common one for lower verbal learners, either at home or among peers.

Because the kind of rich, extended instruction we developed provides a lively verbal environment in which words are explored and played with in highly interactive ways, we believe that the instruction may also have a role in promoting learning of words beyond those in the program. In our initial work, we discussed this hypothesis and labeled the phenomenon *word awareness*. We reasoned that because the children were being inundated with words, and having enjoyable, successful experiences learning them, they might become more aware of new words in their environment, and more likely to expend effort understanding them.

Evidence for word awareness is very limited, however. In our initial study and the replication, both of which lasted from October until March, we administered standardized reading and vocabulary tests as pretests and posttests. For the initial study, children who received our instruction made larger gains on the tests in comparison to a control group. This was not the case for the replication study, however.

Some anecdotal evidence exists for word awareness. On a number of occasions when we were observing the classrooms, children came to us to ask why we had not included certain words in our program, or to give suggestions for other words to include. Two examples of words that children brought to our attention from their own sources were *vigilant* and *crevice*.

Another issue in evaluating whether the rich instruction in our studies helped children to learn words beyond those in the program is to consider what promotes independent word learning. For children to learn words independently they first must notice words in their environment. That is, they must be aware of encountering specific words, notice when newly encountered words appear in subsequent contexts, and notice the ways in which the words are used. Realizing the differences between knowing and not knowing a word assists in word learning also. A learner needs to realize that specific words encountered are unknown, or to what degree they are known.

A third factor in independent learning is the ability to derive word meaning from context, both oral and textual. Although this factor was not present in our programs in any systematic way, the first two factors, which were present, do influence the ability to use context.

The rich instruction in our programs provided children with opportunities, first, to notice words. This was evidenced by the success of the Word Wizard activity, and their sharing of other words both related (e.g., *nutritious* from *nutrition, tyrannosaurus* from *tyrant*) and unrelated to the instructed words. Children also experienced, on a regular basis, being faced with a set of unknown words that, over the course of several days, became well known. Thus, it seems that rich instruction carries good potential for fostering independent word learning.

AN INTERMEDIATE GRADE VOCABULARY PROGRAM

We now turn to a description of the vocabulary program we would design were we teaching in an intermediate grade classroom. The basis for developing such a classroom program would be a deep understanding that certain kinds of experiences in vocabulary have value. Learning an association or brief definition for a word, or meeting a word in an informative context has some pay off (McKeown et al., 1985; Nagy & Herman, this volume). Receiving this kind of information about a word might be seen as an initiating event that begins the process of learning a word. Subsequent encounters with the word may then become more salient, and allow a learner to build up a full understanding of the word. We also know that rich instruction in vocabulary can make a strong contribution to one's understanding and use of specific words (Beck et al., 1982; McKeown et al., 1983). Further, encouragement for learners to extend their word learning beyond the classroom results in even greater facility with the words (McKeown et al., 1985). Finally, because instruction cannot cover all words that children need to know, and because some people are much less efficient word learners than others, it is important to encourage independent word learning. An environment that places emphasis on learning words may encourage this.

With an understanding of these notions from research, we would create a program with several components. One would be rich instruction for a small set of words. Another component would be gimmicks to encourage the use of words being taught outside of the classroom. This encouragement would be extended to include motivation to discover, learn, and use new words other than those introduced in class. We would also introduce lots of words in a narrow way, by creating an association to a definition or synonym. We believe that narrow instruction would be especially likely to lead to further learning when presented in the context of a verbal environment that presented rich and extensive experiences with words as well.

The selection of words for the program and whether they would be taught in a narrow or rich way cannot be determined independent of the classroom curriculum. Rather, those decisions would be made based on classroom lessons, opportunities that arose spontaneously, such as community or news events, and contributions from the children themselves.

The program would not operate from a set of rules about how many words would be taught, how they would be introduced and maintained. Here, we can release ourselves from an experimental paradigm. Rather, the intention would be to establish a way of thinking about words that will lead to the creation of a lively and productive verbal environment. The key to doing this would be to be alert to words in upcoming lessons and elsewhere that we think, based on knowing our students, would be unknown or not well known. Similarly, we would be alert to opportunities to enrich knowledge of words already introduced, to draw relationships between words, and to point out new contexts or different uses for words.

We would lay the groundwork for our vocabulary program by reviewing the lesson materials that we would be using for an upcoming month or two of school. One of the major sources for words are selections from basal reading programs. So we would use those selections as grist for our classroom vocabulary program. We would preview the set of selections that would be encountered for the next month or so of school. For each selection we would be on the lookout for words that seemed important to the central ideas in the selection, but would also identify words that were not necessarily important to the central ideas, yet seemed interesting and generally useful.

To illustrate decisions about the selection and instructional treatment of the words, we provide three examples of dealing with specific reading selections. The selections, a Greek myth, a humorous narrative, and an expository piece, allow us to demonstrate a variety of considerations for vocabulary instruction.

Consider a fourth-grade selection set in ancient Greece about a young woman's haughty attitude toward her weaving prowess. The woman gives no credit to Athena for teaching her to spin. So Athena and she have a contest, and of course, Athena triumphs. The bargain had been that if Athena won, the girl, Arachne, would agree never to weave gain. Seeing how unhappy Arachne is with this outcome, Athena allows her to go on weaving in another form — by turning her into a spider.

Our review of the selection resulted in three sets of words that were related to central ideas. One set contained words that dealt with weaving, such as *loom, flax, warp, woof, skeins, fleece, spindle,* and *dustoff.* A second were words that were associated with ancient Greece, *Athena, Greece,* and *Jupiter.* The third were two words around which the plot revolved, *bargain* and *agreement.* In addition to the three sets of words related to central ideas in the selection, we identified four words as interesting and generally useful, *dwell, boast, stern,* and *marvelous.*

How might we handle these words in view of the variety of vocabulary experiences possible and their differential values? First we look at the setting words (*Athena, Greece,* and *Jupiter*). The amount and kind of instruction that we might provide for these words prior to our fourth-grade children encountering them in this selection depends on what they already know of the ancient Greek gods. Obviously, if we have reason to believe they know a lot, for example, because they had read some of the myths earlier, we would not need to do anything, or at most, mention the setting of the story. But let's assume these children know virtually nothing of ancient Greece. Do we use rich instructional methods to provide a strong backdrop for the selection, or do we provide just enough so that the super power of the gods (they appear from nowhere, they cast spells) is available to the children? The latter would not take much instructional time as fourth graders have a strong schema for super heroes, so Jupiter and Athena could quickly (less than a minute) be related to a well established schema. Yet it would be sufficient for understanding their role in the story.

The decision of whether to introduce the words in a rich or narrow way depends upon what else needs to be done for the selection and whether upcoming instructional content (e.g., some myths will be read; a visit to a museum is scheduled; a social studies unit on Modern Greece is coming) can take advantage of the instructional time that would be needed to establish a strong background.

Now let's move to the longest list of related words, those associated with weaving. Although a good portion of text in the selection is devoted to weaving, and even though it is likely that many fourth graders would not know details of spinning and weaving, such as *woof* and *warp,* we would present these in a very narrow way. Our concern would only be that when the words were encountered in the selection they be processed as "having something to do with weaving and spinning." In contrast, the words we would establish through rich instruction are *bargain* and *agreement.* We have several reasons for doing so. First, they represent the central issue of the story. If readers lacked understanding of a bargain/agreement schema, their comprehension of the story would be severely diminished. Second, the concept of an agreement or bargain is a common plot device in literature. Third, the notions of bargain and agreement are related to many other domains as wide-ranging as everyday human interactions and relations between foreign countries. Thus, bargain and agreement are valuable words to teach for this story and are generative concepts as well.

The interesting and generally useful words, *dwell, boast, stern, marvelous,* are not critical to comprehension if not known. Thus, they could be dealt with either before or after story reading. If before the story, we would not want them to consume much time, so the introduction would be brief and narrow. If after the story, either rich or narrow instruction could be used. The important point about these words is that they would be maintained, used in relation to other general words, and eventually developed in a rich way. Our perspective on these words is that we would be "collecting" them for subsequent use. For example, in selecting them, we were aware that *dwell* relates to *inhabitants,* which occurs in a later selection and *marvelous* relates to the upcoming word *marveled.*

Another selection offers a different kind of example for vocabulary work. The selection, *Pippi Finds a Spink,* is a Pippi Longstocking tale in which Pippi discovers a new word, *spink,* and then searches for a meaning for the word. This selection's conceptual structure, setting, and type of character are likely familiar to children, and thus, in one sense, there is not any critical vocabulary to teach. However, this story represents a situation found frequently in literature, that is, the rich and effective use of language by a good writer. Words such as the following are used: *triumphantly, peculiar, objects, veranda, indignantly, innocent, nations, contagious, needlessly, hoisted, astonishment, tremendous* and *radiant.* Unfamiliarity with these words might not interfere with comprehension of the story, but it could diminish an appreciation for good writing by lessening the impact of effective language use. Another reason for teaching these words is that they are of high general utility. They can be used in many and varied situations, and can be related to other words.

How would the words be taught? Because there are so many of them, we might choose to introduce before reading a subset of those we believe might be least familiar or might add to story enjoyment most. Then after the story all the words would be worked with, likely in a rich way. This would include discussing the contexts from the story in which the words were used. Because of their generative nature, these words would be given attention again, perhaps as part of a weekly vocabulary period, or during the introduction of related words.

A third reading selection exemplifies further issues in selecting and teaching words. This selection is an expository piece about meteors, *Visitors from Space*. The article explains that falling stars are actually meteors, which sometimes fall to earth — in which case they are called meteorites — and create craters. Three words of conceptual importance to the selection are *atmosphere, meteor,* and *meteorite.*

Of the three, *atmosphere* may be the most important to discuss prior to reading, as *meteor* and *meteorite* are explained in text. The selection explains that meteors begin to heat up and then glow as they enter the earth's atmosphere. Without some understanding of what the earth's atmosphere is, and how and where it differs from what lies beyond, comprehension of the selection, and thus of the phenomenon of meteors, would suffer. Another reason to introduce the word *atmosphere* is that it represents a basic scientific concept. An understanding of what the atmosphere is, why and how it affects physical phenomena that occur within it, and how it differs, for example, from what surrounds the moon and other planets is very important to one's knowledge of the scientific domain. The concept of the earth's atmosphere will recur and be built upon as students progress through the science curriculum. So this selection offers a fine opportunity to begin building knowledge of that concept.

We have discussed several selections that offer different kinds of opportunities for vocabulary development. The choice of which words to teach and what kind of attention to give them depends on a variety of factors such as importance to understanding of the selection, relationship to specific domains of knowledge, general utility, and relationship to other lessons and classroom events. A major problem in the vocabulary instruction in basal readers is the egalitarian treatment of all categories of words. For example, in the selection about meteors, the word *atmosphere* is given no greater attention than *completely* or *museum,* which have rather minor roles in the story. In the selection from Greek mythology about Arachne who loved to weave, the word *loom* is given as much attention as *agreement*. *Loom* may be helpful to understand aspects of spinning, but it is a word of low general utility, while *agreement* is central to the entire story as well as being generally useful. Consideration needs to be given to why words are selected for attention and the role they might play in a child's vocabulary repertoire.

Under our program, most words would be taught within the context of the lesson from which they were drawn. In addition to vocabulary work in the context of reading and content area lessons, we would have about a 20- to 30-minute period per week set aside to work on vocabulary. At this time we would review words, present enriching activities, challenge the children to generate contexts for new words, or draw or elicit relationships among words.

Other activities would include those to encourage children to extend their learning beyond the classroom. As with the Word Wizard activity used in our studies, children would be challenged to find uses of taught words, or to use the words themselves, outside of class. A tally would be kept as children brought in evidence.

The notion of working with words outside of class would be extended to words not introduced in class, those that children found on their own. For example, children might be asked to go home and find a word used, such as in the newspaper or a book, that they do not know, and share it with the class. Or children might be asked to bring in a word to "stump the class" and then prepare and teach, with some teacher assistance, a lesson on that word.

We would not underestimate the power of captivating children's interest in words through such gimmicks. We observed, over the course of several studies, how immensely effective the word wizard activity was in getting children to think about and use the taught words. It had the effect of creating a rich verbal environment for children at home as well as in school. This is a characteristic that is lacking for many children who experience slow vocabulary growth.

Research has provided much useful information about vocabulary learning and instruction. What it has *not* provided is a simple formula for optimal instruction, because no such formula can exist. The creation of effective vocabulary instruction calls for a careful crafting of experiences in consideration of specific learning goals, the words being taught, and the characteristics of the learners.

REFERENCES

Beck, I. L., McKeown, M. G., McCaslin, E. S., & Burkes, A. M. (1979). *Instructional dimensions that may affect reading comprehension: Examples from two commercial reading programs*. (LRDC Publication 1979/20). Pittsburgh: University of Pittsburgh, Learning Research and Development Center.

Beck, I. L., Perfetti, C. A., & McKeown, M. G. (1982). Effects of long-term vocabulary instruction on lexical access and reading comprehension. *Journal of Educational Psychology, 74,* 506–521.

Davis, F. B. (1944). Fundamental factors of comprehension in reading. *Psychometrika, 9,* 185–197.

Davis, F. B. (1968). Research in comprehension in reading. *Reading Research Quarterly, 3,* 499–545.

Draper, A. G., & Moeller, G. H. (1971). We think with words (therefore, to improve thinking, teach vocabulary). *Phi Delta Kappan, 52,* 482–484.

Jenkins, J. R., Pany, D., & Schreck, J. (1978). *Vocabulary and reading comprehension: Instructional effects.* (Technical Report 100). Urbana: University of Illinois, Center for the Study of Reading.

Kameenui, E. J., Carnine, D. W., & Freschi, R. (1982). Effects of text construction and instructional procedures for teaching word meanings on comprehension and recall. *Reading Research Quarterly, 17,* 367–388.

McKeown, M. G. (1985). The acquisition of word meaning from context by children of high and low ability. *Reading Research Quarterly, 20,* 482–496.

McKeown, M. G., Beck, I. L., Omanson, R. C., & Perfetti, C. A. (1983). The effects of long-term vocabulary instruction on reading comprehension: A replication. *Journal of Reading Behavior, 15,* 3–18.

McKeown, M. G., Beck, I. L., Omanson, R., & Pople, M. T. (1985). Some effects of the nature and frequency of vocabulary instruction on the knowledge and use of words. *Reading Research Quarterly, 20,* 522–535.

Nagy, W. E., & Anderson, R. C. (1984). How many words are there in printed school English. *Reading Research Quarterly, 19,* 304–330.

Quealy, R. J. (1969). Senior high school students use of contextual aids in reading. *Reading Research Quarterly, 4,* 512–531.

Rankin, E. F., & Overholser, B. M. (1969). Reaction of intermediate grade children to contextual clues. *Journal of Reading Behavior, 1,* 50–73.

Singer, H. A. (1965). A developmental model of speed of reading in grades 3 through 6. *Reading Research Quarterly, 1,* 29–49.

Sternberg, R. J., Powell, J. S., & Kaye, D. B. (1983). Teaching vocabulary-building skills: A contextual approach. In A. C. Wilkinson (Ed.), *Classroom computers and cognitive science* (pp. 122–143). New York: Academic Press.

Thurstone, L. L. (1946). A note on a reanalysis of Davis' reading tests. *Psychometrika, 11,* 185–188.

Tuinman, J. J., & Brady, M. E. (1974). How does vocabulary account for variance on reading comprehension tests? A preliminary instructional analysis. In P. Nacke (Ed.), *Twenty-third national reading conference yearbook* (pp. 176–184). Clemson, SC: The National Reading Conference.

10

The Roles of Instruction in Fostering Vocabulary Development

Michael F. Graves
University of Minnesota

Shortly before or after they celebrate their first birthday, children are likely to utter their first word. Over the 3 months following the appearance of the first word, they may learn an additional 50 words. During this period, children are likely to speak exclusively in 1-word utterances. Then, after accumulating the 50 or so words, they begin stringing words together to form sentences, 2-word sentences at first, then 3-word sentences, and soon longer ones.

Things move rapidly after this. By the time children enter first grade, their phonological systems are largely or fully complete; they can recognize and produce all or all but a few of the sounds in their language. Their syntactic systems, although not as advanced as their phonological systems, are well on their way to maturity; 6-year-olds can understand and produce a large percentage of the nearly infinite number of sentence patterns in the language.

At this same time, as they enter first grade, children's vocabulary development is in one sense similarly impressive. They have learned a substantial number of words, and for many children direct instruction has played an important role in their acquisition of those words. Parents of preschoolers frequently engage in what Brown (1958) calls "the original word game," naming objects for their children and guiding them as they attempt to repeat the names (de Villers & de Villers, 1978).

Although estimates of the number of words first graders know vary tremendously (see Anderson & Freebody, 1981), making it impossible to specify anything like an exact number, Calfee and Drum's (1986) estimate that first graders are likely to know somewhere between 1,000 and 10,000 words is a reasonable but very inexact one. In contrast to the situation with phonology and syntax, then, the first grader still has a long way to go in mastering the vocabulary of the language. Even if the 10,000-word estimate is doubled, the number of words left to learn is still enormous. Although estimates of the size of older children's vocabularies vary even more than do those of younger children's vocabularies, a reliable estimate (Nagy & Anderson, 1984) of the number of different words appearing in the materials children use in school through the 12 years of public schooling puts that number at approximately 100,000 words.

Of course, children do not need to learn all of these words, and they do not learn all of them (see Beck, McKeown, & Omanson, this volume); but they do need to learn some of them. The position taken here is that some of the words students need to learn should be taught directly. Additionally, students need to develop strategies for learning words on their own, and they need to develop an attitude toward words that will encourage them to use these strategies.

Although vocabulary instruction is certainly a part of most elementary reading programs, several studies (Beck, McKeown, McCaslin, & Burkes, 1979; Durkin, 1979; Jenkins & Dixon, 1983; Nagy & Herman, this volume) have suggested that it is frequently a very small part. Durkin, for example, found that out of 4,469 minutes of reading instruction she observed, only 19 minutes were devoted to vocabulary instruction, with an additional 4 minutes being devoted to vocabulary review.

I know of no studies on the amount of vocabulary instruction in secondary schools. However, 14 years of teaching secondary reading courses to in-service teachers, talking to secondary content teachers in a variety of subject areas, and observing secondary classrooms has convinced me that even less vocabulary instruction occurs at that level. More specifically, I believe that anything other than a very brief introduction to some words from an upcoming selection is extremely rare, and that even such brief instruction is quite rare.

My purpose here is to outline a variety of roles that instruction could play in fostering students' vocabulary development. In doing so, I list three goals of vocabulary instruction, consider some subgoals and some of the roles of instruction in reaching those subgoals, and say something about the work that has been done and that I see as needing to be done to clarify the goals and to determine the power of instruction to reach them.

The goals are Learning Words, Learning To Learn Words, and Learning About Words. Although the plan is by no means fully developed and the presentation here is fairly brief, I am hopeful that it can be useful as a beginning description of the sort of vocabulary curriculum that might be presented over the 12 years of elementary and secondary schooling.

LEARNING WORDS

Of the three major goals I have listed, this is the one that currently receives the most attention in schools, and at least until recently it has been the goal that has received the most research attention. Yet even this goal receives a good deal less attention than it deserves, partly at least because the task of learning words is actually a series of tasks that vary markedly depending on the relationship between the learner's knowledge of the word and concept to be taught, and the depth and precision of meaning to be taught. Here, I distinguish six tasks, four of which I have considered in greater detail elsewhere (see Graves, 1984, 1985; Graves & Duin, 1985). The tasks are learning to read known words, learning new meanings for known words, learning new words representing known concepts, learning new words representing new concepts, clarifying and enriching the meanings of known words, and moving words from receptive to expressive vocabularies.

Learning To Read Known Words — *important for low ability readers*

Learning to read known words, words that are already in their oral vocabularies, is the task of the beginning reader; and some direct instruction in such words is part of virtually all beginning reading programs. Chall (this volume) has given some attention to learning to read known words. With the exception of Chall's chapter, the task has received little attention in the present collection because learning such words is a decoding task and the major concern of this volume is with word meanings. Moreover, instruction in recognizing known words in print is presently successful for the majority of students. Average and above-average primary grade students routinely master the sight vocabulary presented in their readers, and by the time they reach fourth grade, they can deal with nearly all of the words in their oral vocabularies when they meet them in print (Graves, 1980). Unfortunately, the same cannot be said for below-average readers; many below-average readers cannot read all of the words in their oral vocabularies. However, because Chall addresses the topic of learning such words and because such words are not the major focus of this volume, I do not consider the matter further here.

Learning New Meanings for Known Words *multiple-meaning words*

The second word-learning task, learning new meanings for words that students already know with one meaning, is one that both authority (e.g., Herber, 1978; Johnson & Pearson, 1984) and empirical evidence (Mason, Kniseley, & Kendall, 1979; Scherr, 1984) testify to as being a potential cause of difficulty. It differs from the task of learning to read known words in that all readers are faced with dealing with polysemous words throughout the 12 years of public school and beyond.

There are at least two sorts of polysemous words. First, many words have a number of common meanings. The words *run* and *head* are frequently cited examples. There are far too many words with common multiple meanings to teach all such words directly; for example, 72% of the words in the Ginn lexicon of 9,000 words have multiple meanings (Johnson & Pearson, 1984). Thus, the major goal in teaching students to deal with such words is to show them that words have multiple meanings rather than to teach them the various meanings of specific words. I discuss this topic in the section on learning about words.

The second sort of polysemous words are words with both common meanings and specialized meanings in particular subject areas. Examples of such words are *product* and *legend*. My belief is that the number of such words is not large; however, data on this body of words would be useful. Whatever the exact number of them, it seems that such words should be directly taught and that teachers in whose classes they arise are the appropriate persons to teach them. Information on the extent to which teachers at various grade levels recognize the existence of such polysemous words and teach them is another sort of data that would be useful.

Learning New Words Representing Known Concepts

The third word-learning task, learning new words that represent known concepts, is in my judgment the largest word-learning task that students face once they leave the primary grades. That is, I believe that the largest percentage of the roughly 100,000 word families that have been estimated to appear in school texts (see Nagy & Anderson, 1984) are words that represent known or easily taught concepts. Examples of such words might be *resent* (meaning "to feel angry") for intermediate grade students, *entice* (meaning "to attract by offering something tempting") for junior high school students, and *languish* (meaning "to lose strength or become listless or depressed") for senior high students. In each case, the word itself is likely to be unknown, but the notion it conveys is likely to be easily within students' grasp.

Because there are so many of these words, the first problem that occurs when we consider teaching them is determining just which of them to teach. Although there is no way of identifying specific words to teach to all students, there are criteria that can lead to reasonable choices. Stated very briefly, these include a word's frequency, probably as listed in Carroll, Davies, and Richman (1971); data on the percentage of students at various grade levels who have been shown to know the word, information that is provided in Dale and O'Rourke (1981); the importance of the word to understanding an upcoming selection; the likelihood that students could learn the upcoming word on their own using their context, structural analysis, or dictionary skills; and the likelihood that the word could be used to further students' skills in using context, structural analysis, or the dictionary.

A second problem that occurs with new words representing known concepts is the matter of how to teach them. The methods that appear to me to have been given the widest recognition by researchers are Beck and her colleagues' intensive instruction (Beck, McKeown, & Omanson, this volume; Beck, Perfetti, McKeown, 1982; McKeown, Beck, Omanson, & Perfetti, 1983; McKeown, Beck, Omanson, & Pople, 1985), Levin and Pressley's keyword method (Pressley, Levin, & Delaney, this volume); Gipe's context method (1979, 1981), and the semantic mapping and semantic feature analysis procedures tested by Johnson and others (Johnson, Toms-Bronowski, & Pittelman, 1982; Levin et al., 1984). It is important to realize, as has not been pointed out until recently, that the procedures have quite different purposes and predictably different outcomes, and any particular procedure should be used only where appropriate. Beck et al.'s procedure, for example, is appropriate for teaching deep and rich word meanings and for fostering students' awareness of what it means to know a word well. The keyword method, on the other hand, does something quite different; it establishes an association between a word and a meaning. I comment further on appropriate uses of some of these methods later in this chapter.

Finally, taken together, the methods mentioned here and most of those used in other research seem to leave a question that has not been adequately addressed. Specifically, the research has seldom dealt with brief teaching techniques such as students simply reading definitions of a set of words. The possible efficacy of brief instruction is suggested in a study by Jenkins, Stein, and Wysocki (1984), who found that a brief exposure to words resulted in more learning from context than no exposure, and in a study by Parker (1984), who found that the frequently maligned procedure of having students look up words in the dictionary and use them in a sentence produced substantial learning. The value of brief instruction is suggested if one considers that brief instruction to be the initial encounter in the series of encounters that are necessary to fully learn a word. And the importance of research on brief teaching procedures is emphasized if, as seems likely to be the case, both individual classroom teachers and producers of basal readers and other texts continue to employ brief teaching procedures.

Learning New Words Representing New Concepts

The fourth word-learning task, learning new words that represent new concepts, is the most difficult word-learning task students face. It is also a task that is sometimes hard to distinguish from that of learning new words representing known concepts. This is the case for two reasons. First, words and the concepts they represent form a continuum. Some words very definitely represent familiar concepts and can be easily explained; others represent somewhat familiar concepts and can be fairly easily explained (at least if they do not have to be explained too fully); and still others represent distinctly new concepts — which may or may not be difficult — and may require a good deal of time and effort to explain (particularly if they do need to be explained fully).

The second reason that the distinction between teaching new words that represent known concepts and new words that represent unknown ones is a fine one is suggested by the parenthetical comment above. That is, the difficulty of teaching a word or concept is influenced by the depth or precision of meaning that needs to be developed. *Fascism,* for example, would represent a new concept for most sixth graders. However, teaching students that fascism is "a type of dictatorship" is certainly radically easier than teaching the full blown concept of FASCISM, and teaching students this brief and incomplete meaning of *fascism* would be a relatively easy task. Such an incomplete meaning, however, would be sufficient for many purposes.

The first problem mentioned with respect to teaching new words representing known concepts, identifying which words to teach, is not nearly as great a concern when words representing new concepts are being considered because there are not as many new concepts that might potentially be taught. The source of words that represent new concepts is the subject matter being taught. Those new concepts that need to be taught are those that represent the major concepts of the subject matter. If the number of new concepts that need to be taught to a particular group of students greatly exceeds the number that can be taught feasibly, then the subject matter is too difficult for those students.

The second problem mentioned with respect to teaching new words representing known concepts, that of what teaching methods to use, is similarly a problem here. There is a large research literature on concept instruction (see Tennyson & Cocchiarella, 1986; Tennyson & Park, 1980), and I do not attempt to review it here. I do want to stress, however, that the teaching procedures used do need to be appropriate to the learning task. The multi-faceted Frayer method (Frayer, Fredrick, & Klausmeier, 1969), for example, is clearly a concept-teaching method. The keyword method, on the other hand, puts all the instructional stress on teaching an association and virtually none of it on teaching or embellishing a word's meaning, and it is thus clearly inappropriate for teaching new concepts.

Clarifying and Enriching the Meanings of Known Words

The next word-learning task, that of clarifying and enriching meanings of already known words, is one that receives little attention in schools. To be sure, students expand the meanings of words they know as they meet words in different contexts. However, the accretion of meaning from context is a slow and by no means certain process, particulary for some students. More direct approaches definitely seem warranted.

The most thoroughly researched and best documented procedure teaching deep and thorough meanings is the intensive instruction developed by Beck and her colleagues. Although it should be noted that enriching the meanings of known words was not the specific goal of this instruction, such procedures as making affective responses to words, noting relationships among both similar and dissimilar words, and encountering words in a variety of contexts are precisely the sorts of procedures needed for enriching word meanings. Results of Beck et al.'s studies have indicated that students gained thorough and deep understanding of the words taught and that students who received more encounters with words than others gained more fluency with the words. And, in fact, Elshout-Mohr and van Daalen-Kaptiejns (this volume) propose a program much like Beck et al.'s for the purpose of enriching the meanings of known words, and suggest that such a program might have a generative effect on learning word meanings and, perhaps, on verbal comprehension more generally.

A second technique useful for clarifying and extending word meanings is the one that Johnson and Pearson (1984) term *semantic feature analysis*. Briefly, the method consists of presenting students with a grid containing a set of related words on one axis and a set of attributes on the other axis. In their initial work with such a grid, students are shown a completed grid. Next, they are asked to fill in a grid, indicating those attributes that belong to each word. Later, they are asked to add to both the list of related words and the list of attributes; and, later yet, they can be asked to create grids. In all cases, there is a good deal of discussion, with much of the discussion devoted to students learning that words differ in a multitude of subtle ways. Johnson, Toms-Bronowski, and Pittelman (1982) have documented the efficacy of semantic feature analysis for teaching new words, but they have not investigated its effectiveness for enriching word meanings. Research on this topic would be a useful addition to the literature.

Moving Words From Receptive to Expressive Vocabularies

The last word-learning task I consider here is that of moving words from students' receptive vocabularies into their expressive ones. Although there is clear evidence that the words used in both speech and writing influence listeners' and readers' perceptions of both the message and its speaker or author (e.g., Bradac, Courtright, Schmidt, & Davies, 1976; Neilsen & Piché, 1981), the task of getting students to actively use the words they learn, like that of honing word meanings, is one that is seldom directly attacked in schools. It is also a task on which there is very little research; in fact, I know of only two studies on the topic.

In one study, Wolfe (1975) found that instruction in a general reading vocabulary increased students' use of words similar in complexity to the words taught in their writing, even though it did not result in students' more frequently using the specific words taught.

The other study, which modeled Beck et al.'s intensive instruction, was conducted by Duin (1983). Duin taught students a set of 10 words that lent themselves to writing a narrative about exploring and then asked students to write an exploring narrative. Results showed that as compared to students who did not receive the instruction, those who did used the words more frequently in their narratives and wrote narratives that were judged to be more structured, have more substance, and be more interesting. Additionally, Duin reported that students seemed to be excited about learning and using words and suggested that a "word awareness" effect similar to that which Beck et al. (this volume) discuss may influence them to pay more attention to their lexical choices in their future writing. One question that remains is that of the effects of repeated instruction of this sort over a period of several years. A related question is whether Beck et al.'s instruction, although not specifically intended to affect speech and writing, might do so.

In addition to using instruction that directly attempts to get students to actively use increasingly sophisticated vocabularies, much of the impetus for students' moving words into their expressive vocabularies seems likely to come as part of their learning to value words, a topic I discuss in the section on learning about words.

LEARNING TO LEARN WORDS

Even if instruction in individual words were as widespread and rich as one could possibly make it, most of the words students learn they must somehow learn independently. This is widely recognized, and some word-learning skills are taught in virtually all reading programs. However, in many instances the skills that are taught are not taught well or thoroughly, instruction is frequently brief and unsystematic, and some skills are not taught at all. Here I consider five skills: using context, learning and using word parts, using the dictionary and thesaurus, developing an approach to dealing with unknown words in context, and developing a personal approach to learning words.

Using Context

Although there is currently some debate about the extent to which students acquire word meanings from encountering words in context (see Jenkins et al., 1984; Nagy, Herman, & Anderson, 1985), most teachers and most researchers would probably agree that using context clues is likely to be one of the most practical means of learning new words. Moreover, use of context clues is taught in virtually every reading program. However, several weaknesses appear to prevent context clue instruction from being as effective as it might be.

One weakness is that the types of context clues being taught are probably not the most effective types to teach. The problem is that some types — for example, contrast clues — occur very rarely in actual materials, whereas other types — for example, experience clues — are so amorphous that they are of no real help to the reader. It seems very likely that the current classification systems, all of which are quite similar, are going to be replaced by the system described by Sternberg (this volume). I believe that Sternberg's system has a tremendous advantage over present systems in that the clues he identifies occur repeatedly in virtually any text and that there are usually several clues to the meaning of any one word. Moreover, the preliminary data Sternberg presents supports the efficacy of his program.

A second weakness of current instruction in context clues is that the time devoted to instruction is a good deal briefer than it probably needs to be. I say this based on my observations of a study in which two colleagues and I (Patberg, Graves, & Stibbe, 1984) taught two types of context clues to fifth-grade students in five 30-minute sessions. Results indicated that the instruction was successful; students improved their ability to use the clues taught to unlock the meanings of novel words. However, two considerations suggest that this week of instruction is only a fraction of the time needed to make students fully competent in using context clues. First, the two types of clues we taught, synonym and contrast clues, are among the easiest to learn. Second, the passages used in the tests provided much richer clues than normal texts, which frequently contain only vague and partial clues to the meanings of unfamiliar words. I can only speculate about how much time might be needed for thorough instruction in using context clues, but thoroughly teaching intermediate and secondary grade students to use context clues seems likely to require several weeks of initial instruction and a good deal of periodic review. Again, I suspect that most programs provide much less time than this.

A third weakness of most current instruction in context clues is that the instruction consists of a brief explanation of clue types and the task coupled with students being required to practice the task. As Sternberg points out and as his preliminary data indicate, teaching students the process of using context clues and teaching them about factors that affect the usefulness of clues are important parts of teaching students to use context. More generally, effective use of context clues, like effective learning of most difficult tasks, is likely to be best facilitated by instruction that employs explicit teacher explanations (see Roehler & Duffy, 1984) and incorporates the principles of teaching effectiveness and active teaching (see Good, 1983). The Patberg et al. study represents an initial attempt at providing this sort of instruction.

Learning and Using Word Parts

As is the case with context clues, virtually all students now receive some instruction in word parts. However, even more than is the case with context clues, the instruction they receive frequently has a number of weaknesses.

The major weaknesses, or at least those that need to be dealt with first, are curricular. A situation that Stotsky (1976) pointed out with respect to prefixes — that there is a good deal of confusion about what prefixes are and consequently about teaching them — appears to hold for other word parts as well. Thus, the first thing that is needed is full description and consideration of the sorts of elements that might be taught. A likely list would include inflectional suffixes, derivational suffixes, prefixes attached to regular English words, prefixes attached to non-English roots, and non-English roots themselves. What needs to be particularly considered is the extent to which each type of element is likely to contribute toward students identifying a word's meaning. For example, inflectional suffixes carry only grammatical meaning and are thus of little or no help in determining word meanings. On the other hand, some derivational suffixes, for example, -less, carry a clear lexical meaning while others, for example, -ty, clearly indicate a part of speech, but have a much less clear lexical meaning. Suffixes such as -ty are likely to be of little use in determining word meanings.

Once the types of elements and their potential value in revealing word meanings are described, criteria for identifying the specific elements of each type that need to be taught must be established, and the specific elements to be taught must be identified. This position is in sharp contrast with that taken by Pressley, Levin, and McDaniel (this volume), who indicate that there are 3,000–4,000 common roots and affixes in English and suggest that learning these would be a manageable task. My belief is that learning anything like this number of word parts would only be feasible and fruitful for some college-bound students. I suspect that a set of word parts to be taught to typical elementary and even secondary school students ought to include something closer to 100 elements.

Unfortunately, most current suggestions for identifying word parts to be taught are not very valuable. For example, arguing on the basis of consistency of meaning, Deighton (1959) lists 10 prefixes worth teaching, 2 of which, apo- and equi-, appear in fewer than 10 words in the Carroll et al. (1971) word frequency list. Similarly, Dale, O'Rourke, and Bamman (1971) list well over 1,000 roots to teach, some of which appear in only one or two words in the Carroll et al. list. However, promising work in identifying word elements to be taught is currently being conducted by White and Speidel (in preparation). For example, these researchers have shown that nearly half of the prefixed words in the Carroll et al. word frequency list begin with one of four negation prefixes: *un-, in-* (not), *dis-*, and *non-*. Here are four prefixes that are clearly worth teaching.

In addition to decisions about what word parts to teach, decisions must be made about the order in which word parts are taught, the grades at which they are taught, and the grades at which they are reviewed. Although the listing of word parts just given — inflectional suffixes, derivational suffixes, prefixes attached to regular English words, prefixes attached to non-English roots, and non-English roots themselves — constitutes an order that is generally logical, an optimal order would not be this neat and orderly; for example, some prefixes (concrete and easily definable ones such as *un-*) should almost certainly be taught before some suffixes (abstract ones such as *-ion*). Deciding on grade levels for teaching specific word parts is partly a matter of arbitrarily establishing certain grade levels for certain elements, and partly a matter of deciding when and for what sorts of students certain elements might be useful. For example, instruction in non-English roots may be appropriate only at the high school level, and only for some students.

Finally, as is the case with context clues, effective instructional procedures, procedures consistent with principles of teaching effectiveness and active teaching and employing explicit teacher talk need to be developed. Nicol, Graves, and Slater (1984) describe a successful attempt to teach a set of prefixes using instruction that is generally consistent with these principles. And Pressley et al. (this volume) mention a study in which root words were successfully taught to college students and indicate that additional work in teaching word parts is underway.

Using the Dictionary and Thesaurus

As is the case with both context clues and word parts, students routinely receive some instruction in using the dictionary. Elementary schools provide instruction in alphabetizing, in using guide words, in using pronunciation keys, and, perhaps, in choosing meanings appropriate for the context in which one finds a word. However, I do not believe that many programs go much beyond this or that such instruction is sufficient for teaching students to effectively use the second most popular book in the English language.

Exactly what students need to know regarding the dictionary varies a great deal from one grade to another. Possibly the most important thing students need to learn is which dictionaries are appropriate for them. Students also need to know a number of things about the particular dictionary they use: what the entries for individual words contain and how they are arranged, what aids to its use the dictionary provides, and what features beyond the basic word list the dictionary includes. Much of the important information appears in the front matter of the dictionaries themselves, but it is very seldom read, and simply asking students to read it is hardly sufficient instruction. Thus direct instruction in how to use specific dictionaries is needed. Finally, less utilitarian but important in generating interest in the dictionary is information found in books about dictionaries; for example, some students at least might be intrigued by the fact that the *Oxford English Dictionary* was such a mammoth undertaking that 70 years and three editors passed away before it was finally published.

Students also need direct instruction in using the thesaurus. Such instruction is worthwhile because the thesaurus is used for a somewhat different purpose than is the dictionary. In general, the dictionary is used when a word has already been identified — when we have read it and want to be certain of its meaning or when we are considering using it in writing and want to check its meaning or its spelling. A thesaurus, on the other hand, is much more likely to be used when we are looking for a word to use. We use a thesaurus when we have something to say but want a new way of saying it. Getting students in the habit of using a thesaurus is a step toward getting them to enlarge their active vocabularies.

Developing an Approach to Dealing with Unknown Words

If students are going to get maximum benefit from what they learn about context clues, word parts, and the dictionary and thesaurus, they need a definite strategy for dealing with unknown words when they encounter them in their reading. The following approach, based on suggestions by Calfee and Drum (1986) and Sternberg, Powell, and Kaye (1983), is an example of such a strategy.

1. Recognize that an unknown word has occurred.
2. Make a preliminary judgment about the importance of the unknown word to understanding the passage.
3. Attempt to infer the meaning of the unknown word from the context preceding it.
4. Read on. Attempt to infer the meaning of the unknown word from the context following it.
5. Make a second judgment about the importance of the unknown word to understanding the passage.
6. Attempt to infer the meaning of the unknown word by looking at the word parts.
7. Make a third judgment about the importance of the unknown word to understanding the passage.
8. Turn to the dictionary or another resource.

This, of course, is only one approach; a variety of others are possible. Also, it needs to be recognized that teaching students to use such an approach is a major task; even initiating the strategy—recognizing that an unknown word has occurred—can be a big step for some students. However, in keeping with the current emphasis on the importance of metacognition (e.g., Brown, Campione, & Day, 1981) and on being explicit about what we ask of students (e.g., Roehler & Duffy, 1984), it seems extremely important to give students definite strategies such as this one rather than assuming that they will develop such strategies on their own.

Adopting a Personal Approach to Building Vocabulary

As I noted at the beginning of this section, regardless of how much instruction we do in schools, students will actually do most of their word learning independently. It therefore makes sense to encourage students to adopt personal plans to expand their vocabularies over time. Options include learning word parts, looking up novel words and keeping a file of them, making a commitment to learn a word a day and actually using those words, making a commitment to use the thesaurus when writing, using vocabulary building books, doing crossword puzzles, and playing word games of various sorts. Although it is undoubtedly the case that some of these approaches are intrinsically better than others, what probably matters is that a student will use an approach rather than that it is the best one. Thus, information on the approaches students will and will not use would be helpful.

LEARNING ABOUT WORDS

Of the three major goals I have listed, this is the one that currently receives the least attention. In fact, I suspect that this goal receives almost no deliberate attention and very little incidental attention in most schools and classrooms. Moreover, I know of very little research, theory, or even speculation on the topic. Nevertheless, I believe learning about words has the potential for being an extremely important part of a comprehensive vocabulary program. Here, I consider five topics—learning what it means to know a word, learning that word meanings vary and how they vary, recognizing and manipulating relationships among words and their referents, learning to recognize and use figurative language, and learning to value words.

Learning What It Means To Know a Word

This, of course, is an extremely ambitious goal. As Calfee and Drum (1986) point out, the question has baffled philosophers throughout history. Although the question is not likely to be fully answered in the near future, and perhaps will never be fully answered, investigators are beginning to describe the different sorts of word knowledge. In this volume, the chapters by Curtis, Elshout-Mohr and van Daalen-Kapteijns, and Beck et al. each include consideration of some aspects of what it means to know a word. Other investigators have also considered the question. For example, Dale and O'Rourke (1981), whose views strongly influence Curtis's chapter, list four levels of word knowledge: never having seen the word before, recognizing it as a word but not recognizing its meaning, knowing the contexts in which it is used but not its meaning, and knowing its full meaning. Calfee and Drum (1986), to give another example, note that word knowledge involves such diverse skills as the appreciation of metaphor, analogy, and word play, as well as the ability to recognize synonyms, define words, and use them expressively.

Although this brief consideration can provide only a glimpse of the many ways and levels at which one can know a word, it is at least suggestive of some of the things that we might like to impart to students. Further work in this area, in addition to pursuing questions of what it means to know a word, should probably include attempts to determine students' metacognitive knowledge of their word knowledge at various ages and ability levels. One might also investigate the effects of direct attempts at fostering such metacognitive knowledge.

Learning That Word Meanings Vary and How They Vary

What students need to learn about polysemy is almost as straightforward as what they need to learn about what it means to know a word is abstract. Nevertheless, because polysemy is so ubiquitous a phenomenon, it definitely deserves attention. I have already pointed out much of what I think students need to learn about polysemy in the discussion of multiple meaning words in the section of the chapter on learning new meanings for known words. Students need to learn that a great many words have multiple meanings, that polysemous words can constitute a source of difficulty in their reading, and that some words have specialized meanings in particular subject areas. Additionally, they need to realize that the same word can be instantiated with quite different meanings in different contexts. It seems likely that the first three of these concepts could be taught fairly easily, but that the fourth one would be more difficult to teach and would need to be taught at a later grade level.

Recognizing and Manipulating Relationships Among Words

Given the centrality of the notion of conceptual networks to current cognitive theory, it is not surprising that several suggestions have been made for instruction aimed at highlighting and manipulating relationships among words (e.g., Calfee, 1981; Johnson & Pearson, 1984). Additionally, work with synonyms, antonyms, classification, and the like is a part of many basal programs. Also, some of the empirical work already mentioned—that by Beck and her associates (e.g., Beck et al., 1982), that by Johnson et al. (1982), and that by Levin et al. (1984)—has presented instruction involving relationships. However, this work has not focused on teaching relationships; instead it has focused on teaching the words. Systematic research on the effects of instruction dealing with relationships among words on students' understanding of the relationships themselves and conceptual networks in which they operate seems definitely called for. For example, with respect to synonymy, it seems likely that elementary grade children would profit from instruction which stressed that, although synonyms have about the same meaning, they rarely have precisely the same meaning and that as either readers or writers children need to appreciate the different nuances of meaning in synonyms such as *push* and *nudge* or ones such as *angry* and *furious*.

The conceptual and research task needed to develop strong programs in teaching relationships among words would seem to be quite similar to that needed to develop strong programs in teaching word parts. That is, the possible relationships need to be specified, the purposes of teaching each relationship need to be clearly defined, the order for teaching the relationships and the grade and ability levels at which they might most profitably be taught have to be identified, and procedures for teaching need to be devised and tested.

Learning To Recognize and Use Figurative Language

Some attention to figurative language is currently a part of all school programs. However, a comprehensive instructional program would go considerably beyond what is done in most schools. First, the full range of images, figurative language, and word play should be dealt with. This would include—but not necessarily be limited to—simile, metaphor, personification, allusion, synecdoche, meiosis, hyperbole, riddles, and puns. Second, these devices need to be formally introduced and taught, periodically reviewed, pointed out in the speech and writing of others, and encouraged in students' own speech and writing. It needs to be made very clear that such devices are not solely the province of poets and litterateurs. Third, and in keeping with this last point, it needs to be made clear that the responsibility for pointing out and encouraging the use of such devices extends well beyond English teachers. Metaphor and allusion, for example, are vital parts of much good social science writing, and good journalistic writing is often filled with images, figures, and word play. The *New York Times,* for example, recently noted that "Balloons have become a high-flying business and sell at inflated prices," and observed that "Ever since the apple episode, delving into secret knowledge has been a risky business."

Learning to Value Words

This is almost certainly the most etheral of the goals I am suggesting. It may also be the most important, for if students do not come to truly value words, there is little chance that they will seriously care about learning them or using them with precision. The approach to achieving this goal seems to me to be straightforward, although difficult to effect. Students need models of clear, vivid, and precise diction in what they read and what they hear. They also need models who demonstrate concern for words. Teachers—teachers from kindergarten through graduate school—can serve as such models.

Teachers can influence students by themselves using clear, vivid, and precise diction. They can routinely point out adroit use of words in the speech and writing students encounter, and in students' own speech and writing. They can bring up interesting facts about words, and they can make direct references to the importance of words.

As an example of the sort of attitude, commitment, and skill that teachers can demonstrate, I quote from a class handout distributed at the beginning of each semester by Garrard Beck, a former teacher at Washburn High School in Minneapolis. For 18 years, from 1962 when he began the course until 1980 when he retired, Mr. Beck taught a one-semester course titled Word Study. Originating as a substitute for Senior English, a required course for seniors who were not taking any other English courses, Word Study became an elective and grew from a single section to five sections. It also grew into both a major part of Mr. Beck's life and an institution at the school.

> As a firm believer in the credo that one lives in his head or not at all, I view a knowledge of words as a means to this end and as a sine qua non of life. Every word you know is a window upon the world, and the desideratum of the struggle is to emerge from one's cellular self into a mansion of many rooms and many windows. Words are labels for the things we see and the things we feel. Without such labels we are lost, or at least confused. A certain, that is, an assured knowledge of words gives us at least a fighting chance to bring some semblance of order to the ineluctable insinuation of chaos. It might be perversely stated that man's claim to fame is his extensive and complex utilization of his thumb and his tongue, by which he has removed himself by an uncomfortable and questionable distance from his Darwinian cousins. How many of us have stood in front of the cages of chimps and gorillas, and felt uneasy about the chasm and the kinship that lay between us. And how often has the same feeling arisen when there are no bars between us, when the superficial appearances are identical or nearly so. Words make the difference: which words we use, how we understand them, and how we intend them to be understood. This—and only this rationale and device—will, in time, obtain for us the elusive genius which we insistently call humanity. A multitude of animals are more beautiful than we are, stronger, shrewder, kinder, longer-lived, less-troubled. Our unique distinction has yet to

be claimed, but, when it is, it will be essentially verbal. That is to say, the way out of the jungle is via a reasonable harmony between the word and the reality it identifies.

CONCLUDING REMARKS

Like Mr. Beck, I see the goal of achieving "a reasonable harmony between the word and the reality it identifies" as vitally important. Also, in keeping with Mr. Beck, I view instruction as having a vital role in achieving this goal. In all, I have listed 16 areas in which instruction can play a part in fostering vocabulary development. This much is obvious. In these concluding remarks, I want to make three points that are perhaps not as obvious, and that I believe are worth stressing.

First, the plan described is intended to be a long-term and comprehensive one that would be implemented across the 12 years of public schooling and that would involve the majority of teachers and administrators in a district. Bringing such a plan into existence would require the sort of commitment, coordination, and cooperation that is difficult to secure. Yet I believe that the same sort of commitment, coordination, and cooperation is necessary for strong programs in almost any area of the curriculum; and thus I do not believe that it is unrealistic or inappropriate to seek such support for a vocabulary program.

Second, it needs to be recognized that instruction directed at any one of the three goals fosters achievement of the others as well. Thus, for example, instruction that teaches students individual words strengthens the likelihood that they will learn other words from context, and instruction that teaches students to value words is likely to promote both their learning individual words and their learning ways to learn words. Additionally, it seems worth noting that the instruction is directed at both cognitive and affective learning and that these two sorts of learning can serve to reinforce each other.

Finally, I want to point out that as I consider the various roles that instruction can play in vocabulary development, the instruction I envision is in the majority of cases teacher-directed, active teaching that involves a good deal of explicit teacher talk. Dittoed sheets and workbooks would play a small part in the program, and asking students to complete tasks without first clearly showing them how to complete those tasks would play almost no part whatsoever. Additionally, as I consider the instruction, I envision teachers who themselves appreciate words and the English language more generally, who are knowledgeable about language, and who are precise in their diction and articulate in their speech and writing. Without such teachers, the plan outlined here would be of no value; with such teachers, it can become far more than anything that can be put down on paper.

REFERENCES

Anderson, R. C., & Freebody, P. (1981). Vocabulary knowledge. In J. Guthrie (Ed.), *Comprehension and teaching: Research reviews* (pp. 77–117). Newark, DE: International Reading Association.

Beck, I. L., McKeown, M. G., McCaslin, E. S., & Burkes, A. M. (1979). *Instructional dimensions that may affect reading comprehension: Examples from two commercial reading programs* (LRDC Publication No. 1979-20). Pittsburgh: University of Pittsburgh, Learning Research and Development Center.

Beck, I. L., Perfetti, C. A., & McKeown, M. G. (1982). The effects of long-term vocabulary instruction on lexical access and reading comprehension. *Journal of Educational Psychology, 74,* 506–521.

Bradac, J. J., Courtright, J. A., Schmidt, G., & Davies, R. A. (1976). The effects of perceived status and linguistic diversity upon judgments of speaker attributes and message effectiveness. *The Journal of Psychology, 93,* 213–220.

Brown, R. (1958). *Words and things.* New York: Free Press.

Brown, A. L., Campione, J. C., & Day, J. D. (1981). Learning to learn: On training students to learn from texts. *Educational Researcher, 10* (2), 14–21.

Calfee, R. C. (1981). *The book: Components of reading instruction.* Unpublished manuscript, Stanford University.

Calfee, R. C., & Drum, P. A. (1986). Research on teaching reading. In M. C. Wittrock, (Ed.), *Handbook of research on teaching* (3rd ed., pp. 804–849). New York: Macmillian.

Carroll, J. B., Davies, P., & Richman, B. (1971). *The American Heritage word frequency book.* New York: Houghton Mifflin.

Dale, E., & O'Rourke, J. (1981). *The living word vocabulary.* Chicago: World Book–Childcraft.

Dale, E., O'Rourke, J., & Bamman, H. A. (1971). *Techniques of teaching vocabulary.* Menlo Park, CA: Benjamin/Cummings.

Deighton, L. C. (1959). *Vocabulary development in the classroom.* New York: Columbia University Press.

de Villiers, J. G., & de Villiers, P. A. (1978). *Language acquisition.* Cambridge, MA: Harvard University Press.

Duin, A. L. (1983). *Effects of intensive writing instruction on a specific writing task.* Unpublished master's thesis, University of Minnesota, Minneapolis.

Durkin, D. (1979). What classroom observations reveal about reading instruction. *Reading Research Quarterly, 14,* 481–533.

Frayer, D. A., Fredrick, W. C., & Klausmeier, H. J. (1969). *A schema for testing the level of concept mastery* (Working Paper No. 16). Madison, WI: Wisconsin Research and Development Center for Cognitive Learning.

Gipe, J. P. (1979). Investigating techniques for teaching word meanings. *Reading Research Quarterly, 14,* 624–644.

Gipe, J. P. (1981, April). *Investigation of techniques for teaching new words.* Paper presented at the meeting of the American Educational Research Association, Los Angeles, CA.

Good, T. L. (1983, April). *Classroom research: A decade of progress.* Paper presented at the meeting of the American Educational Research Association, Montreal.

Graves, M. F. (1980, April). *A quantitative and qualitative study of students' reading vocabularies.* Paper presented at the meeting of the American Educational Research Association, Boston, MA.

Graves, M. F. (1984). Selecting vocabulary to teach in the intermediate and secondary grades. In J. Flood (Ed.), *Promoting reading comprehension* (pp. 245–260). Newark, DE: International Reading Association.

Graves, M. F. (1985). *A word is a word.* New York: Scholastic.

Graves, M. F., & Duin, A. L. (1985). Building students' expressive vocabularies. *Educational Perspectives, 23*(1), 4-10.

Herber, H. L. (1978). *Teaching reading in content areas* (2nd ed.). Englewood Cliffs, NJ: Prentice-Hall.

Jenkins, J. R., & Dixon, R. (1983). Vocabulary learning. *Contemporary Educational Psychology, 8,* 237-260.

Jenkins, J. R., Stein, M. L., & Wysocki, K. (1984). Learning vocabulary through reading. *American Educational Research Journal, 21,* 767-787.

Johnson, D. D., & Pearson, P. D. (1984). *Teaching reading comprehension (2nd ed.). New York: Holt, Rinehart & Winston.*

Johnson, D. D., Toms-Bronowski, S., & Pittelman, S. D. (1982). *An investigation of the effectiveness of semantic mapping and semantic feature analysis with intermediate grade level children* (Program Report No. 83-3). Madison, WI: Wisconsin Center for Education Research.

Levin, J. R., Johnson, D. D., Pittelman, S. D., Levin, K. M., Shriberg, L. K., Toms-Bronowski, S., & Hayes, B. L. (1984). A comparison of semantic- and mnemonic-based vocabulary-learning strategies. *Reading Psychology, 5,* 1-16.

Mason, J. M., Kniseley, E., & Kendall, J. (1979). Effects of polysememous words on sentence comprehension. *Reading Research Quarterly, 15,* 49-65.

McKeown, M. G., Beck, I. L., Omanson, R. C., & Perfetti, C. A. (1983). The effects of long-term vocabulary instruction on reading comprehension: A replication. *Journal of Reading Behavior, 15,* 3-18.

McKeown, M. G., Beck, I. L., Omanson, R. C., & Pople, M. T. (1985). *Some effects of the nature and frequency of vocabulary instruction on the knowledge and use of words. Reading Research Quarterly, 20,* 522-535.

Nagy, W. E., & Anderson, R. C. (1984). How many words are there in printed school English? *Reading Research Quarterly, 19,* 304-330.

Nagy, W. E., Herman, P. A., & Anderson, R. C. (1985). Learning words from context. *Reading Research Quarterly, 20,* 233-253.

Neilsen, L., & Piche, G. L. (1981). The influence of headed nominal complexity and lexical choice on teacher's evaluation of writing. *Research in the Teaching of English, 15,* 65-73.

Nicol, J. A., Graves, M. F., & Slater, W. H. (1984). *Building vocabulary through prefix instruction.* Unpublished paper, University of Minnesota, Minneapolis.

Parker, S. L. (1984). *A comparison of four types of initial vocabulary instruction.* Unpublished master's thesis, University of Minnesota, Minneapolis.

Patberg, J. P., Graves, M. F., & Stibbe, M. A. (1984). Effects of active teaching and practice in facilitating students' use of context clues. In J. A. Niles & L. A. Harris (Eds.), *Changing perspectives in research in reading/language processing and instruction* (pp. 146-151). Rochester, NY: National Reading Conference.

Pressley, M., Levin, J. R., & Delaney, H. D. (1982). The mnemonic keyword method. *Review of Educational Research, 52,* 61-91.

Roehler, L. R., & Duffy, G. G. (1984). *Direct explanation of comprehension processes.* In G. G. Duffy, L. R. Roehler, & J. A. Mason (Eds.), *Comprehension instruction: Perspectives and suggestions* (pp. 265-280). New York: Longman.

Scherr, R. (1984). *Effects of polysemous words on sentence comprehension: A replication and extension.* Unpublished paper, University of Maryland, College Park.

Sternberg, R. J., Powell, J. S., & Kaye, D. B. (1983). Teaching vocabulary-building skills: A contextual approach. In A. C. Wilkinson, (Ed.), *Classroom computers and cognitive science* (pp. 121-143). New York: Academic Press.

Stotsky, S. L. (1976). *Toward more systematic development of children's reading vocabulary in developmental reading programs for the middle to upper elementary grades.* Unpublished doctoral dissertation, Harvard University.

Tennyson, R. D., & Cocchiarella, M. U. (1986). An empirically based instructional design theory for teaching concepts. *Review of Educational Research, 56*, 40–71.

Tennyson, R. D., & Park, O. (1980). The teaching of concepts: A review of instructional design research literature. *Review of Educational Research, 50*, 55–70.

White, T. G., & Speidel, G. E. (in preparation). *Children's knowledge of prefixes, suffixes, and root words.*

Wolfe, R. F. (1975). *An examination of the effects of teaching a reading vocabulary upon writing vocabulary in student compositions.* Unpublished doctoral dissertation, University of Maryland, College Park.

Author Index

A

Abelson, R. P., 55, *71*
Aborn, M., 82, *85*
Ackerman, R. P., 81, *87*
Actkinson, T. R., 144, *145*
Ahlfors, G., 119, *124*
Ahmad, F., 111, 116, 120, *126, 127*
Ahmed, M., 116, *126*
Alvermann, D. E., 143, *144*
Ames, W. S., 83, 84, *85*
Anderson, J. R., 76, *85*
Anderson, R. C., *15, 16,* 20, 21, 22, 25, 26, 27, 28, *33, 34, 35,* 37, 39, 40, 42, 43, 45, 47, 48, 49, *50, 51,* 74, 76, 80, 81, 83, *85, 86, 87,* 120, *126,* 129, 130, 131, 132, 137, 140, 144, *144, 145,* 155, *163,* 165, 166, 168, 173, *182, 183*
Anderson, T. H., 144, *144*
Anglin, J. M., 82, *85*
Armbruster, B. B., 143, 144, *144*
Atkinson, R. C., 109, *124*
Aulls, M., 81, *85*
Aurentz, J., 110, *124*

B

Baldwin, R., 24, 26, 32, *34*
Bamman, H. A., 174, *182*
Barron, R.R., 143, *144*
Batterman, N., 65, *70*

Baumann, J. F., 39, 40, 41, 46, 48, *51*
Beck, I. L., 12, *15,* 23, 25, 30, 32, *34, 35,* 66, 67, 68, *69,* 129, 130, 133, 140, 142, *144, 145,* 150, 152, 153, 158, *162, 163,* 166, 169, 179, *182, 183*
Begg, G., 81, *87*
Beishuizen, J. J., 69, *70*
Bellezza, F. S., 109, 113, *124, 127*
Bensoussan, M., 122, *124*
Berry, J. K., 95, *105,* 110, 112, 113, 117, *125, 127*
Bertino, M., 81, *86*
Bettelheim, B., 9, *15*
Beuhring, T., 115, *124*
Bird, L. B., 78, *86*
Bishop, S. L., 109, *127*
Bispo, J. G., 110, *127*
Bolinger, D., 77, *86*
Bond, G. L., 38, *51*
Borkowski, J. G., 111, *126*
Bourne, L. E., 116, *125*
Boyes-Braem, P., 67, *70*
Boyle, O., 142, 144, *145*
Brackfeld, G. I., 108, *126*
Bradac, J. J., 171, *182*
Brady, M. E., 47, *51,* 148, *163*
Brandenburg, G., 22, *34*
Bransford, J. D., 28, 29, *34, 55, 69,* 116, *126*
Brown, A. L., 177, *182*
Brown, R., 165, *182*

Bruner, J. S., 108, *126*

Bryant, S. L., 95, *105,* 110, 111, 114, *126, 127*

Burkes, A. M., 140, *145,* 153, *162,* 166, *182*

C

Calfee, R. C., 77, 78, *86,* 165, 176, 177, 178, 179, *182*

Campbell, E. Q., 14, *15*

Campione, J. C., 177, *182*

Carnine, D. W., 30, *34,* 142, 143, *145,* 148, 153, *163*

Carpenter, P. A., 82, *86*

Carroll, B. A., 80, 82, 84, *86, 87,* 121, *124*

Carroll, J. B., 1, *6,* 20, *34,* 37, 39, 40, *50,* 74, *86,* 168, 174, *182*

Chall, J. S., 7, 8, 10, 11, 12, 13, 14, *15, 16,* 20, *34,* 38, 45, 47, 49, *50, 51*

Chapman, R., 108, *124*

Chen, C. C., 81, *87*

Chomsky, C., 13, *16*

Churchill, G. G., 108, *126*

Clark, J. M., 110, *126*

Cocchiarella, M. V., 170, *184*

Cohen, B., 62, *70*

Coleman, J. S., 14, *16*

Collins, J. M., 46, *50*

Collins, K. W., 144, *145*

Conard, S., 14, *15*

Courtright, J. A., 171, *182*

Coyle, G., 142, 143, *145*

Crafton, L., 31, *34*

Craik, F. I. M., 119, *124*

Crist, R. L., 119, *124*

Cronbach, L. J., 37, 44, 45, 47, 49, *50,* 85, *86*

Cuff, N., 22, *34*

Cureton, E. E., 38, *51*

Curley, R., 76, *86*

Curtis, M. E., 44, 46, *50,* 55, 65, *70*

Cykowski, F., 110, *125*

D

Dale, E., 1, *6,* 8, 10, 11, 12, 13, *16,* 41, 42, 43, 45, 46, 48, *51,* 168, 174, 178, *182*

Danilovics, P., 110, *125*

Dansereau, D. F., 144, *145*

Darch, C., 142, *145*

Davies, P., 20, *34,* 39, 40, *50,* 168, 174, *182*

Davies, R. A., 171, *182*

Davis, F. B., 27, *34,* 37, 40, *51,* 147, *163*

Davis, G., 142, *145*

Davis, K., 142, *145*

Day, J. D., 177, *182*

Deighton, L., 25, *34,* 174, *182*

Delaney, H. D., 25, *35,* 109, 110, *126,* 169, *183*

Dennis-Rounds, J., 111, *126*

Desrochers, A., 109, 110, *126*

deVilliers, J. G., 165, *182*

deVilliers, P. A., 165, *182*

Dickinson, D., 109, *127*

Digdon, N., 110, 111, *126*

Dirkzwager, A., 69, *70*

Dixon, R. C., 24, *34,* 107, *124,* 133, 134, 140, 142, *145,* 166, *183*

Dolch, E. W., 38, 41, 42, *51,* 78, *86*

Dooling, D., 28, 29, *34*

Draper, A. G., 23, *34,* 148, *163*

Dretzke, B. J., 111, 115, 116, *125*

Drum, P. A., 77, 79, 80, 82, 84, *86, 87,* 121, *124,* 165, 176, 177, 178, *182*

Duffy, G. G., 173, 177, *183*

Duin, A. L., 167, 172, *182, 183*

Dulin, K., 81, *86*

Dupuy, H., 22, *34*

Durkin, D., 23, *34,* 140, *145,* 166, *182*

E

Eckerson, L. D., 7, *16*

Elivian, J., 78, 81, *86*

Ellis, A. M., 144, *145*

Elshout, J. J., 53, 54, 55, 58, 64, *70*

Elshout-Mohr, M., 55, 58, 60, 65, *70,* 82

Emans, R., 81, *86*

Engelmann, S., 142, 143, *145*

Evans, S. H., 144, *145*

F

Fairbanks, M., 20, 25, 28, 30, *35*

Farr, R., 37, *51*

Feifel, H., 8, *16,* 45, *51*

Feldman, K. V., 62, *70*

Ferguson, G. A., 54, *70*

Finn, P. J., 82, *86*

Fokkema, S. D., 69, *70*

Franks, J. J., 116, *126*

Frayer, D. A., 170, *182*

Fredrick, W. C., 170, *182*

Freebody, P., 10, 12, *15,* 20, 27, 28, *33,* 37, 42, 43, 45, 47, 49, *50,* 74, 81, 85, *129,* 130, 131, 137, *144,* 165, *182*

Freschi, R., 30, *34,* 142, *145,* 148, 153, *163*

Friedman, A., 116, *125*

G

Gallagher, M., 20, 28, 29, 31, *35*
Gates, A. I., 38, *51*
Ghatala, E. S., 110, 111, 112, 113, *125, 126, 127*
Gipe, J. P., 119, *124,* 142, *145,* 169, *182*
Gitomer, D. H., 46, *50*
Glaser, R., 46, *50,* 55, 65, *70*
Good, T. L., 174, *182*
Goodman, K. S., 9, *16,* 78, *86*
Goodman, Y., 9, *16*
Graves, M. F., 75, *86,* 167, 173, 175, *182, 183*
Gray, W. D., 67, *70*
Gray, W. S., 11, *16,* 24, *34,* 47, *51*
Green, B. F., 38, *51*
Guilford, J. P., 55, *70*

H

Halff, H. M., 83, *86*
Hall, J. W., 117, *127*
Hanf, M. B., 144, *145*
Hare, S. Z., 119, *124*
Harris, A. J., 41, *51,* 64, *70*
Harris, S., 14, *15*
Hayes, B. L., 112, 113, *125,* 169, 179, *183*
Hayes-Roth, B., 62, *70*
Herber, H. L., 167, *183*
Herman, P. A., 25, 26, *34, 35,* 76, 80, 81, *87,* 173, *183*
Herold, C., 11, *16*
Hershey, M. M., 109, *127*
Hiebert, E. H., 10, 12, *15*
Hobson, C. J., 14, *15*
Hoffman, J. V., 82, *86*
Holly, C. D., 144, *145*
Holmes, E., 11, *16,* 24, *34,* 47, *51*
Hope, D. J., 110, *127*
Hunt, E. J., 74, *86*
Hyde, T. S., 119, *124*

J

Jacobson, M. D., 41, *51*
Jenkins, J. J., 119, *124*
Jenkins, J. R., 24, 32, *34,* 47, *51,* 76, 80, *86,* 107, 121, *124,* 133, 134, 140, 142, *145,* 148, 153, *163,* 166, 169, 172, *183*
Jensen, A. R., 74, *86*
Johnson, D. D., 10, 12, *16,* 39, 40, 41, *51,* 107, 111, 112, 113, 114, 123, *124, 125,* 167, 168, 169, 171, 179, *183*

Johnson, D. M., 114, *124*
Johnson, M. D., 67, *70*
Johnson, M. K., 28, 29, *34,* 55, *69*
Johnson-Laird, P. N., 68, *70*
Juel, C., 23, *35*
Just, M. A., 82, *86*

K

Kameenui, E. J., 30, *34,* 142, 143, *145,* 148, 153, *163*
Kaplan, E., 8, *16,* 58, 62, 68, *71,* 82, *87,* 108, *127*
Kaye, D. B., 74, 82, *87,* 107, 108, 111, 112, 114, 115, 116, 117, 118, 121, *127,* 156, *163,* 176, *183*
Keil, F. C., 65, *70*
Kellerman, D. K., 81, *86*
Kendall, J., 167, *183*
Kibby, M. W., 38, *51*
Kirkpatrick, E., 22, *34*
Kirkpatrick, J. J., 38, *51*
Klare, G. R., 11, *16,* 45, *51*
Klausmeier, H. J., 62, *70,* 170, *182*
Klein, G. A., 81, *86*
Klein, H., 81, *86*
Kniseley, E., 167, *183*
Konopak, B. C., 76, 80, *86*
Kruglov, L. P., 45, *51*
Kuczaj, S. A., II, 77, *86*
Kuhn, T. S., 130, *145*
Kuiper, N. A., 95, *105,* 110, 111, 114, *127*

L

Lachman, R., 28, 29, *34*
Lafrance, M. S., 108, *126*
Laufer, B., 122, 123, *124*
Leeds, D., 38, 41, 42, *51*
Levin, J. R., 25, *35,* 95, *105,* 109, 110, 111, 112, 113, 114, 115, 116, 117, 120, 122, 123, *124, 125, 126, 127,* 169, 179, *183*
Levin, K. M., 112, 113, *125,* 169, 179, *183*
Lewis, N., 108, *125*
Litowitz, B., 82, *87*
Long, G. L., 144, *145*
Lorge, I., 7, 8, 12, *16,* 20, *34,* 38, 45, 49, *51*
Lutz, K. B., 108, *127*
Lyons, J., 73, *87*

M

MacNamara, J., 59, *70*
Madison, J., 80, 82, *87*

Margosein, C. M., 25, *34*
Marshall, J. C., 59, *70*
Mason, J. M., 167, *183*
Masson, M. E., 119, *125*
Mastropieri, M. A., 110, 116, *125, 127*
Matthews, M. M., 10, *16*
McCaslin, E., 25, 32, *34,* 140, *145,* 153, *162,* 166, *182*
McCormick, C. B., 95, *105,* 109, 110, 111, 112, 113, 115, *125, 127*
McCullough, C., 74, *87*
McDaniel, M. A., 110, 114, 116, 118, 119, *125*
McDonald, B. A., 144, *145*
McGivern, J. E., 110, 111, 115, 116, *125*
McKeown, M. G., 12, *15,* 23, 25, 30, 32, *34, 35,* 66, 67, 68, *69,* 129, 130, 133, 140, 142, *144, 145,* 150, 152, 153, 156, 158, *162, 163,* 166, 169, 179, *182, 183*
McPartland, J., 14, *16*
Mervis, C. B., 67, *70*
Mezynski, K., 129, 130, 131, 140, *145*
Michener, S., 95, 110, 111, 114, *125, 127*
Miller, G. A., 68, *70,* 74, 75, 77, *87*
Miller, G. E., 95, *105,* 110, 111, 112, 113, 116, 117, *125, 127,*
Moe, A. J., 7, 8, *16,* 39, 40, 41, *51*
Moeller, G. H., 23, *34,* 148, *163*
Moerk, E. L., 108, *125*
Mood, A. M., 14, *16*
Morris, C. D., 116, *126*
Morris, W., 74, *87*
Murphy, G. L., 62, *70*

N

Nagy, W. E., 13, *16,* 20, 21, 22, 25, 26, *34, 35,* 39, 40, *51,* 76, 80, 81, *87,* 120, *126,* 155, *163,* 166, 168, 173, *183*
Nakamura, G. V., 110, *127*
Neilsen, L., 171, *183*
Nelson, K., 82, *87*
Nelson, T. O., 119, *126*
Nicol, J. A., 175, *183*
Ninio, A., 108, *126*
Nitsch, K. E., 59, *70*
Novick, S., 68, *70*
Nussbaum, J., 68, *70*

O

O'Brien, K. L., 108, *126*
Omanson, R. C., 30, *35,* 150, 152, 158, *163,* 169, *183*

O'Rourke, J., 12, 13, *16,* 41, 42, 46, 48, *51,* 168, 174, 178, *182*
Ortony, A., 83, *86*
O'Sullivan, J. T., 111, *126*
Overholser, B. M., 81, *87,* 156, *163*

P

Paivio, A., 109, 110, *126*
Pany, D., 47, *51,* 142, *145,* 148, 153, *163*
Papert, S., 68, *70*
Park, O., 170, *184*
Parker, S. L., 169, *183*
Pascarella, E. T., 25, *34*
Patberg, J. P., 173, *183*
Pearson, P. D., 10, 12, *16,* 20, 25, 26, 28, 29, 31, *34, 35,* 48, *50,* 107, 111, 114, 123, *124,* 167, 168, 171, 179, *183*
Perfetti, C. A., 10, 12, *15, 16,* 23, 30, *34, 35,* 66, 67, 68, *69,* 129, 130, 133, 142, *144,* 150, 158, *163,* 169, 179, *182, 183*
Petrone, J. M., 119, *124*
Petty, W. T., 11, *16,* 75, *87*
Pflaum, S. W., 25, *34*
Piche, G. L., 171, *183*
Pittelman, S. D., 112, 113, *125,* 169, 171, 179, *183*
Pople, M. T., 152, *163,* 169, *183*
Powell, J. S., 74, 82, *87,* 91, 97, *105,* 107, 108, 111, 112, 114, 115, 116, 117, 118, 120, 121, *127,* 142, *145,* 156, *163,* 176, *183*
Pressley, M., 25, *35,* 95, *105,* 109, 110, 111, 112, 113, 114, 116, 117, 119, 120, 122, 123, *125, 126, 127,* 169, *183*

Q, R

Quealy, R. J., 83, 84, *87,* 121, *127,* 156, *163*
Rankin, E. G., 81, *87,* 156, *163*
Ray, K., 110, 111, *126*
Ray, M., 108, *127*
Razik, T., 1, *6*
Resnick, L. B., 69, *70*
Richman, B., 20, *34,* 39, 40, *50,* 168, 174, *182*
Robinson, A. H., 81, *87*
Robinson, F. P., 78, *87*
Robinson, H., 24, *35*
Roehler, L. R., 173, 177, *183*
Rohwer, W. D., Jr., 109, *127*
Rosch, E., 67, *70*
Rosenshine, B., 12, *16*
Roser, N., 23, *35*

Ross, K. A., 112, 113, *127*
Rubeck, P., 81, *87*
Rubenstein, H., 82, *85*
Rubin, D. C., 82, *87*
Ruddell, R., 142, 144, *145*
Russell, D. H., 38, 45, *51*

S

Saadeh, I. Q., 45, *51*
Sachs, H., 25, *35*
Samuel, J., 109, *127*
Samuels, S. J., 81, *87*
Schank, R. C., 55, *71*
Schatz, E., 24, 32, *34*
Scherr, R., 167, *183*
Schmeck, R. R., 55, 64, *71*
Schmidt, G., 171, *182*
Schreck, J., 47, *51*, 148, 153, *163*
Schvanveldt, R., 81, *87*
Scott, J. A., 10, 12, *15*
Scruggs, T. E., 110, 115, *125, 127*
Sears, D., 77, *86*
Seashore, H. G., 38, 40, *51*
Seashore, R. H., 7, *16*
Semlear, T., 81, *87*
Shriberg, L. K., 110, 111, 112, 113, *125,* 169, 179, *183*
Shular, J., 108, *127*
Silbert, J., 142, *145*
Sim, D. D., 122, 123, *124*
Sinclair, C., 120, *127*
Singer, H. A., 147, *163*
Sipay, E. R., 64, *70*
Slater, W. H., 175, *183*
Smith, F., 7, *16*
Smith, M., 22, 23, *35*
Smith, R. W. L., 120, *127*
Snow, C., 14, *15*
Speidel, G. E., 174, *184*
Stahl, S. A., 11, 12, *16,* 20, 25, 28, 30, *35,* 47, *50*
Stallings, J., 12, *16*
Stein, M. L., 32, *34,* 76, 81, *86,* 121, *124,* 134, 142, *145,* 169, 173, *183*
Sternberg, R. J., 55, *71,* 74, 82, *87,* 91, 94, 97, 104, *105,* 107, 108, 111, 112, 114, 115, 116, 117, 118, 120, 121, *127,* 142, *145,* 156, *163,* 176, *183*
Stibbe, M. A., 173, *183*
Stoll, E., 11, *16*
Stotsky, S. L., 12, *16,* 174, *183*

Stratton, R. P., 114, *124*
Swaby, B., 29, *35*
Sweeney, C. A., 113, *127*

T

Tennyson, R. D., 170, *184*
Terman, L. M., 10, *17*
Tetewsky, S. J., 94, *105*
Thomas, E., 24, *35*
Thorndike, E. L., 74, *87*
Thorndike, R. L., 11, *16,* 37, *51*
Thorndyke, P. W., 63, *71*
Thurstone, L., 27, *35,* 53, *71,* 147, *163*
Tillman, V. P., 116, 118, 119, *125*
Toms-Bronowski, S., 112, 113, *125,* 169, 171, 179, *183*
Toye, A. R., 110, *127*
Traver, R., 58, *71*
Tuinman, J. J., 47, *51,* 148, *163*
Tulving, E., 119, *124*

V

van Daalen-Kapteijns, M. M., 55, 58, 60, 64, 65, *70,* 82, *86*
Van der Veer, G. C., 69, *70*
Vining, S. K., 119, *126*

W

Wagner, R. K., 104, *105*
Watson, J. D., 129, *145*
Watson, R., 82, *87*
Wechsler, D., 10, *16*
Weinfeld, F., 14, *16*
Werner; H., 8, *16,* 58, 62, 68, *71,* 82, *87,* 108, *127*
Wesman, A. G., 38, 40, *51*
White, T. G., 174, *184*
Whyte, G., 108, *127*
Wilkinson, I. A. G., 10, 12, *15*
William, S., 144, *145*
Wolfe, R. F., 172, *184*
Woo, G., 120, *127*
Wysocki, K., 32, *34,* 76, 81, *86,* 121, *124,* 134, 142, *145,* 169, 173, *183*

Y, Z

York, R. L., 14, *16*
Zelan, K., 9, *15*

Subject Index

A

Access hypothesis, 131
Accuracy, 68, 148
Affixes, 81, 174, 175, *see also* Context cues
Aptitude hypothesis, 131
Associative learning, *see* Keyword method
Automaticity, 57, 68, 104, 131, 148

B, C

Bilinguals, 14, 15
Code-emphasis method, *see* Phonics
Cognitive processes
  components, in word acquisition, 60–63
  knowledge acquisition, 91, 95–97, 101
  process training, 98–103
Cohesion, 77
Comprehension, 27–32, 40, 45–46, 49, 90,
    130–139, 147–151
Concept-teaching, 169, 170
Computer-assisted instruction, 69
Context
  and comprehension, 31
  cues, 82, 83, 91, 92, 98–101, 117, 120, 121,
    134, 135, 173
  incremental learning, 25
  linguistic, 81–84
  moderating variables, 92–94, 98–102
  oral vs. written, 24–26

  prior knowledge, 78–81
  and semantic ambiguity, 55, 57, 64
  situational, 75–77
  topical, 77, 78
  and word recognition, 9
  vs. direct instruction, 12–14, 140

D

Decoding , *see* Word recognition
Decontextualization, 61, 62, 103, 104
Diagnosis, 45–47
Dictionary use, 175, 176
Direct instruction, 11–13, 19, 23, 31, 32, 40,
    140, *see also* Keyword method

E, F

Explicit instruction, *see* Direct instruction
Expressive knowledge, 133, 171, 172
Figurative language, 179
Fluency, *see* Automaticity
Frayer method, *see* Concept-teaching

I

Incidental learning, *see* Context
Individual differences
  context, use of, 26, 81, 82
  and keyword method, 110

metacognition, 78, 79
vocabulary, 23, 45–48, 62–64, 115
Information processing, *see also* Cognitive
    processes
memory limitations, 54–57, 64
Instructional design, 49, 50, 132, 138, 139,
    149, 162
Instrumentalist hypothesis, 28, 47, 131, *see
    also* Direct instruction
Intelligence tests, 10

K

Keyword method
    applicability, 110, 169
    vs. contextual method, 94, 95, 111–120
Knowledge-based approach, 29, 30
Knowledge hypothesis, 28, 131, *see also*
    Schema

L, M

Language experience, 9
Metacognition, 78, 79, 157, 172–181
Minorities, low income, 14, 15
Mnemonics, *see* Keyword method
Morphemes, 82, 83, *see also* Context cues

P

Phonics, 9, 10, 12
Polysemy, 167, 168, 170, 178
Prefixes, 174, 175, *see also* Context cues

R

Readability, 11, 45
Recall, cued vs. free, 117, 118, 134, 135

Receptive knowledge, 133, 134, 171, 172
Rich instruction, 147–162, 169–171

S, T

Schema, 28–30, 63, 64, 77, 78
Semantic feature analysis, 171
Semantic groups, 149, 178, 179
Semantic mapping, 143, 144, 169
Sight method, 10, 13
Strategies, 176, 177, *see also* Cognitive
    processes
Structure-of-Intellect model, 55
Suffixes, 174, 175, *see also* Context Cues
Synonomy, 179
Syntax, 14, 81–84
Thesaurus use, 176
Total language approach, 9

V

Vocabulary assessment, 37–49, 135, 136
Vocabulary depth, 43, 46, 47, 68, 75, 76,
    79–81, 133–135, 148, 155, 177, 178
Vocabulary growth, 8, 21–23, 26, 45, 46, 165
Vocabulary size, 7, 8, 20–27

W

Word form, 38, *see also* Context cues
Word frequency, 20, 38–42
    and difficulty, 41
    and learning, 66, 82, 149–155
Word recognition, 8–15, 43, 76, 167, *see also*
    Phonics
Writing, 171–172